Bleachy-Haired Honky Bitch

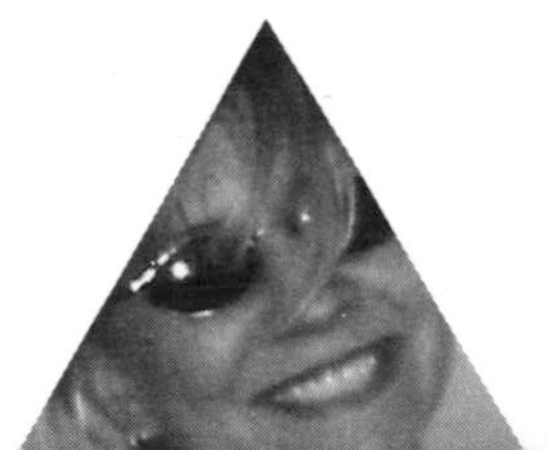

HOLLIS GILLESPI

ReganBooks
Celebrating Ten Bestselling Years
An Imprint of HarperCollins*Publishers*

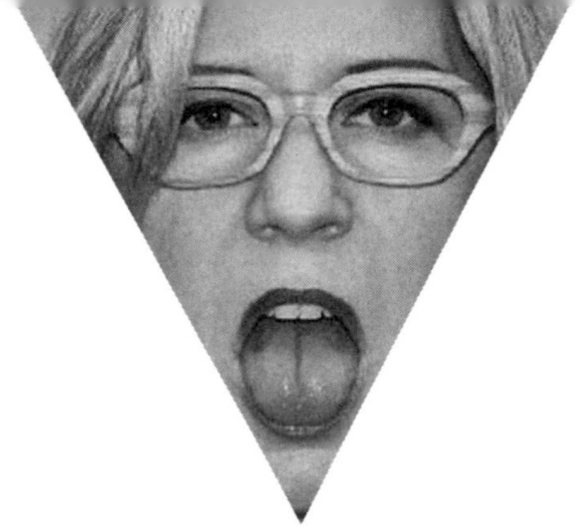

Bleachy-Haired Honky Bitch

Tales from a Bad Neighborhood

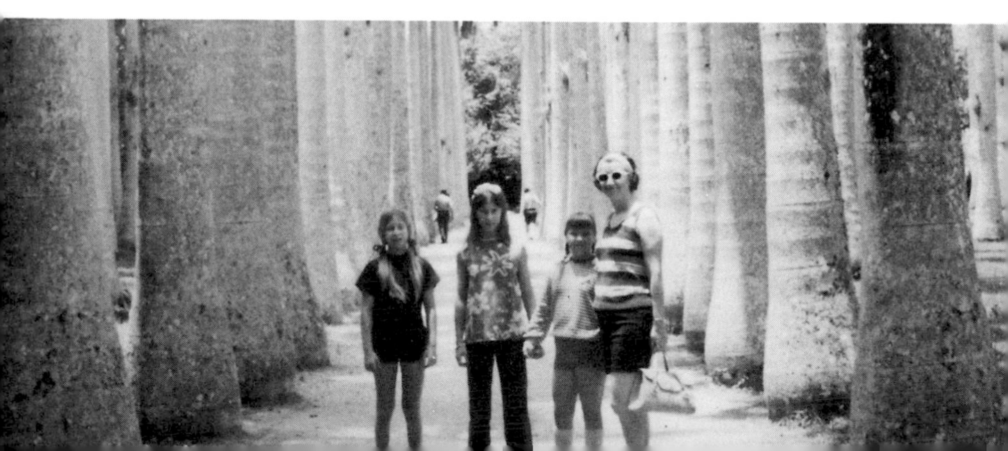

Photography credits: pages i, 1, 73 courtesy of Michelle Hogan;
page ii courtesy of Ron MacDonald;
pages iii (top), 3, 8, 80, 158 courtesy of Lary Blodgett;
pages iii (bottom), v, 4, 5, 6, 22, 50, 67, 70, 74, 79 (top and bottom), 84, 104, 107, 135, 138, 139, 162, 165, 195, 198, 199, 217, 232, 236, 241, 275 courtesy of Hollis Gillespie;
pages 119, 120, 121, 155 courtesy of Daniel Troppy;
page 172 courtesy of Kimberly Kislig.

A hardcover edition of this book was published in 2004 by ReganBooks, an imprint of HarperCollins Publishers.

For information address HarperCollins Publishers Inc.,
10 East 53rd Street, New York, NY 10022.

HarperCollins books may be purchased for educational, business, or sales promotional use.
For information please write: Special Markets Department, HarperCollins Publishers Inc., 10 East 53rd Street, New York, NY 10022.

FIRST PAPERBACK EDITION PUBLISHED 2005

Designed by Kate Nichols

The Library of Congress has cataloged the hardcover edition as follows:

Gillespie, Hollis.

Bleachy-haired honky bitch : tales from a bad neighborhood / Hollis Gillespie.—1st ed.

p. cm.

ISBN 0-06-056198-X

1. Gillespie, Hollis. 2. Journalists—United States—Biography. I. Title.

PN4874.G385A3 2004

070.92—dc22

[B]

2003049503

ISBN 0-06-056199-8 (pbk.)

05 06 07 08 09 WBC/RRD 10 9 8 7 6 5 4 3 2

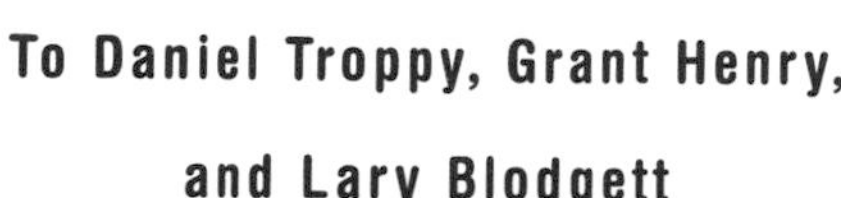

To Daniel Troppy, Grant Henry,

and Lary Blodgett

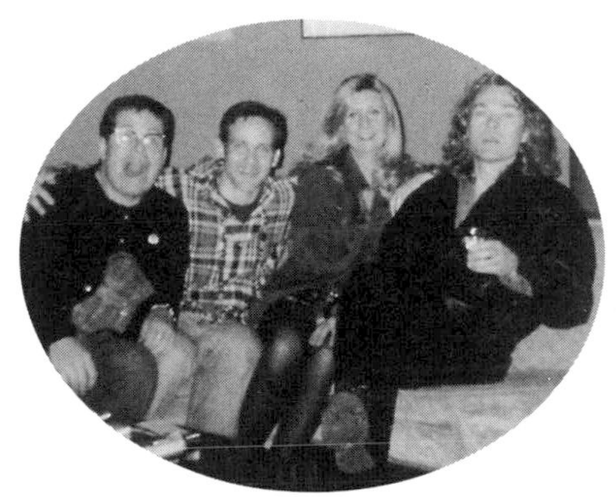

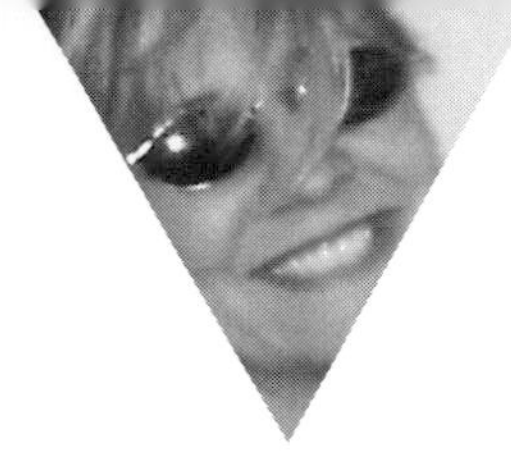

Introduction

Thank God you bought this book. Seriously. But even so, to this day I've yet to trust the notion it's not necessary to break your ass to make a buck, so as I write this I'm still employed at my blue-collar job, and my hands are still calloused from lugging stuff. I haven't thrown away my flight attendant badge and sensible shoes yet and, even scarier, probably never will. The other day my supervisor asked me when I was going to quit, seeing as how I'm a famous writer now and all. I told him, "I ain't quittin' 'til they pry the peanuts from my cold, dead fingers, fucker!"

The funny thing is I didn't know I was writing a book when I started this. Most people have a book lying around in their heads. I, literally, had this one lying around on my closet floor. The chapters were encased in stacks of journals I'd kept while I was going through the complete crap fest that becomes most young adulthoods fraught with loss and other pain, though with me it started earlier than normal. I don't think I would have survived if I hadn't sat down with a pen and paper (laptops were, like, eleven thousand dollars back then), opened an artery, and just let the poison out every chance I got.

Most of those chances came while I was on layovers. I had faked my way into becoming a German translator in addition to my job as a flight attendant, and every week I flew to one of three countries—Germany, Austria, or Switzerland—and it was in those places, absent any good primetime TV or other mental enemas to feed my need for distraction, where the terror of the truth would hit and I'd have to write. It was a compulsion, an awful compulsion. (Please understand, though, this is not a book about flying so much as it is about getting grounded.)

Then two guys, Patrick Best and Steve Hedberg, publishers of *Poets, Artists & Madmen* in Atlanta, saw something in my stuff, a spark or something, I don't know. I'm just glad they were looking where I wasn't. They began running my pieces in their paper, and it all took off from there, especially after Sara Sarasohn, producer of NPR's *All Things Considered*, began airing my commentaries on her program.

I should mention that nearly everything in this book is true, so long as truth can be trusted to my recollection. A few names have been changed to protect the guilty, but in truth, most of the guilty not only insisted I use their names but also that I spell them correctly and include their phone numbers.

One more thing: I didn't really call my supervisor "fucker" that day, because if I had, he could have canned my ass like a truckload of tuna. But because of you and lots like you who bought this masterpiece of mine, I am without a doubt absolutely almost positive, kinda, that it hardly would have mattered. So thank God, and thank you too.

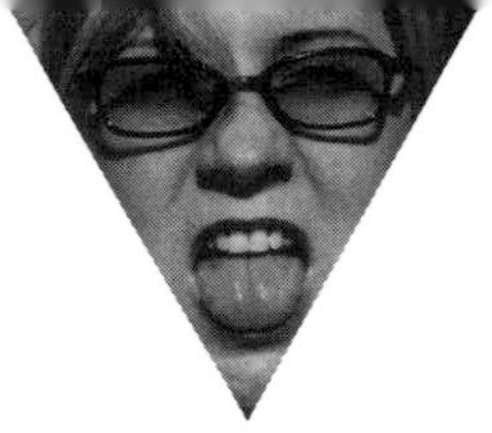

Hellish Gargoyle

If nothing else, at least I'm living up to my name these days, because I just discovered that in German—make that bad German—my first name means "hellish."

And my last name is even worse. In German, my last name means "gargoyle." You would think I would have known about this sooner, because I've been a bad German interpreter for twelve years now, but you'd be surprised at how long you can interact within another culture and still keep your knowledge of it neatly limited. Take my mother, who was subcontracted to build missiles for the Swiss in the late eighties. We lived in Zurich for two years, and the only German word she learned was *ja*. She couldn't even pronounce "Waikiki," but in my eyes she compensated for her lack of knowledge in this area by the fact that she had a job making bombs.

As an interpreter, my dealings in Germany have mostly been

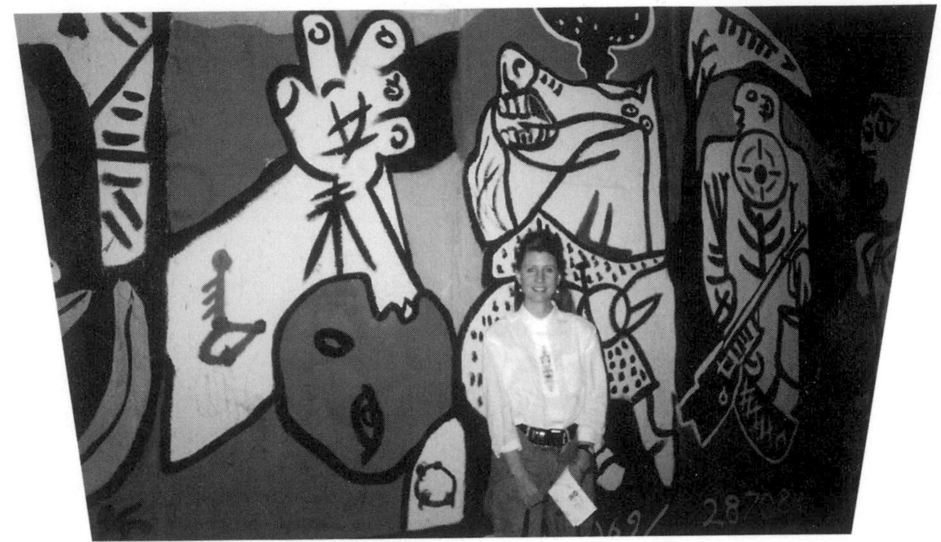

In front of the Berlin Wall, 1991

polite business relations, so I've never had the need to say the word "hellish" to these people—not unless I was introducing myself anyway.

You'd think I'd be better at the whole communication thing, considering I'm an official foreign-language interpreter. Fortunately for me I represent people who have no idea I'm using a very broad interpretation of the word "interpreter" to describe my services. As far as they know, I'm translating their words with sparkling precision, but luckily the Germans are pretty tolerant of non-natives who attempt their language, so the interactions usually go off smoothly. Once, an American doctor directed me to ask a German patient when she had had her last bowel movement, and I dutifully turned to the woman and asked her, essentially, "Madame, when was the last time you went to the toilet solidly?"

She answered my question and laughed. My clients must think I am very clever, as I am always making people laugh in their native languages. It is apparently even funnier because I have perfect pronunciation, and I can turn to a German pharmacist and say without a hint of an accent, "It would please me greatly to purchase medicine for my fluid nostrils," or to a Spanish taxi driver, while searching for the metal end of the over-the-shoulder safety strap, and tell him, "Pardon me, but I am missing the penis of my seatbelt," or to an Austrian hotel clerk regarding a beautiful fountain nearby, "Is it possible to acquire a room with a view of the urinating castle?"

It must be hilarious to hear these massacred phrases spoken with the determined clarity of a cowbell. People gather around me and ask me to repeat myself. "Tell us again about the storm in your stomach," they say, after I translate my account of Montezuma's revenge, "especially the part about your exploding ass."

I used to be ashamed at what a bad interpreter I was, until I realized that I get my meaning across, and isn't that the whole point? And there are people out there who actually think I'm good at this. They *request* me. Every time my work takes me to Europe I still feel giddy, like a stowaway, as if I've been able to stave off discovery long enough to fake my way across the Atlantic one more time. Once, while in Munich, I happily hopped along the river's edge. It was sunny and warm, and I'd just bought a bag of olives at

The Berlin Wall

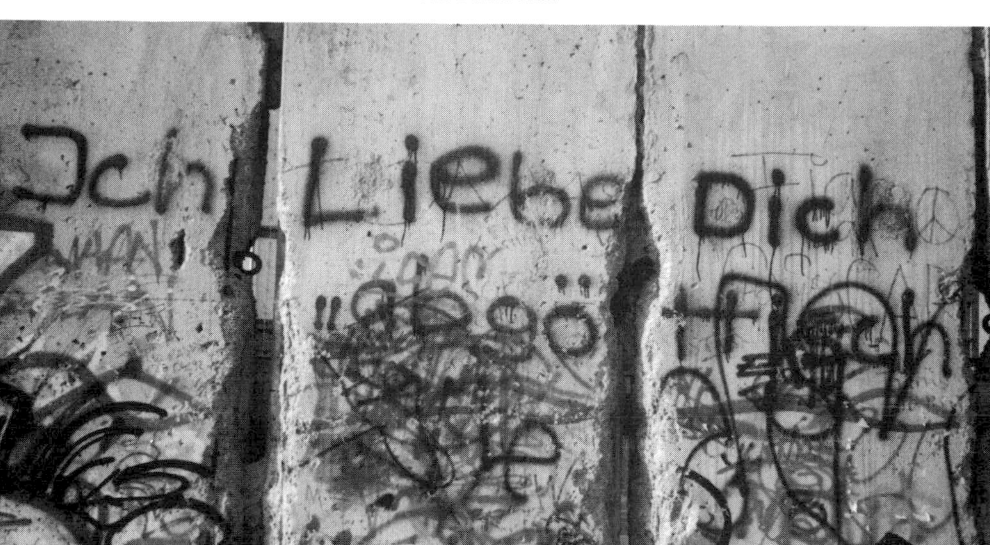

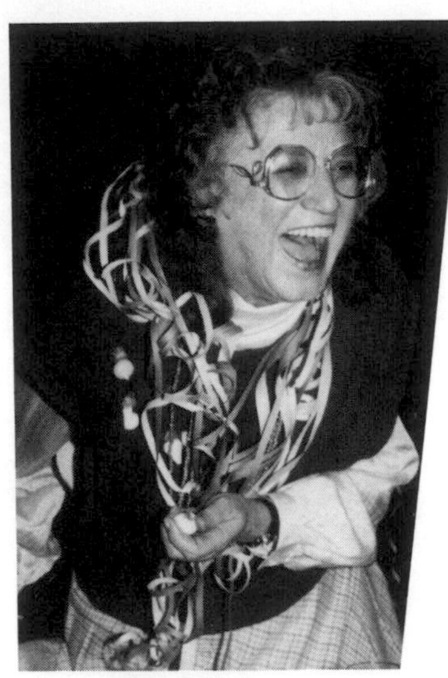

My mother in Zurich, 1987

an outdoor market. They were the right kind too—pitted—and I was able to request them by clearly stating, "It would please me to have a hundred grams of the big, boneless black ones."

But it fell to a Polish hairdresser to finally enlighten me about my name. I'd been in Munich for a week, participating in a study program that would stuff this half-forgotten, guttural language back into my brain in order to retain my interpreter status, and after class one day I ducked into a salon on Sendlingerstrasse to see if anyone there had time to bleach the hell out of my hair.

I always figured Germany would be a good place to score some good hair highlights. Anyone who's ever been there can see that all the local women make it their mission to look like they were born and raised on a California beach. Unlike them, though, I actually was born and raised on a California beach, though thirteen years of Atlanta living has seriously eroded my surfer-girl image.

The Polish hairdresser's name was Barbara, and I didn't even need an appointment. She simply ushered me to a chair and started slapping some high-test rotgut on my roots. This was my kind of place. In Atlanta, the hairdressers always talk me into new color treatments recently invented by a team of twelve scientists toiling under a glass dome in Finland. The result is usually okay, I guess, but my hair never ends up blond enough. "Can't we dispense with this fancy crap?" I always ask. "Don't you have anything back there strong enough to burn the barnacles off a boat?"

American colorists always ignore me and commence their subtle application of a fancy new product. But not Barbara. Barbara's own hair had been bleached so blonde and so bright that, if you had an idea to gawk straight at her head, it would be safer to do it from under one of those protective helmets that welders wear. Her own German was bad, but better than mine, because at least she knew the meaning of my first name. She laughed when she heard it, "You come from Hell, *ja?*"

It wasn't until my scalp was practically bleeding that she finally removed the foils and rinsed the solution from my hair, which, by the way, didn't fare too well. Much of it had burned off at the roots, leaving little bald patches, and the streaks that remained were as white as lab mice. I would classify the results as less than successful: My scalp looked like it had been bitten by electric eels. I wanted to get out of there fast so that I could assess the damage privately and see if actual sobbing was called for. In my haste, I forgot my umbrella, which prompted Barbara to dash after me down the busy street.

I tried to ignore her but it wasn't happening. She was calling out my name sweetly, my full name, which she'd read from my credit card, and people were beginning to stop and look around, their curious eyes eventually settling on me. There was nothing else for me to do, so I simply turned and took my place in the world. "Over here, Barbara," I answered her. She trotted to my side as I stood there, bleach-blond locks and all.

"Hellish Gargoyle," she smiled, "here you are."

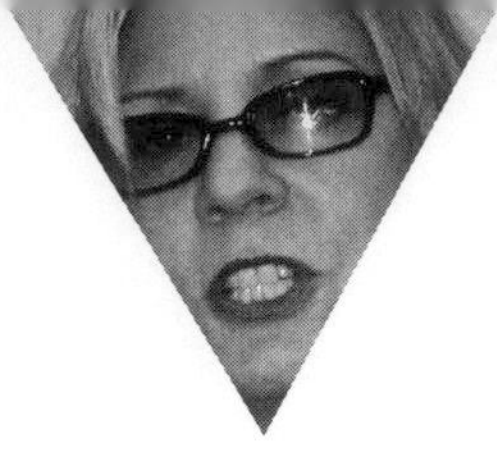

Suicidal Tendencies

My friend Lary keeps offering to shoot me again, and not like the last time either. This time, he says, he'll actually put some effort into aiming the gun—at my head, even—and probably not miss. "At the worst you'll end up a vegetable, but it's not like you'll have to be aware of it."

I've stopped bothering to remind him I don't want to die. Sometimes I still get mad at him for shooting at me the first time. The bullet hit a brick and could have ricocheted into my throat or something, and I might have died horribly, flopping like an octopus in a private ocean of my blood. "You were breaking into my house," Lary likes to point out. It's just his reflex, he says, to start shooting when someone shatters his window. I can't believe that to this day he tries to blame me for his broken window just because I tossed a rock through it.

He's to blame, of course. If he had a doorbell like a normal person I wouldn't have to throw stuff at his house to alert him to my presence. He claims he wasn't really aiming at me anyway, because if he had been, I'd be dead right now, and he would've had to bury me in the giant concrete bay he's building along his property line so he can plant a wall of bamboo stalks to keep all the ice-cream colored houses next door out of sight.

He acts as if it would have been a *hassle,* a big, huge burden to have to dispose of my body. Does he not remember his own instructions to me in the event of his death? How I'm supposed to push his corpse out of a helicopter at a high altitude with his cat strapped to his chest? On top of that I have to aim for a suburban cul-de-sac because he wants to end up impaled on a swing set. One last fright for the neighborhood kids, he says. Plus, since he doesn't even care if his cat outlives him, I'm supposed to strap her, scratching and hissing, to his dead chest. Now how's *that* for a burden?

Our friends Daniel and Grant, on the other hand, refuse to let me be the executor of their living wills. They know I will never pull the plug, even if there is nothing left but their head in a fishbowl. They're probably afraid I'll go senile and beat them with their own feeding tubes until I tire out. Instead, they are each other's informal executors, with explicit instructions to euthanatize the other when the need for adult diapers comes into play, which I think is excessive. "You might *like* the diapers," I try to reason. "Jesus, don't just *die,*" I plead, but they just laugh as if they're looking forward to it.

It's the burden of it all, I suppose. People have different thresholds for dealing with death, and some have none at all. I think it has to do with your heart, and whether you follow its wishes. I used to work in the copy office of a city magazine alongside three bitter old acid vats who treated me like an unwanted weight because they had to teach me the intricacies of an outdated system that they themselves made sure to keep complicated in order to postpone their own obsolescence. When they weren't resenting me, they resented one another, and it killed me that I didn't fit in. The one closest to my age was twice my age, a woman named Eugenia with bulbous, thyroid eyes and a limitless collection of those spangle earrings you buy at bad craft shows.

She'd been working there longer than the lives of a lot of rock stars, and when she left to start her own novelty toilet-paper company (you could order rolls emblazoned with pictures of your ex-boyfriend's face or the like), she was heralded as if she were an escaped hostage and sent off with a fond farewell that consisted of copious drinking during lunch hour.

But the toilet-paper venture didn't work out for her. She was back within months, broke both financially and spiritually. In her absence the editors had learned they didn't need to replace her, so when she asked to return they fired me to make room. At the time I felt defeated, but I've since realized that Eugenia was simply returning to her lair like a sick elephant, because there is more than one way to die, and this was hers. My last image of Eugenia is watching her approach her old desk like it was the electric chair.

I try instead to remember her during her farewell celebration when, in a moment of booze-induced camaraderie, she told me how happy she was to leave the office because she feared she'd be trapped there forever like a corpse in a crypt. Then she brandished a company picture taken more than a decade earlier, when her hair fell long and thick in a braid down her back. The image was a far cry from the liver-spot-mottled, boozy-breath wretch who pinched the photo with her thumb and ring finger to better accommodate the lit cigarette habitually occupying her dried-out hoof. I truly hated her, and she truly hated me, but at that moment she was about to embark on an exploration, choosing to bear the burden of her aspiration rather than let it dissipate without a trace, and I have to respect her for that, because at that moment she was free, free to let the world literally wipe its ass on her dream.

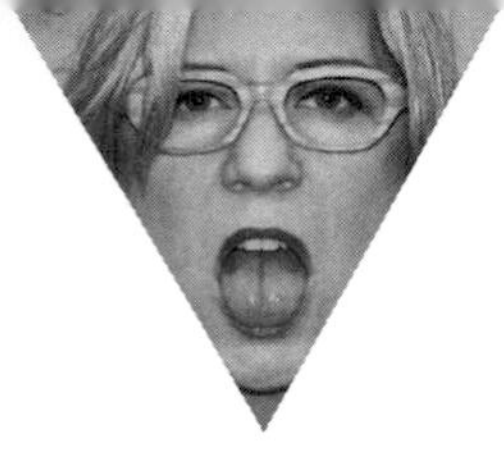

Fear of Dreams

I have to respect Eugenia for that, because one of my biggest fears is going broke. I mean *bad* broke, like living-in-an-abandoned-truck-on-a-mattress-made-of-old-bathrobes broke. I just don't know how well I'd fare, having to burn little piles of pet hair and shredded floor mats to keep warm, having to lick the inside of discarded sandwich wrappers to stay alive, having to scrape myself with rusty Brillo pads to abate the itch factor from various parasites. The prospect just looms there in my life, promising such discomfort.

But here's something funny about fears: They morph. Like last year when I happened across a documentary on that twenty-three-year-old porn star named Savannah, who shot her own head off because she cut her face in a car wreck and thought her career was over. A life like hers would be worse than being broke, not because she was a porn star, which is bad enough (I can't think of a harder job than having sex, *all day*, with a succession of penises the size of sewage pipes), but because a team of documentary filmmakers chronicled her entire cocaine-addicted flea-fleck of a life and didn't come up with a single redeeming moment in it. Not one, just a succession of cockwagging heavy-metal musicians and dickless video directors who had used her like a toilet seat and later talked about how "vulnerable" she was. Even her own mother had only this to say: "I guess she made a good adult-film star."

So now that's my biggest fear: to be unredeemed because I spent most of my life whoring away my quality time. Like I've always worked a plethora of pointless part-time jobs for money because I'm used to thinking that if it were up to my writing income alone, I'd be living in a house that I built myself out of four sticks and a stained tablecloth. Because writing is not what I do for money. Writing is what I do because I'm cursed and can't help it. There are other things I do for money.

Like the time I was a copy editor for that city magazine. My job was to pasteurize the creativity out of every article that came across my desk so they'd all sound the same by the time they went to print. I was fired because, among other things, the concentration level of my coworkers was lowered by my loud laughter. Then I worked as a managing editor at an art publication, which wouldn't have been so bad if my boss hadn't been such a volcanic bitch. She funded the magazine with her father's money and her own savings culled from her former job selling piece-of-crap Peter Max lithographs out of, I think, the trunk of her car. She used to answer her own phone with three different accents so callers would think they were being threaded through a bevy of receptionists. After six months she fired me because she stopped by the office at ten o'clock one Sunday night and saw that I wasn't there.

After that I applied for, and was offered, a job as a skycap at the San Diego airport. I regret turning it down. But it's not the money I miss (skycaps make a ton), I regret my pride. I didn't want to encounter past enemies or old flames at the airport on their way somewhere exciting, while I, in my belted uniform, lugged their bags. I wish I weren't so proud. It would make life a lot easier. I could just work my blue-collar job and not long for something better. I could look at the sky and just see the stars, not be begging the heavens for a break.

But as I said before, I am cursed. It runs in the family. My father used to come home drunk and blather to my mother about making it big. "I can do it," he'd slur. He was gonna open a hot dog joint called the Frank 'n' Stein, or he was gonna patent the world's most wondrous key chain design, or he was gonna write a bestseller about being a used-car salesman. "I can," he'd mumble before passing out in his cigarette-burned La-Z-Boy. "I know," my mother would answer, and in the morning she'd head to work and he'd nurse his hangover.

I still wonder what that taught me, other than to feel oddly ashamed that I want to be better than I am, that I want to stop being suffocated by my safety nets and finally reach for what I've dreamed about. I want to stop fearing there's some kind of cosmic Carol Merrill about to show me I traded everything for what's behind curtain number 3, and when the curtain opens years from now, there I'll be—a failed drunk in a La-Z-Boy lamenting about how I could've become a skycap. God, that's scary, but if that's what the future holds—me in a La-Z-Boy—then I hope I'm sitting there content with having tried. I just want to have tried. What's worse, after all, a dream that never comes true or never admitting you dream at all?

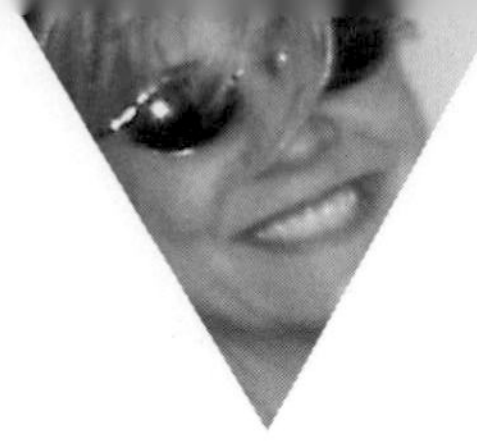

Everybody's Mother

When I was a kid, I thought everybody's mother made bombs. I thought everybody's mother left in the morning before the rest of the house was awake, then came home at night with a government badge clipped to their lapel with "Top Security Clearance" printed above their picture. I thought everybody's mother walked through the door when the day was done, collapsed on a Herculon-upholstered recliner, and smoked Salem menthols with her wig askew while her kids melted down an entire stick of butter to pour over the popcorn they made themselves for dinner. I was nine when I realized my mother was literally the only one like her.

But I didn't brag about it or anything, even though her job would have carried some major weight on the playground. "My mother has probably killed *thousands* of people," I could have boasted, though it probably wouldn't have been true, because the only thing I remember my mother saying about the weapons she made was how poorly they performed at the missile-testing site, but it's not like anyone could have proven me wrong. Plus, even a bad weapon—especially a bad bomb—can wreak a lot of havoc.

My mother was always careful to clarify that she didn't make nuclear bombs, rather she designed conventional defense bombs, trying to drill home the notion that if people were killed with one of her bombs, it was because they deserved it. She never said those very words, but I got the idea it was important to her that people not view her as a *mad* missile scientist, but rather as a passive one, a just-a-Joe-with-a-job-to-do kind of missile scientist.

She was happiest when she was working on rockets, probably because rockets usually don't kill people unless by accident. When we moved to Melbourne Beach, Florida, when I was nine, it was so she could work on the last *Apollo* moon launch. My father was employed then, selling trailers, and our other family car was a massive motor home called the "Amigo." On the night of the last launch, we drove it to the beach and parked there, waiting with the rest of the citizens in what appeared to be a townwide tailgate party.

The rocket was supposed to take off in the late afternoon, but didn't until nearly midnight. My mother was not at all surprised. At that time, my older brother, a budding tennis prodigy, had been left behind in California to live with another family in an attempt on my parents' part to provide him a sense of continuity as he finished high school and, hopefully, earned a full college scholarship. My two sisters and I had yet to show any such promise, and that night we were sleeping in the motor home when my father finally rousted us to view the launch. Until then my parents had been sitting in lawn chairs on the shore the whole time, drinking cans of Budweiser with our neighbors. "This is a historic occasion, aren't you excited?" a lady asked me, her hooch breath just about cremating my corneas. I recognized her as someone else's mother, a neighbor who once knocked on our door to complain about my habit of decorating the pointy cactus-like plant in her front yard with wads of used chewing gum. But tonight all was forgiven in this booze-induced benevolence.

Drunk parents were no novelty to me, and so it wasn't enough to keep me awake. My father did though. "Goddammit!" he hollered. "This is an important goddamn moment and I'll be goddamned if you worthless goddamn ungrateful brats sleep through it!" Then he flicked each of us in the head with his middle finger, which was heavy as lead, so the effect was like getting hit in the skull with a roll of quarters.

I stared sullenly at the dark horizon. The crowd quieted, and soon a flame flickered far off in the darkness, and from that another flame broke free and rose into the sky like a falling star in reverse, then it disappeared behind clouds. The spectacle lasted perhaps thirty seconds and then it was over, signifying the end of my mother's foray into designing instruments of discovery rather than destruction. Soon she would have to return to making bombs. That night, however, the crowd around me was still gasping with wonder when I asked to go back to sleep.

My father, angered by his children's lack of awe, ordered everyone back into the cavernous motor home, threw the lawn chairs in after us, and popped another Budweiser before getting behind the wheel. On the way home, I dozed in the back as the Amigo lurched unsteadily along at high speed. I remember thinking we would be fine if we crashed, because this was a very big motor home, much bigger than the other vehicles on the road. Nothing we hit could hurt us, not even a house. Yes, we were fine. It was everyone else who was in danger.

I suppose it was an expected mind-set for a child whose mother made bombs, but I'm almost ashamed to admit how long I used that kind of reasoning in my life.

As we lurched along, my mother did not seem to mind being lost—not that time anyway. I remember seeing my parents, two lone figures each in a big bucket seat, separated by a massive Naugahyde console. My father must have taken a wrong turn somewhere. "Where *am* I?" he muttered to himself as my mother sat oblivious beside him.

Years later, it would be the other way around: One morning, as he lay oblivious in bed, she stood in the bathroom and looked in the mirror, searching for a trace of the woman she had once been. When she was younger, she had wanted to be a beautician but had become a weapons designer instead. She was woefully bad at cosmetology—when she used to practice on my sisters and me, we would always end up looking like open-casket cadavers in a group funeral—whereas she excelled at math, which was hard for her to admit. When it fell to her to earn a living once my father's aversion to employment became obvious, she reluctantly relied on her un–hoped for talent and went to work for IBM, falling into the job like other mothers fall into cashiering at coffee shops. From there she learned to build computers and then to build bombs for the government.

My mother had been designing missiles for a few decades until that morning when she awoke and could no longer recognize herself. She had started out so long ago with the simple dream of making people beautiful, and here she was, making bombs instead. We were living back in California then, though we moved so often it's hard to keep track of which house it was. I do remember the lone figure of my father, asleep in their king-sized bed, blind to the lone figure of my forty-six-year-old mother crying in the bathroom over their double vanity. "Where did I go?" she sobbed, her hand flat against the glass. "Where *am* I?" Watching her, I wanted to tell her I could see her just fine, but even then I knew that was not the answer she needed.

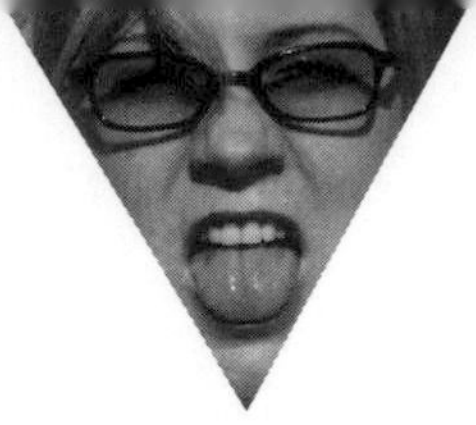

Changing Values

Last week I lucked into a truckload of German Easter eggs. Their value is immeasurable because I use them to bribe Lary into fixing the odyssey of exposed wires and dislodged plaster that passes for my apartment. Normally Lary can't resist these eggs, because they come with a plastic capsule in the center that contains an intricate toy, proof that Lary is really nothing but a fermented adolescent under all that irritable exterior, but unfortunately for me he's in hiding lately on account of his stalker. That says a lot about this person, his stalker, because not many people have the power to diminish the value of German Easter eggs in Lary's eyes.

Even though I personally have never seen Lary's stalker, I hear accounts from those who have ("She has fake tits as big as Liberty Bells!"), so I believe it when he says she exists. He leaves town for weeks at a time these days, and when he does come home he stays at a friend's until it's time to take another job and then he's gone again. He tells me to "be really careful" when I go feed his cat. Now I figure something's got to be wrong because the two things Lary truly values are his cat and his solitude, and something is keeping him from both. So I have to commend this stalker's technique, because Lary's desire to avoid her is greater than his longing for either his pet or his privacy. When you think about it, it's a very effective method of exerting power over a person—to find out what they value and devise a way to deprive them of it.

It doesn't always work. Take my father and his designer shoes, for example. Though he was largely jobless, my father nonetheless would not have been caught without his designer shoes, which he buffed and cared for like two prized Pekingese. They made his stride purposeful, so that when he walked into his favorite bar, his friends would take him for a man of standing. This image of himself became endangered when my mother left us and took her income with her. His attempt to gain some power during the divorce was to threaten to sue for custody of me and my sisters, assuming that—faced with the possible loss of something she really valued—my mother would instantly acquiesce and return home. He was wrong.

"You want the kids? Take them," she said, forcing my father to acknowledge that he couldn't. He backed down, and the divorce concluded with my father cutting his children loose and my mother cutting him a check that promised to keep him in modest supply of designer shoes for a few years yet.

Ever since then I've marveled at what an effective method of self-protection it is to divest yourself of the things that matter to you. If you can't control your need to cling to these things, you'll be controlled by the threat of losing them. Lary put the things he values on hiatus in order to bore his stalker into not bothering him. She's already moved to another state, and I hear she's reduced her harassments to intermittent episodes in which she spends the night in a rental car in his driveway. My guess is she'll soon quit altogether, because Lary's devaluation of the things he normally holds dear effectively took her weapon away.

My father died soon after the divorce. I attended his funeral with my mother, and as my father lay in state, she noticed immediately that his shoes were ugly and not name brand, so she accused the funeral director of stealing his real pair. My father had been working a new job selling used cars, and his coworkers in attendance insisted those were the shoes he always wore. They said he'd been saving money for a deposit on a bigger apartment, so when his daughters visited they wouldn't have to sleep on a trundle bed in his living room.

My mother excused herself. The rest of the funeral she spent in the ladies' lounge, where she might not have sobbed so loudly if she'd known we could hear her through the wall. I think she was remembering that aborted custody battle and how they both had been wrong regarding what the other most valued.

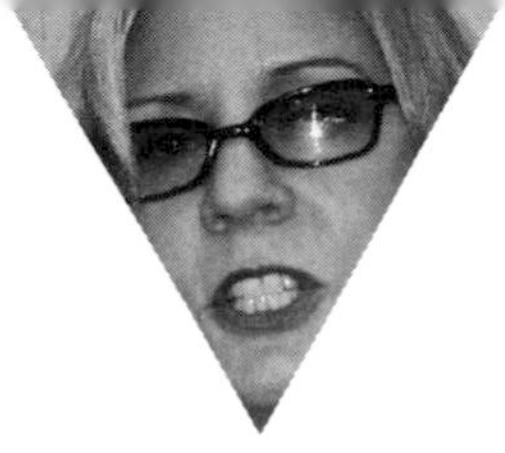

Poisoned Fish

I'd just like to state for the record that I didn't deliberately try to poison my mother when I was six. God, if you believed my siblings, sometimes you'd think I was Lucifer's little minion growing up, what with the fact that I had a pack-a-day smoking habit by the time I was twelve and that once, when I was very young, like *five,* I killed a puppy with a tennis racket, but you have to let me explain this stuff. For example, the cigarette addiction was just a natural extension of my heritage, since both my parents puffed like living chimneys and by the time I was a year old I already had lungs that looked like two used tea bags. I remember once my brother accidentally ate a cigarette ash and spent the rest of the afternoon rubbing his tongue on the carpet under the coffee table to get the taste out of his mouth. That's just how our house was: so steeped in smoke you could send signals. I didn't even have to buy my own cigarettes, I just kyped them from the cartons my parents kept strewn about the house.

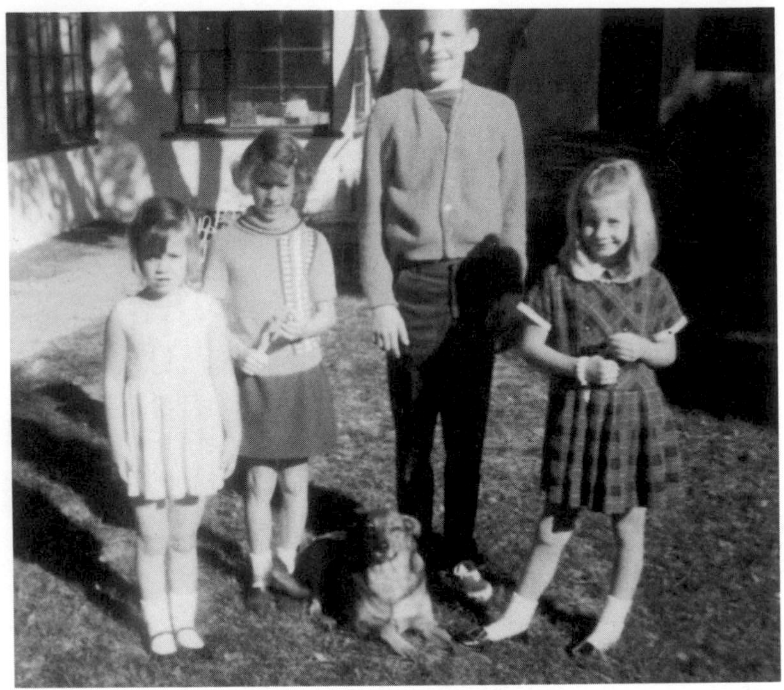

Kim, Cheryl, Jim, and me with Echo

That my parents didn't notice packs at a time were missing is just testimony to the hugeness of their own habit (I myself quit at thirteen). That they died young should not have been a shock—it was anyway, of course, but it shouldn't have been. For the record, I didn't have anything to do with it.

And the puppy. It's not like I hacked it to death. Jesus God, get that out of your mind. The puppy was from a litter our dog Echo birthed under the big wooden desk in my brother's bedroom. One day I thought it would be fun to place one of them on the end of a tennis racket and flip it around, but I stopped as soon as my brother demonstrated to me how the puppy wasn't enjoying it by beating me over the head with a can of artificial snow. "When puppies whine that means they're crying," he said, "like how you cry when I do this": *thwack.* Weeks later the guy who adopted the puppy came back and demanded another one because the first one was faulty on account of how it died days after he brought it home. I always blamed myself, thinking it never fully recovered from the flipping, though for all we knew the man was taking the puppies straight from our house to a cosmetics testing facility. So it's possible I had nothing to do with that death either.

You could almost talk yourself into believing that I was an ideal child, if not for the time when I was six and gave my mother, as a present, poisoned fish wrapped in toilet paper. That my intentions were good is only slightly less incredible than the fact that my mother understood them to be so, and therefore didn't mete out her harshest punishment, which was to shove my whole head into a kitchen sink full of soapy dishwater until I coughed for air. I had collected the fish, dead and floating, from a polluted tributary behind the park after I overheard my parents arguing about money. At the time, my father had quit his job again, and my mother was between contracts, and there was no money to put food on the table, she said. Later I presented the fish, wrapped in paper from the public toilet, to my mother. "Food for the table," I said proudly.

My mother was never one to cry much—except once when I returned home after she had officially reported me missing when I had stopped at the cinema on my way home to watch *My Fair Lady,* a movie that lasts about five days in duration. But she didn't this time, though I was worried she would when I saw her face as I handed her the dead fish. Instead, she gently took the fish straight from my hands to the trash pail and thanked me graciously as she washed my palms. Absent any alcohol to kill the germs, she opted to rinse my hands with warm water and lighter fluid. I swelled with self-importance at the officious undertaking, as I noticed that she took extreme care to first extinguish her cigarette.

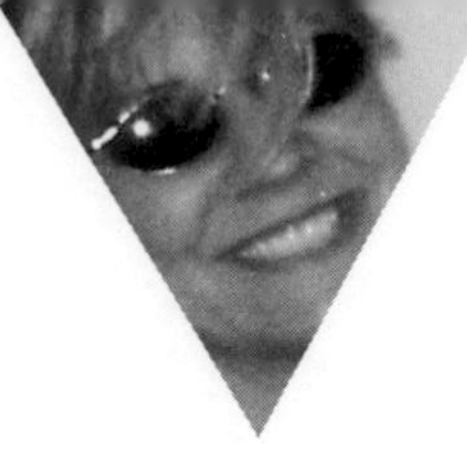

One Word

My friends and I are making our movie debut in a film called *Fuck Fight Pray,* or, to put it in the words of the independent director here filming all day, "F-U-C-K! Action!" His name is Darren, and every time he spells out that one word I wonder if I should even bother trying to calm our neighbors by noting that we're not making porno, and that this is an "art" film slated to be entered in Sundance (or at least in the annual Musical-Spoons Jamboree—probably). The movie is being crafted by creative young visualists with dreams and stuff. But why bother, when Daniel is out back bragging to the neighbors that he has a nude scene, and they believe him.

"Full frontal!" he shouts.

The movie is a beautiful tri-part cinematic observance, and this segment in particular is about a young woman contemplating a crossroads in her life after receiving a marriage proposal. In one segment, Daniel and I play a bickering married couple, and in our scene all you see are the backs of our heads, but even then I bet you can tell we come across as naturally as two big fake breasts. The reason we were picked to appear in the film is because—this is important—when asked if they could come festoon our places with props and film equipment, we answered with one word, "'kay!"

Then we heard the title. When I ask Darren why he spells it out—rather than simply saying it—while calling the scenes, he says it's because he doesn't want to use harsh language in case children are nearby. "F-U-C-K!" he recites. "Action!"

I'm amused that he has a problem with that one word, seeing as how he cowrote the script. I have a bigger problem with euphemisms. There was once a local liquor store appropriately nicknamed "Horny Pete's," because the proprietor once tried to molest a seven-year-old girl, who escaped and ran screaming all the way home clutching her mother's Salem menthols, which was the reason she had been dispatched on the errand in the first place. When she got home she handed over the cigarettes and commenced bawling her eyes out. "What the hell happened to you?" her mother asked, lighting up.

"He . . . he . . . he," the girl blubbered, *"he pulled down his pants!"*

"He pulled down his pants?" the mother shrieked, and she wasn't even thinking about the owner of the liquor store; she was thinking about a neighborhood kid known for pissing in public. When she heard that a grown man had flashed her daughter, her anger was so palpable that the smoke shooting from her nostrils was not from her cigarette. "We're going to the police, and we're gonna get that goddamn sick prick arrested," and they drove to the station.

That girl was me, and I'll never forget the female police officer who took my statement. She had hair like Ethel Mertz and absurdly arched, penciled-in eyebrows. My mother waited outside the room while the officer asked me to tell her exactly what had happened. I told them that, before flashing me, the liquor store owner had tried to provide me with a little porno lesson by showing me pictures of couples in the throes of copulation, and he repeatedly used the word "fuck" along with all its conjugations. The officer, though, was uncomfortable with that word and asked me to substitute it with the phrase "make love."

"Every time you need to say that one word," she explained patiently, "stop yourself and say 'make love' instead."

So I did. When we finished I was led back to my mother, who was assured that they would "lock his perverted ass up," as she herself put it. On the way home I told her about the word substitutions the officer had requested of me while transcribing the statement. Upon hearing this she slammed the brakes so hard she needed to make that "mom arm save" maneuver to keep my un-seatbelted upper half from doing a face plant in the dashboard. Without saying a word, she drove straight back to the station, took my hand, and marched us up to the officer's desk.

"Excuse me," she stated loudly. The officer looked up, and my mother continued. "He did not say 'make love.' Do you understand me? 'Love' has nothing to do with this. I don't want my daughter associating what happened to her today with the word 'love,' am I making myself clear? I would like the statement to be completely accurate."

"It's just one word," the officer tried to argue.

"The *correct* word is 'fuck'—do you understand that? Now write it down." She hovered while the officer rifled through her desk to retrieve a pen. "F-U-C-K," my mother recited loudly, and we didn't leave until she was satisfied that the statement, in all its conjugations, clearly reflected that one word.

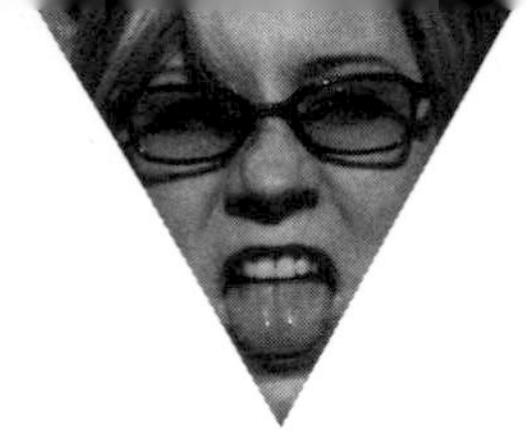

Not the End of the World

When Lary shot at me the first time, I could tell he was secretly glad I didn't die. It could have been an easy accident, my death, it could have been one of those "oh, fuck" moments that happen in an eye blink that you spend the rest of your wretched life wishing you could take back. I mean, if you were a normal person. Lary, on the other hand, keeps wishing he could take back the moment in which his compassion led his aim astray.

I take issue with that. I don't ever really remember wanting to die, but Lary insists his remorse is for my sake, claiming that I have since been begging to be put out of my misery. Take the time I called him, completely suicidal, according to him, years ago. I remember the incident, but needless to say our recollections differ. For one, it was he who called *me,* and this is exactly the conversation:

Him: "What's up?"

Me (typically frustrated and hyperbolic): "Goddammit. I'm totally on the ledge, ready to jump."

Him: "Well, what's *stoppin'* ya?"

I was speaking figuratively, goddammit, because my window didn't even have a ledge, as I was living on the first floor of a renovated telephone factory. It was 10:30 in the morning and the world had ended already. This doesn't usually happen until evening, after I have envisioned myself barefoot and stringy haired, collecting tin cans with callused hands that have yellow fingernails as thick as nickels. I envision scabs all over my body as well, though I don't know where they came from, but I am definitely scabby in these nightmares, probably from sleeping on concrete.

These panic attacks, in which I foresee myself living under a freeway overpass, are nothing new to me: I've been having them for, well, ever. We were renters, my family, and during my entire childhood we moved around like a pack of traveling circus-sideshow workers. My earliest memories are of hiding among moving boxes to get away from my parents, whose ferocious fights inevitably overflowed menacingly upon my siblings and me. We moved every single year because my parents were notoriously cheap and refused to renew any lease that called for an increase in rent. Sometimes we moved because my mother scored government contract work designing missiles for the military. But since contracts come to an end, one week we'd be living in a palace, the next in a trailer two miles north of the Tijuana border. We were never actually homeless—or perhaps that's all we *ever* were. But times have changed, or I hope they have, because after a childhood of transience, my dream is to own my own home.

There's nothing like trying to buy a house to trigger a big case of homelessness panic. Maybe it's because my friend Grant keeps reminding me daily that if I bought a house I could lose it—like *that!*—because of my credit card debt. Here's the story: After graduating college I took my fertile, virgin credit history and used it to collect charge cards like key-chain charms. *This is great!* I thought. *Who needs to earn actual cash when all you have to do is flash one of these?* Too bad you're expected to pay back those balances, and not with a check so rubbery you can wrap your boyfriend's dick with it in a pinch. After defaulting on every balance, I eventually agreed to a minimum payment plan that promised I'd be debt-free in only eight hundred years. Before I began to aspire to home ownership, this debt and I coexisted in blissful symbiosis. I made the minimum monthly payments on my giant balances, and the credit agencies never made a fuss about it, and they still don't. But Grant explained to me that I have "credit cancer," and that my outstanding credit card balance is a big financial tumor festering quietly until the day it becomes a five-headed hell-dog of a disease and *infects everything I own and takes away my home*. It was nicer not knowing this, back when I had both a big bank account *and* a big outstanding credit card balance. It hadn't occurred to me to use one to diminish the other, but now, after I've siphoned off my bank account to cure myself of credit cancer, I'm as broke as I've always been, minus the comforting illusion of prosperity.

So if, as I fear, I'm going to be homeless, I should get comfortable with it. As it happens I've actually had some practice. One night, years ago, in New Orleans my whole family was homeless because the Le Richelieu hotel got our reservations mixed up, having scheduled our arrival for noon on the following day, instead of midnight that night. All the other hotels in New Orleans were booked solid, and the Le Richelieu (remember that name: LE RICHELIEU), unsympathetic to our situation, kicked all of us, a mother and her three daughters, into the street, in the middle of the night.

"Well, it's not the end of the world," my mother sighed as we set out to wander the French Quarter until sunrise. At 3 A.M. we encountered an off-duty waitress on her way home from work. She took us in, and we slept on the floor of her living room. The next morning she wouldn't even let us buy her breakfast. So we checked into our hotel, and that night we returned to her restaurant and requested her section. My mother tipped her $125, which is almost unheard of from a homeless person, especially a notoriously cheap one with the shower curtain from our hotel room stuffed into her purse.

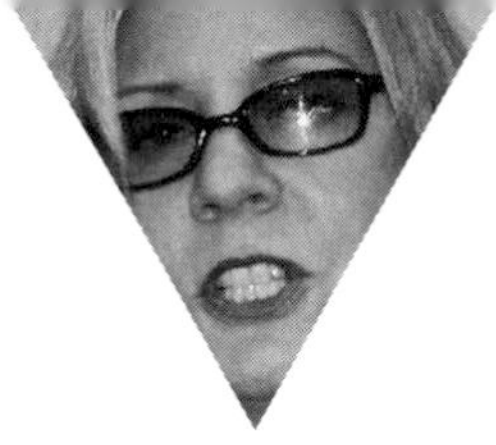

Stealing Home

You would think that having a klepto in the family would be fun, but my mother could never steal the right things. For instance, what was with the *pool cues*? She collected pool cues like souvenir spoons, yet she couldn't shoot a game to save herself from a jail sentence. In fact, I never once saw my mother play billiards, yet we always had pool cues piled in our house like giant pick-up sticks.

This freaky theft fetish started after she left my father and moved into one of those apartment complexes catering to broken lives, the kind that offers fully furnished units stylishly decorated to look like bank lobbies. These places are usually stuffed with other finger-snapping separated people pretending to be ecstatic about their situations, and there is always a community billiard room.

That's when the pool cue fetish began. She also liked to steal lawn furniture and potted plants, but that was probably because, after the divorce was final, she moved to the beach in San Diego, where it's taken for granted that people's patios are to be routinely looted like Korean convenience stores. Out there, if it's on your patio and not locked down, it's considered you don't really want it anyway, and the people who take the stuff almost think they're doing you a service, like clearing dirty plates off your table at a restaurant.

"Let me get that out of your way," my mother thought every time she passed an unsecured beach chair. You'd think the chairs would have piled up in our house as well, like the pool cues, but her own patio was unrestricted, and her hot lawn furniture was stolen back from her almost as soon as she could arrange it in a welcoming pattern on her deck.

I once watched a news program that profiled bands of thieving women who wore really loose muumuus and could, for instance, walk out of a department store with a TV between their knees. I remember thinking, "Why can't Mom steal stuff like that?" Instead, what did we have? Pool cues, shower curtains, hotel-room keys, an entire sleeve of those individually wrapped little soaps from an airplane lavatory. Don't ask me how, but she once stole a six-deck card shoe from a casino blackjack table. Do you know the sleight of hand required to steal off the top of a casino table? You practically need to be David Copperfield to pull that off.

"Why didn't you take the row of hundred-dollar chips *right next* to the card shoe?" I asked.

"Are you kidding?" she blustered, eyes wide. "That would be *stealing*."

Mom had been stealing ever since I could remember. Whenever we moved, she would take something from the old place with her: sink fixtures, switch-plate covers, cabinet doors, a fireplace mantel. It got to the point where we needed a separate truck just to haul all the dismembered parts of our past residences.

The pool cues were an enduring mystery though. Why would she take them, when she never played pool in her life? Everything else she could have at least used, even though most of it she never did. After she passed away we found a pink toilet seat she took from a hotel in New Orleans. My sisters and I, on the other hand, learned to play pool like prison parolees. We started young, back in grade school when we walked to my father's favorite bar after class so we wouldn't be home unsupervised while my mother was at work. We racked the balls while my dad belted beers and joked with the other regulars, and when the clock struck 5 P.M. we went home to greet my mother.

She used to argue with him, saying that a bar was a bad place to bring up children, and why couldn't we spend that time at a park or a pizza joint or somewhere more wholesome? "They like it there!" her husband would holler. "They've got pool, air hockey, Pong! It's paradise!"

Later, after she left him and we went to stay with her, she began presenting us with the pool cues. "I want you to feel at home," she told us. It was the first time I saw her nervous.

So maybe it does make sense, the pool cues and all. Looking back at all the parts she stole from our past homes, it almost got to the point where we didn't need a new place at all, just walls to hold all the pieces of the old places together. Maybe that's why she took all that random stuff—the bathroom medicine cabinets, the curtain rods, the doorknobs, the *stairs* (she actually took a wrought-iron spiral staircase once)—maybe she was simply, little by little, trying to steal us a home of our own.

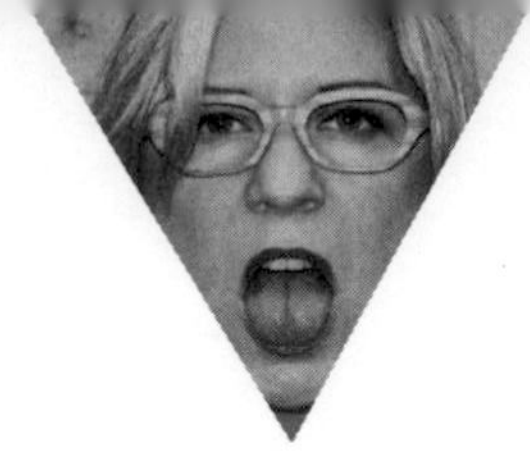

The Happiest Man Alive

Lary insists he saved my life that day on the phone during one of my more memorable homelessness panics, but now he says he's convinced suicide would have been the better option, hence his recurring offers to shoot me. But I think he's secretly glad I decline them, because who else would he find to feed his fleabag cat while he's away?

Not Grant, that's for sure. Grant doesn't do cats, not since he baby-sat mine overnight one time and wouldn't let her sleep on his head. Grant has a head like a nest of autumn leaves, cobwebs and all, and you can't blame cats for wanting to sleep on it, but Grant says he was traumatized by waking up in the middle of the night with a cat on his head, and all I can say to that is "yeah, right," because Grant has awakened to a lot worse, believe me. Sometimes I wonder if he is in some kind of personal contest to see what nightmare might be next to him when he opens his eyes in the morning. After picking up some slag from the Heretic, where he goes every week on "Lights Out" night, when everybody blindly balls each other in pitch-blackness, Grant would even sleep with his hand in a fist so as to hinder his watch from being stolen in the night. It didn't work, so now he wears a cheap watch from Target and sleeps with his hands relaxed. Actually *sleeps*.

"I wonder that I'm alive," Grant says with a smile.

See? I keep telling Lary that *Grant* is the one he should be worried about, not me, given Grant's alarming lack of concern over his survival in dangerous situations. For example, I don't think it's exactly *safe* to be traipsing off into the woods with a trio of Mexican military cadets. But that's Grant. He likes to hit on heterosexual men too, another dangerous endeavor. Sometimes I think the only reason Grant has heterosexual male friends at all is because he's hoping one day to pounce on one in a weak moment and turn them to his side. He sincerely thinks all men are gay, except our friend Chris, but I know Grant is just saying that because Chris gets his hair cut for five dollars at a place on Metropolitan Parkway with a sign out front that advertises "Fades and Braids." No self-respecting gay man alive would appear in public with haircuts that bad. Even Grant, with his cobwebs, keeps his curls in methodically gelled disarray. It's just the bad haircut that keeps Chris from being fair game for Grant, and it's a good thing too, because Chris would probably kill him if he tried anything.

So, if you ask me, it's Grant who is suicidal, not me, since he's always offering it as an alternative whenever I ask him anything. The other day I called to tell him I was having a hard time finding curtains big enough to cover the clerestory windows in my loft. "What do I do?" I implored.

"Suicide," he said.

Obviously, Grant needs help. I thought this phase would pass, but it just gets worse. Once I called him to see what he was doing. "Nothing," he said, "I got no dreams, no goals, no aspirations . . . I'm the happiest man alive."

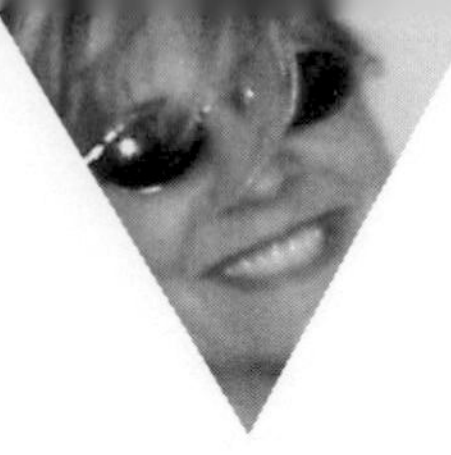

Curse of Financial Fools

So now I'm cursed with some kind of property clock, as opposed to the biological type. I can just feel it *tick, tick, ticking* until I'm old and it's too late to amass the fortune I always figured it would take to make a down payment. And regarding money, I take after my mother, who spent hers unwisely, as opposed to my father, who didn't make any at all and also spent my mother's money unwisely. I started work when I was fourteen, making $1.75 an hour as a trainee at Baskin-Robbins, and spent my entire first paycheck on a puka-shell necklace. A few months later I was fired for being morose. I'd just seen the movie *Jaws,* which affected me deeply, and I would spend most of my shifts sitting on top of the reach-in freezer wondering aloud what it would feel like to be bit in half by a shark. It didn't help that my boss, Mrs. Beeson, had an amputated index finger on her right hand. Missing body parts always stoke the fire of an adolescent's imagination.

Later, of course, I got that job at the magazine. People who know me now laugh when they hear I used to have an office job, and that I used to share that office, which was the size of a guest bedroom, with three crusty copy editors: one an overbearing sexual pervert and two others who smoked like walking sausage factories. Our hate for one another was so thick it was almost nourishing, but it all ended for me quietly one day after I watched my boss eat a bowl of soup. It was that simple.

The other magazine employees had normal work schedules, but my department was different. For example, on the day my brother was hospitalized for emergency heart surgery, I was reprimanded for having spent only eight hours at the office before leaving to be with him. "You really need to get back here and help us finish this work," the senior copy editor said into my answering machine that night. He had big lips and a body like a seven-foot bowling pin. He used to play bongo drums for a defunct sixties band called Big Fat Momma. The time of that message was 10:21 P.M. A month later he sent me an odd but purely obscene e-mail about how he liked to stir chocolate fondue with his schlong. The e-mail's last word was "creeeeeamy."

They liked to tell me my laughter lowered their concentration level, until I said it was a good trade-off since their smoking lowered my life expectancy. My coworker Eugenia was as fond of her cigarettes as was our immediate boss, who would fervently puff away while devoting an entire day investigating whether "corn stick" was one word, two words, or hyphenated. Me, I felt it would be more fun to spend the day ripping out my own kidneys with a rusty crowbar, so it didn't take them long to turn on me.

They were gathering evidence to get me canned while I was gathering momentum to make their lives miserable. But one day I saw my boss sitting at his desk holding a big, shallow bowl of beef vegetable soup. It wasn't an uncommon sight—for fifteen years I don't think that man ever left his office for lunch hour—so I don't know why it affected me so profoundly that day in particular. It just did. He dipped the spoon into the bowl, slowly scooped away from himself, and then slowly lifted the spoon to his lips. Hunched like he was, the psoriasis scabs on his scalp showed through his thinning hair. I had considered him mean, petty, unforgiving, and unfair—but then I saw him with that soup, and I had to leave.

I went outside, sat in my car, and sobbed. After a while, a woman from the sales department came up and said something to me through the window. She had misinterpreted my tears and meant to comfort me. "From the first day we saw you in that office," she said, "we've all been saying you don't fit in." She meant it as a compliment.

I've had other jobs—coat-check girl on the docked *Queen Mary* in Los Angeles, beef-log sample giver at Swiss Colony, and waitress on the graveyard shift at a coffee shop in San Diego when I was seventeen. I remember that one in particular because of the night a drunk reached up and pinched my nipple through my uniform while I poured him a cup of coffee. Nearby sat the owner of a mid-scale Mexican restaurant located down the street. He regularly stopped in for eggs and an English muffin after his place closed for the night. His restaurant had regular hours and a better clientele, so I approached him and asked for a job, figuring a healthier environment would do me some good. His response was to tell me I was lucky to have the job I had, which caused me to become more angry at him than I was at the nipple-pinching dickwit, because it's a fathomless insult to tell an idealistic teenager she is "lucky" to make a living that includes having to tolerate being pawed by wasted pigs. In response to his remark, I sat the coffee pot down on his omelet, took off my apron, and left.

In keeping with the curse of financial foolery I inherited from my parents, I spent the money I made during this period on rounds of margaritas for my friends and dates at the Del Mar racetrack. My recently divorced mother bought a sleek Datsun 260Z, even though she couldn't drive it because she had broken her left foot while hang gliding in Mexico a month earlier. She could have used that money as a down payment on the beachfront condo we were renting at the time, but sixty thousand dollars was "laughably expensive" for a place with only two bedrooms, she said. Today that place is worth half a million.

These days I still lack knowledge of what to do with money other than pay bills and buy more rounds, but lately I've been having a hankering for "holdings," even though I'm not sure I know what those are. I dream of owning a home of my own. I mean that literally too. In my dreams I'm always checking out houses, assessing their cabinets and ceiling height, their "curb appeal." None of them are ever right, and I hate it when I have those dreams. I wish I would find a fucking house, even if it's just in my head, but I keep moving from empty house to empty house and all of them are somehow off, like the view to the beach is blocked or the street out front is too busy or there are *no doors*. God, I hate those dreams, which always make me feel like I'll always be homeless.

But then that feeling fades and eventually I'll start dreaming different dreams, like I'll start thinking maybe I can pull it off, this homeownership thing. Maybe I could clean up my credit, save some money, and one day actually own a home of my own. Maybe I will, after all, outlive a gypsy fortune-teller's recent assessment of me: "You have no trouble acquiring money," she said as she peered into my palm, "you just have trouble keeping it." Then she charged me twenty-five dollars.

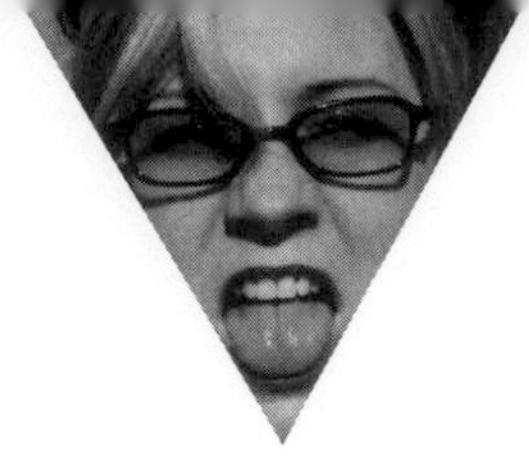

Eight Naked Strangers

Recently I was staring at eight naked strangers. One of them was so deeply tanned I'd taken to calling her "Suitcase Face," another had a body like a pail of paste, another had tits so fake she could use them to caulk bathtub tile. And the men were *really* laughable. One had a gut so big it hung down low enough to cover up all his naughty bits, and another had no ass at all, just this weird concavity where his butt should have been.

They were splayed out by the pool, marinating themselves in sunlight like sacrifices offered up to the cancer gods. I hope they didn't see me up there gawking at them through my window, appreciating one of the perks of scoring a room that overlooked the hotel sundeck on a rare sweltering day in Switzerland. "How did that lady live to be a hundred?" I asked myself, eyeing a wizened twig whose skin had baked into beef jerky. Surely, with all that sun exposure, she'd have grown a sarcomatous tumor the size of a Siamese twin by now. But then I realized she might not be that old after all—it could just be the aging effects of the sun. It ages you, doesn't it? And the nakedness. The nakedness probably didn't help.

I remember being naked in public only once. Notice I say "remember," because Lary swears six years ago he practically had to tackle me to keep me from stripping on the streets in Prague, which makes no sense at all to me. I remember nothing like that happening that night, though I do remember Lary trying to convince a gay Czech street hustler that I was a pre-op transsexual, telling him I'd be happy to drop my pants to prove it. I don't remember this striptease he claimed I performed, though the next morning I did notice that the spaghetti straps on my blouse were ripped. But that could have happened a number of ways, like during the drunken "hump dance" I did on the bar with some circus performers.

I've been naked in public before, just not always knowingly. In college I once went dancing with a handsome frat boy, and I wore black lace stockings under a dress of airy material that buttoned down the entire length of my back. I remember noticing all these people watching me as I shimmied on the dance floor, and here I thought it must be because I looked so damn hot. I discovered later, though, that my groping date had earlier undone almost all the buttons down my back. So the whole time these people were not watching me because I looked so damn hot, they were staring at me because my tatty ass was hanging out the back of my dress. It took me an entire decade to stop dying of embarrassment over that.

But there is more than one kind of nakedness, because that is nothing compared to the state of nakedness I was suffering when I met Lary. Back when I first moved to Atlanta, when I was lonely and worked at a clique-afflicted coffeehouse because I had no better way to waste my time, I could not possibly have been more miserable, and I don't think I had a single damn friend except Lary. I'd met him months earlier at the wedding of his ex-girlfriend, a lovely person he was a fool to let slip away, but if Lary is not foolish he is not himself. Thank God. We bonded like a broken teacup, Lary and

I, all the freaky shards of our damaged personalities fitting together to form the bride of Frankenstein, but by that time Lary had already grown the crab shell he likes to keep around his heart.

I was a different story; I was all out there. I was fresh from just having lost everything: my last parent, my live-in boyfriend, my home, my youthful incorruptibility, the last remnant of my ragged optimism, and my ability to keep it all inside and covered up. God, I was as shattered as a wrecked windshield and just as transparent, and I wore it like the opposite of a bulletproof vest, wide open and just too much to conceal. My state of wretchedness leaked out of me for everyone to see.

I swear, it was like the ass of my emotions was always hanging out. I was a shipwreck; fascinating from a distance but you wouldn't want to be *in* one. I hadn't built the emotional damn yet, didn't even know how, and about four minutes into a conversation with me people would literally begin to *back away* from the flood.

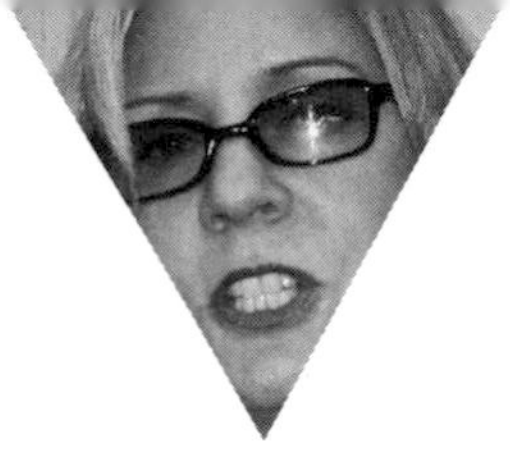

The *Perfect* Father

Like I've always said, there are advantages to being the daughter of an alcoholic trailer salesman. For example, I learned how to make the perfect Bloody Mary before I turned ten. My father didn't teach me—he favored beer, as evidenced by his favorite hat fashioned from flattened Budweiser cans bound together by blue yarn. No, it was a bartender named Kitty who taught me. "Angel," she'd say as she lined up the various canisters needed to concoct the drink, "this here is the *perfect* Bloody Mary."

Kitty worked at the Thin Lizzy in Costa Mesa, where my father hung out. Kitty had the cackle laugh of a chain-smoker and bleached hair that was teased into a beehive helmet. She shot the breeze with my father while I drank Shirley Temples, ate potato chips, and perfected my pool game. My father didn't play pool but placed bets on me nonetheless. The secret ingredient in a perfect

Bloody Mary, by the way, is one dissolved cube of beef bouillon. My father hated Bloody Marys.

"Making more red vomit, Kitty?" he'd say.

"Get the hell out of here, you useless sack o' crap," laughed Kitty, who was quite crusty. She always made my father chuckle. It didn't work for me, though, because later—thinking I had the green light from Kitty—I myself jokingly called him a useless sack of crap and his response was to beat the crap out of me. My mistake, I think, was that I was not handing him a beer when I said it.

There are other benefits to being the daughter of an alcoholic trailer salesman, such as wisdom. For example, my father always kept packets of peanuts scattered about the front seat of our family Fairlane. He once told me conspiratorially that peanuts mask booze breath better than peppermint gum. That there is knowledge, if you ask me.

He would always put me in the front seat of the car and insist that I not wear a seatbelt. "You don't want to wear a seatbelt," he said, "because if you're strapped in, you can't get thrown clear of the wreckage. It's always better to get thrown clear," and he'd finish by waving his arm in a sweeping motion, as if to indicate that, at the moment of impact, my prepubescent body would fly out the window and float down on a distant patch of cushy clover.

"Because blue-eyed angels don't die in car wrecks," he'd say, "they get thrown clear."

My mother disagreed with him. "With that logic," she would yell at him, "you should just let her sit outside on the hood of the car, because that's where she's gonna end up anyway." But still I sat, unstrapped, eating peanuts and laughing as my father ran red lights and popped curbs.

He once ran over a lady's foot, but that's because she deserved it, he said. "Anyway, she's walking fine," he observed as we watched her scramble away. I was impressed with how fast she could run with that limp.

The main benefit to being the daughter of an alcoholic trailer salesman was the trailers themselves. My dad's trailers were nicer than our houses, and we preferred campgrounds that were more like concrete parking lots, with "hookups," whatever those are (I just know we always drove around until we found a campsite that offered them).

My father let me cook on our camp-outs, and one night I put the steaks on the grill when the coals were too hot, so the meat caught fire. The flames shot so high I thought pigeons would fall—fully charred—from the sky. I frantically doused the grill with a bucket of water, and when the smoke cleared the steaks were covered in ash. So I speared each one, hosed them off, then refired the grill and started over. My father watched the whole process from his lawn chair, Bud cans both on his head and in his hand. He barely raised a brow.

"Angel," he said later when I served him dinner, "this here is the *perfect* steak."

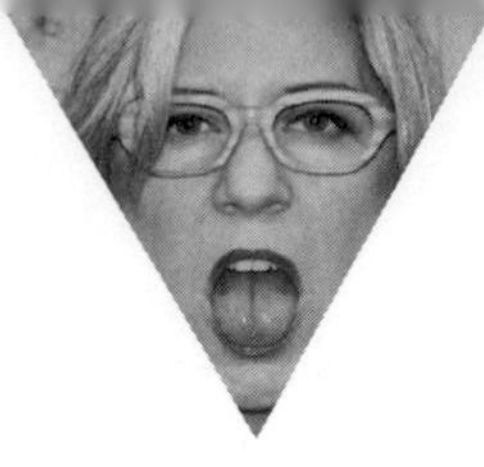

Drowning

My little sister was saved by our dog once. She was on her way to the pool in our apartment complex and, since she was only eleven months old, faced certain death, no doubt. I was just three myself, but I remember that day, as I do the day my parents brought her home after she was born. "Look what we found in the hospital parking lot!" my father exclaimed that morning, wheeling the carriage into the room. That is about all I remember of that day, except for the fact that I never got a good look at the baby. People were constantly crowded around her carriage like car wreck witnesses, and she was so swathed in cotton she might as well have been a bundle of underwear. I couldn't figure out the fuss, but the fuss soon dissipated. I mean, this was my mother's fourth kid, after all. I was her third.

The day Kimberly came home from the hospital, while my father was joking with the well-meaning neighbors and the extended family members with whom we were still on speaking terms, my mother sat alone on the patio, smoking her fourth menthol that morning. "Did you hear what I said, honey?" my father called out to her above the hearty guffaws of the visitors. She nodded and waved from the other side of the sliding glass door, mouthing the words "parking lot." Most likely she had heard it before, another of my father's well-worn shticks, which he probably pulled out and performed at all their previous spawnings. "Look what we found in the parking lot," my father repeated, slapping his knee.

I don't remember how my sister, eleven months later, actually came to *be* in a parking lot, alone and unnoticed by all except our smart mutt Echo, but she would have had to crawl across one to get to the pool. Evidently Echo stood between my sister and the water and barked so menacingly that it kept my sister from advancing. This drew the attention of our neighbor, a large Hawaiian lady with flared nostrils and black hair piled in a bun as big as a bicycle seat on top of her head. The scene startled her out of the hammock she had hung in her living room, and she bustled over to our place to knock on our open door and tell my father that my baby sister was at that moment being attacked by a dog down by the pool.

My father darted past her and across the parking lot, where he saw Echo holding vigil near the pool's edge, where my sister wailed like a frustrated little seal, unable to reach the water and commence drowning. I'm told there was no tearful clutching of my sister to my father's chest or anything, no shower of kisses on her cherished face and precious blond head. No, he simply took her by the hand and led her back home, where he opened another Budweiser and fashioned a barricade out of dining room chairs to keep my sister's wanderings isolated to the area between his feet on the ottoman and his favorite game show on TV.

After that my mother insisted that Echo sleep inside with us, rather than on the patio behind the sliding glass door, even though it meant that our home became so infested with jumping fleas you could actually *see* them en masse like a little dusky cloud that always stayed at ankle level above our carpet. It was two years after saving my sister that Echo gave birth to the litter of puppies under the big wooden desk in my brother's bedroom. They were sweet little mutts like their mother, with coats of red fur that would turn wiry one day.

Then came the afternoon I thought it would be fun to place one of them on the end of a tennis racket and flip it like a furry little burger. When, weeks later, the guy who adopted it demanded another one because that one had died, my mother told me not to blame myself. "Some puppies don't make it," she said with little sentiment.

Echo, though, was a different story. That dog became a conduit for my mother's sanity, a loving presence in the midst of an often unloving marriage fraught with blame and broken dreams. Often I would find my mother asleep on the couch in the morning, clutching Echo like a life preserver. When Echo died a decade later, it was my mother who found her curled up in the garage, under the big wooden desk that used to belong to my brother. She closed the door and wouldn't let us come inside. My sisters and I hovered by the door waiting, but my mother stayed in there all morning, holding vigil over our old mutt Echo, the sweet old dog that saved people from drowning.

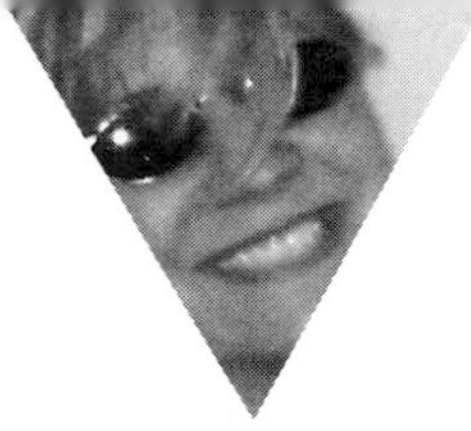

Piercing Experience

I'm not suicidal, but sometimes I look around and wonder if I need any more evidence that I'm wasting my life. I don't date. My three best friends are men, none of them romantic prospects (except possibly for each other). Two of them, Daniel and Grant, are addicted to colonics and take great pleasure in calling me with daily updates detailing their stool consistency. The other, Lary, drives a rusty BMW with big, plastic, biblical characters stolen from a lawn nativity scene sitting upright in the backseat like cab passengers. One of our favorite things to do together is go to the Clermont Lounge, where the strippers are all flawed in the most amazing ways. One is so fat we've nicknamed her "Butterball." Another has so many tattoos she doesn't even look naked when she's naked. Another is the survivor of a botched boob job and had to have her implants removed, so now her tits just dangle there, withered, like two turkey wattles.

We pass out money and sit there, completely certain that we're

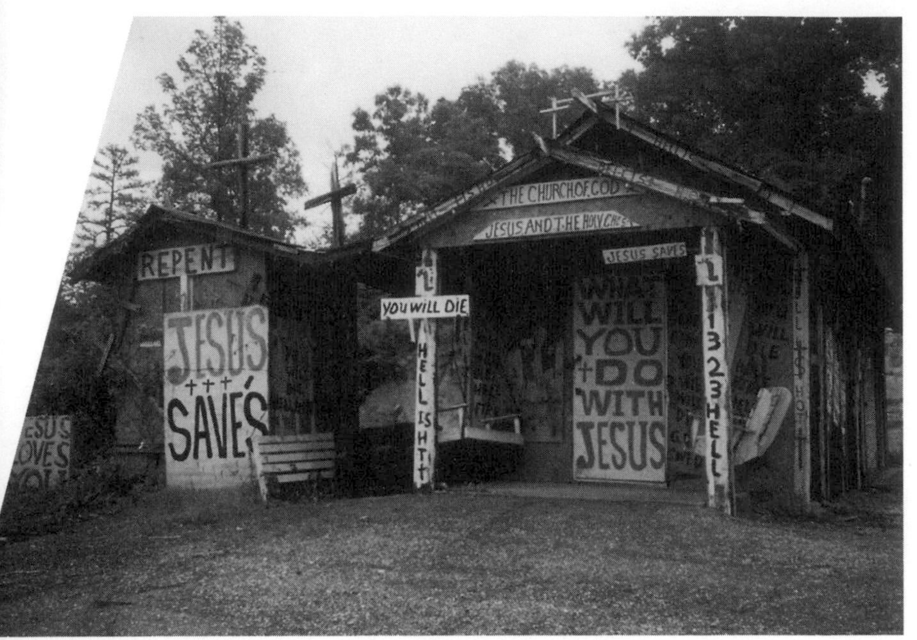

Roadside religious signs

safe from meeting anyone remotely right for us. Sometimes a girlfriend will advise me to get away from these guys, to move to more conservative Sandy Springs and live in a stylish apartment building, which is known as an outpost for single airline pilots, rather than the renovated telephone factory where I now reside. But then I look at my job, which is artist/writer/photographer/flight attendant/foreign-language interpreter, and my office, which is decorated with plywood signs stolen from the roadside, and the bumper sticker on my car, which reads "Teenage Prostitute to the Stars," and I realize, *Oh my God, I belong with these people!* So I've resigned myself to my place with them, and with that resignation I figure I might as well get myself pierced.

The first time I saw body piercing I was in Amsterdam browsing through titles in the self-mutilation section of a bookstore when I came across a picture of a woman who looked like she had her vagina impaled on the contents of an entire toolbox. After seeing that, it was a few days before I could unclench my knees. After that, the last place I figured I'd find myself was in a piercing parlor sitting in some kind of modified dental chair with—and maybe my memory is exaggerated here—*stirrups,* looking at a woman with hair like a nest of festering albino tarantulas. But there she was, coming at me with a spike bigger than the kind cavemen used to kill bison, and there I was, clasping Grant's hand so tight he pulled away a lobster claw.

As piercings go, mine isn't that exotic. It's in plain view, on the inside of my ear, which means there's no hardware clanking around in my underwear. Every once in a while some stranger standing next to me in line will hiss, "Did that hurt?" In which case I get to turn around with my usual aplomb and say, "Hell yes it hurt! I could have given birth to a full-grown grizzly bear and it wouldn't have hurt half as much! Jesus God, 'course it hurt! And the *swelling!* I had a head like Elephant Man for two weeks! And that's not even considering the 'crust' factor!"

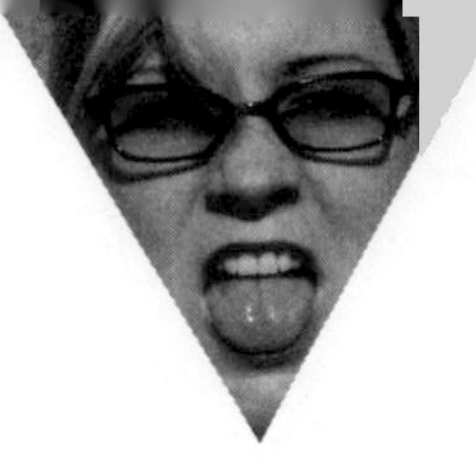

The Most Merciless Weapon

A lug wrench makes a decent weapon. I know this because I used to carry one in my glove compartment back when I drove my ancient Volkswagen, which cost me two hundred dollars and was held together by duct tape and silicone tile caulking. The car ran out of gas often back then because, like me, the gas gauge wasn't working at the time. Hence I was stranded a lot, and I'd hike the highway to the nearest phone clutching my lug wrench in case I'd need to drive it like a metal stake through the skull of a passing serial killer.

"Nobody's gonna leave my murdered carcass splayed on the roadside for early-morning joggers to trip across!" I'd tell myself as I stomped along. "I'm not gonna be lying there dead with every orifice violated, not me, because I've got this, you know, *thing* here, this metal whatever-it-is. So, yeah, I'd like to see somebody try something, especially now that I've decided constant practice swings are in order until I reach a safe destination."

I'd walk along, throwing random jabs, spinning around, thinking I heard something. "Who's there?" I'd hiss. "Take *that!*" And I'd continue to lunge about like a hallucinating heroin addict, because they're out there, people who want to hurt you, and you have to be prepared.

Gather your weapons. Lary carries a gun in his glove compartment. I don't know how comfortable I am with that because I really think a lug wrench would do fine. I've never had to hit anyone with mine, but I bet it would hurt. My mother once fought off a biker in New Orleans with a broken souvenir Hurricane glass from Pat O'Brien's. He wasn't actually trying to kill us or anything, the biker, in fact he was simply riding his Harley really slow and it kind of looked like he might have been leering in our direction. So my mother waved the weapon at him as he went by, and he kept going.

Looking back, you'd think my mother could have done better than a broken glass, seeing as how she made her living designing defense weapons. She probably also could have done better than to serve her kids bowls of Halloween candy for breakfast too, but at the time I thought it was great, and by first period I had such a sugar buzz I could bend spoons with my brain.

My father didn't like us eating candy for breakfast, but he slept late because it took a lot of energy to charm people into buying him beers at his favorite bar all night. Sometimes, though, he'd make it a point to rise early and force-feed us something weird like Welsh rarebit topped with capers or whatever. He put capers on everything, and pearl onions. He liked to experiment with different cuisines, creating complicated entrées like oyster soufflé and homemade rabbit-bladder sausage and stuff, with capers and pearl onions everywhere.

He might as well have been asking us to eat battery acid, I mean that's how eagerly we anticipated his dinners. We became experts at squirreling food in our pockets to feed to the dog on bathroom breaks. Sometimes my father would throw his hands up in exasperation at our philistine palates, then it would fall upon my mother to make her famous tamale pie from a box, which required nothing more complicated than browning a pound of burger meat. We feasted on it like famine victims while my father stood in the corner of the kitchen and chain-smoked.

Once he went on a failed bread-baking binge, which resulted in about thirty loaves as dense as bricks wrapped in tinfoil that he kept by the kitchen door. I remember thinking those would make good weapons, and I planned to use them on any rapists attempting to invade the homestead.

A few months after my mother left us, she forced my father to leave our family apartment, having reached her limit, I suppose, when it came to paying his rent. After that she didn't immediately move back in with us herself, opting to live out the lease on her temporary pad instead. During this time, whether my father was living with us or not, my sisters and I almost always ate dinner with my mother at her groovy singles apartment complex, chowing down on char-grilled hot dogs at the sleazy poolside "mixers." But before my mother kicked him out, my father still cooked us dinners every night back at our family home in anticipation of our appearance, and I remember seeing their cold remnants in the kitchen the next morning, intact except for the small portions missing he had served himself. Once I noticed he'd made us a tamale pie, but not from a box, and he'd topped it with capers and pearl onions. Looking back, I wish we could have pretended we liked some of his meals, but when you're young your weapon is honesty, which is perhaps the most merciless of them all.

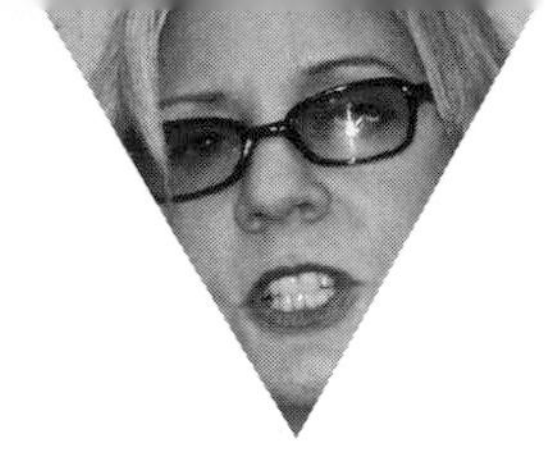

Dance of Life

Lary and I went to a nightclub the other night and he, as usual, stayed across the room in case I felt like dancing, not that I ever do anymore. There is no actual physical restraint keeping me from dancing—like a broken javelin imbedded in my head, for instance—so technically I suppose you could say I am capable of dancing. In college I used to quasi-dance. It was the eighties, and I was a quivering, cocaine-fueled blur that needed to expend energy. Once the burden of tuition fees had forced me to drop my drug habit, though, I rarely danced again, instead isolating my spasmodic outbursts to those times when I was blotto and inexplicably overconfident. Ten years ago, exceptionally soused, I actually tried to charm Lary into dancing with me, figuring heavy flirting was in order.

"Goddammit, you crusty pocket of butt rot," I slurred, "get out there on the dance floor with me."

Lary doesn't "do" dancing. And even if a comet passed within four feet of his head, creating a magnetic force that completely altered his physical aura and infused all the molecules in his body with a jolt of electrons responsive to sound waves that caused his toe to begin tapping to a beat, he would *still* never dance with me. He has seen me dance, and when I dance, he says, I look like a mental patient swatting at imaginary insects.

That's not to say there weren't times when I thought I was hot. Under the delusional influence of youth and the correct bucketload of alcohol, I could convince myself I was tearing up the floor, that people were actually clearing the way to get a better look at the physical wizardry of my technique, and that a spotlight was actually descending upon me from above because the DJ had discerned that my incredible ability to boogie was the standard to which everyone in the club should aspire.

God, I'm gorgeous, I remember thinking at those times. *I'm young and beautiful and free and unfettered and I could fucking fly if I wanted, just take off and catch a wave and surf the world with my mermaid hair and my wide eyes, and I can reach with my goddamn twenty-two-year-old fingers and wrap my hands around the heart of the universe and run with my arms outstretched across a field of feathery daffodils forever and everyone here knows it.*

But then I grew up and learned that I have the internal rhythm of a well-used med-school cadaver. So I try not to dance too much anymore, because I have faced the reality of my limits, unlike this woman I saw at a club while I was in college. She was drunk and had stringy hair, partaking in some after-office celebration and undulating like an offbeat walrus all over the dance floor. You could tell she thought she was hot, when really she was out of place, deluded by booze into thinking she was as lithe as an acrobat, as desirable as a runway model, her face radiating a pathetic, misplaced elation. Watching her, I held her in the highest contempt, and my eyes bored rays of hate into her private little capsule of complete joy. I resolved to never end up like her, to never be caught dancing with all the grace of a plastered parent crashing her kids' sock hop.

I am amazed at how often I think of that woman now. Images of her constantly flash into my mind. I remember her black dress, and her cascade of brassy, bleached hair, her jubilation, and her complete conviction that she was incandescent. Sometimes I feel the same revulsion I felt at the time. *She should have faced the reality of her limits.*

But other times it's different. *Look at her go,* I observe, as the image plays over in my head, and the woman forever dances awkwardly on, her jowls wagging in a beatific grin, her toneless upper arms waddling at odds with the music. I want to recapture the same pity and conceit I felt when I first saw her, the conviction that she is trespassing on undeserved territory, but I'm unable to muster that old feeling. Instead, as the phantom woman does a few lunging twirls and then faces full on the camera lens of my memory—her eyes alight and her arms outstretched—I have to catch my breath because she is so beautiful.

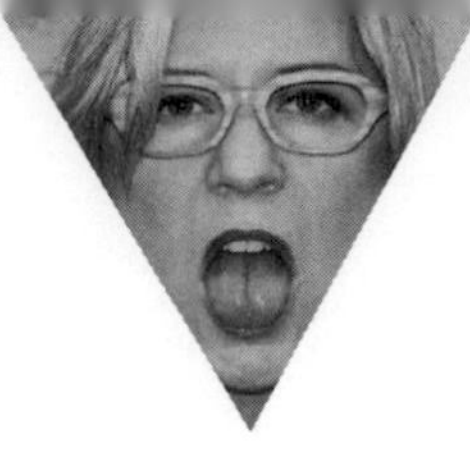

Something Caught

I just got popped for speeding on the way home. Daniel was in the car, and not until the officer was gone did we figure out the perfect way to get out of a speeding ticket: You pretend you have something caught in your throat, and then ask the police officer to kindly use his penis to help dislodge it. Lary says that would work if he were a police officer, but probably not if he were the perpetrator.

Like he should worry. Lary is almost immune to police. I couldn't even get the police to handcuff him when he was shooting at people running through the parking lot that abuts his backyard. Granted, they were burglars Lary had caught in the act of robbing his house, but I don't see how the police could have known that at first. I figured I'd at least get to see a SWAT showdown before matters got sorted. But no, Lary says they told him not to miss next time, and to just drag the bodies from the parking lot onto his property, thereby reinforcing a self-defense scenario.

"What about the trail of blood?" Lary sensibly asked them.

"We won't see it," Lary says they answered.

Daniel and I don't enjoy that kind of privilege when it comes to police, so we're basically law abiding, except for the occasional traffic ticket, and we wouldn't get those if not for Freedom Parkway. The police swarm like hornets around that stretch of road, which appears to be a seamless offshoot from the freeway, except for a thirty-five mph limit. When you exit onto the parkway, it's practically impossible *not* to speed. You have to brake as if approaching a barricade, and most people don't bother. A lot get caught.

I got caught, and I hate that "caught" feeling. I hate it when you're flying along, enjoying life, and something stops you cold, sucking all the fun out of everything. For example, the other day I was in New York, on Canal Street, where I had intended to buy a truckload of fake handbags and other designer knockoffs that, to me, are the total ass end of tacky, but evidently they're precious to image pussies back home who are too poor to afford the real thing. I thought I could cash in on that. I mean, what better way to make a buck than to bilk vain people? But while I was at the hotel asking the concierge for directions, a woman at the reception counter next to me casually mentioned that she personally "boycotts" Canal Street.

"Why?" I asked.

"Sweatshop labor," is all she needed to say.

Oh, Christ. Until then I'd been in a happy state of amnesia about the fact that those knockoffs are pumped out by sweatshop workers. I went anyway, though, thinking maybe the guilt would just dissipate as I packed up bagloads of the fake booty and fenced it back home.

I thought about calling Daniel to see if he'd sanction profiting from the misery of immigrants and children. He was busy working on his art opening at the Marcia Wood Gallery, his first since he figured out years ago that he had to stop pumping out fake shit and start creating the real thing, expressing what's really in his heart.

That was when all his unexpressed creativity was caught in his chest like a big fish bone because he was too inhibited to let it loose. Today, let me tell you, he has let it loose.

You never know with him. He just might have shouted, "Crack the whip on those overworked adolescent asses, honey!" He's capable of being quite salty sometimes. To this day, he swears that Pearl, his goldfish, died accidentally when . . . let's face it, it's pretty hard to accidentally grind your goldfish up in the garbage disposal. And when he and his boyfriend Mitch decided to move in together, Daniel seriously suggested a good way to accommodate Mitch's cat would be to close her up miles away in a rented storage compartment.

I didn't call him after all. It wouldn't have mattered what he said. I knew I couldn't cope with the image of little fingers toiling away in an underventilated misery pit when they should be off experiencing the more conventional misery of grade school. So I headed empty-handed back to the subway station. In the center of the crowded platform was a street performer belting out a song, one of those emotional country ballads, and the guy really let loose with his voice. I stood there with the rest of the crowd, envying him. *God, I wish I could do that,* I thought. I wish so badly to be able to let loose with my voice. I wished it so strongly I even started to see it. *Wow, look at me,* I thought. Look at me *singing,* look at me *dancing,* look at me jumping, running, *soaring.* Look at me standing up and shouting out what's in my heart! Then I could feel it welling up. I swear I could feel it coming out! I could feel myself *flying along!*

Then the train came and cut me off. I boarded it with the rest of the horde, having been reverted back to my basic self, having been stopped cold again, with nothing in my hands but something caught in my heart.

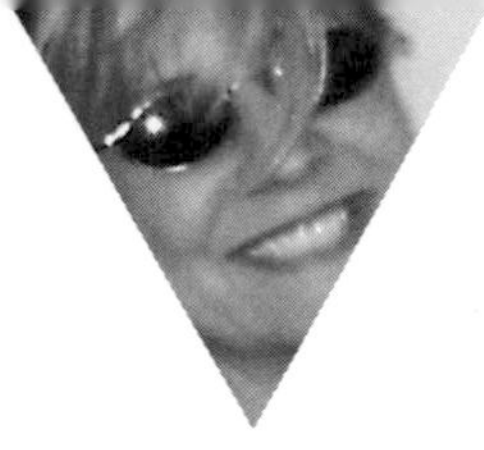

I Can Fly

Isn't there some kind of age limit on acid trips? You'd think that by the time you turn forty or so you'd graduate to *prescribed* drugs and become a legitimate, respectable junkie like a few First Lady runners-up I could name. But Lary is at least five hundred years old—or older than me anyway, not that you'd ever know it by his behavior, which landed him in the hospital yesterday with a concussion and cracked ribs and probably brain damage too, not that you'd be able to tell right off. Essentially what happened is that Lary took acid, climbed the scaffolding inside his warehouse, and flung himself headfirst off the top just like a junkie. His account will differ from mine because I was not actually there, but since he was all hopped up on drugs neither was he if you think about it. Still, he insists he slipped and did not fling himself, and that he did not climb the scaffolding because of a bad trip but because of his bad roof, which is falling down and needs to be fixed.

"Don't give me that," I said. "You thought you could fly, didn't you?"

Lary knows I'm afraid of acid, because as a kid I totally bought into that tax-funded traveling sideshow of ex-addicts who used to visit grade schools and host antidrug rallies, which essentially entailed freaking everybody out with stories of their former junkie escapades. These were not just trite little tales about hippies who thought they could fly. No. For example, one guy took the microphone and told the audience about his drug buddy who had a bad trip one day and barfed out his entire tongue onto the floor. That's right, one second his friend was fine with his tongue attached to the back of his throat and everything, then he took some drugs and *bleh,* there his whole tongue was on the linoleum, raw and quivering like a piece of liver.

Looking back, I realize that's probably not even possible (right?), but for an eight-year-old it painted a pretty graphic picture of what to avoid, and now I can at least look at myself and say I didn't end up a tongueless junkie. Too bad I couldn't, at least in part, extend the same compliment to my best friend. In all, I'm really glad Lary didn't die, because knowing the condition of his place, a fall like that could have easily meant impaling his brain on a big railroad spike. We're pretty close, considering we have little in common. He is the oldest in a brood of ten siblings falteringly brought up by a severely God-fearing mother and a philandering father, and I am the middle kid from a much smaller family that was headed by my mother, an atheist missile scientist and part-time petty klepto with broken aspirations of becoming a beautician, and my father, a boozing unemployed trailer salesman who once had huge dreams for himself, only his fears turned out to be much bigger.

Lary once told me he spent very little time at home while growing up, instead choosing to wander the woods behind his house. That's how I like to picture him, as a child running with his arms outstretched in total solitude, gleeful to be free of the emotional oppression of his home. My own home held a similar aversion for me as a kid. At first, my chain-smoking parents fought with the ferocity of rival tigers, each blaming the other for the fizzle their hopes and dreams had become, but as the years passed, that anger hardened into a calcified weight that simply hung there in our house, hidden in the constant blanket of cigarette smoke over our heads.

I used to wait until the middle of the night to escape. After my parents fell asleep, I'd sneak out and run barefoot through our neighbor's vast front lawn. When it was warm I'd unbutton my flannel shirt and just run in the quiet night, back and forth under the moonlight, with my shirt flapping behind me like a little cape, my face hardly able to contain my utter joy.

Then, one morning, my father awoke, rheumy-eyed and shaking. "I saw you in the grass last night," he said angrily. I was immediately terrified, certain he'd mete out his usual punishment, which was to clout me across the ass with the lid of a tin flour canister we kept in the kitchen, but instead he stopped and just stood there. Through the smoke of his cigarette I saw his face suddenly fall as if broken by the weight of all his mistakes, all the steps he took or was too timid to take. But these had nonetheless led him here, to this messy house, confronting an errant child he'd watched gallop barefoot under a full moon in the middle of the night. Looking back, I wish I had taken his whiskered, tortured face in my hands, but I didn't. Instead, I am left with the memory of how he stopped and shook his head, and ran his twitching fingers through his thinning hair. I remember his eyes, his booze-addled eyes, suddenly beseeching for something just outside his reach.

"I saw you," he said again, softly, "and you were flying."

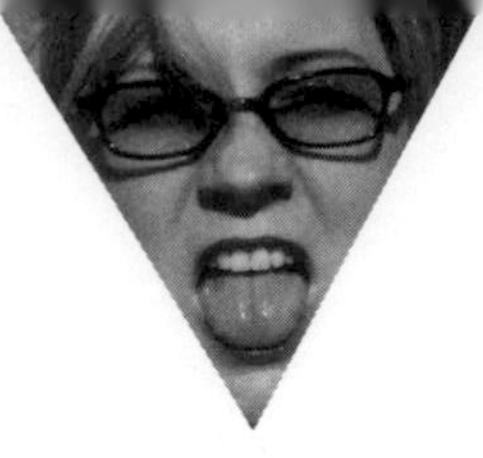

Big Dix

I once spent five days in Vienna as part of my job, and the whole time I had the flu, so I was hostage to a hotel room with a TV that offered only two English-speaking channels, one of which was a pay-per-view porno station. It featured a movie about marauding sex zombies who appeared to be the victims of a horny hypnotist. They ran around rutting everything in sight, until everyone just melded together into a hump of grunting flesh that was stuck together like an undulating, sweaty M.C. Escher painting.

At least I think that's what it was about. The plot was a little unclear, because I could only watch three minutes at a time before the film was automatically charged to my room. Seeing as how the American dollar is so valueless in Europe that people are using it to stuff up peepholes in pay toilets these days, I figured the U.S. currency equivalent of one in-room porn film fest roughly matched the price of a healthy human kidney on the black market.

So because of my reluctance to fork over the dough, it became more of a porn peep show, really, but it got me to thinking: Do men really think women *want* to have sex with a penis the size of a sewage pipe? Do they think we look at someone who could pass for a human tripod and actually say to ourselves, "Oh, wow, won't it be fun to rearrange my inner organs with that thing?!?" Do they think we just can't wait to get our hands on some guy with a penis so huge he would need a blood transfusion if he got aroused?

Judging from this movie (and, I'm sorry, I'm not going to watch eighty more to back up my theory), where the men who sprouted fleshy telephone poles from their pants looked like they were having a great time and the women looked like they were getting clubbed to death, my answer would be: I guess so.

I bet it's because of the average hetero male mentality when it comes to breasts, in which boobs big enough to be seen with the naked eye from passing aircraft are a real treat, that men never believe us when we say size doesn't matter. But think of it this way: During sex, breasts are basically there to provide something to play with. If that were the only purpose of penises, maybe the colossal-equals-boffo theory would apply. But here's a reminder: Penises have to *fit* somewhere. Remember? So, average man, the average woman doesn't salivate at the sight of a penis the size of a ham shank. Our typical reaction would be to calmly excuse ourselves, go to the bathroom, and climb out the window. I'm pretty sure of that.

Most women don't want to feel like they've been trampled on by buffalo after having sex. Afterward a lot of us would just like to be able to walk away from the experience with . . . well, we'd just like to be able to walk.

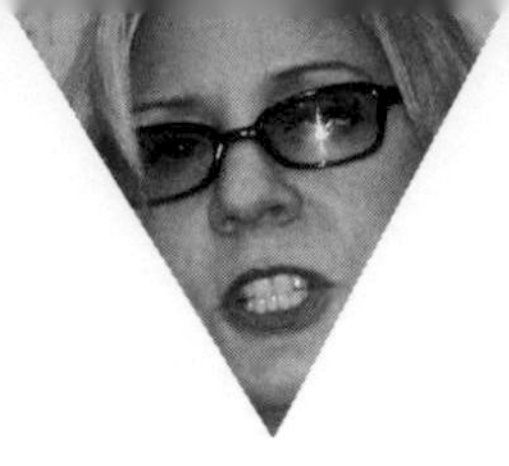

Bona Fide Fag Status

For years Daniel, Grant, and I have lusted after the same hot bicycle cop in Virginia-Highland. Maybe you've seen him, the one with tan arms like carved marble emerging from his short-sleeved uniform. At first sight of him, Grant practically soared out of his seat and stuck himself to the window of the coffeehouse like a wet piece of putty. And he wasn't even really *gay* yet (well, of course he was always gay, but at that time he was trapped way in the back of the closet behind an ex-wife, a present wife, a daughter, and a dog named Ellie May). It wasn't just a closet for Grant, it was a cocoon—but when that cop walked by, Grant didn't just come out, he flew out and flapped around the room on opal-colored wings. He was free! After that, the only time his feet touched the ground was to get his toenails painted by that poor Korean girl on Ponce de Leon Avenue. (I say "poor" because you should see Grant's feet, they're *hooves*.)

I had known Grant before he wore his bona fide fag status like the feathered headdress that it is, but not for that long. His heteroness only overlapped with our friendship by a couple months, and during that time our relationship had been as chaste as kindergarten paste. It wasn't until later, when Grant had finally gotten in touch with his inner impishness, that I'd occasionally have to call him and ask, "Was that your *tongue* in my mouth last night?" Grant's tongue is in everyone's mouth these days—it's practically his signature handshake. Somehow his roguery is always forgivable. Once he came back from Barcelona and, in front of almost all our friends, handed me a bunch of bestiality porn he bought at a Spanish yard sale and bellowed, "When I saw this I thought *Hollis*!"

Grant was always sort of quasisafe as a man, what danger there was not being the sexual kind, not really, not to me anyway. He has carried me home blotto drunk a couple times, and despite the free rein that gave him, the worst thing he ever did was raid my kitchen and eat all the leftover packs of airplane peanuts I'd planned to hand out at Halloween that year. So imagine my surprise when he e-mailed me a few days ago to say he was furious at me for forgetting that we once slept together.

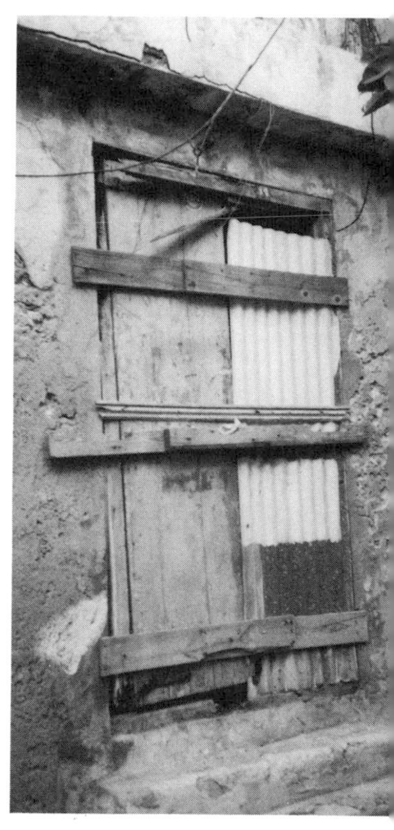

Isla Mujeres

"Oh, c'mon!" I have to scream. "We never slept together!"

This is embarrassing for a couple reasons. Grant and I had been communicating via mutual friends' e-mail because he is trying to be retired again, this time on a tiny island off the coast of Cancún called Isla Mujeres. Grant's e-mails reach me fine, but for some reason I can't get through to him from my address, so I have to write him from other people's computers, and sometimes he replies along the same route. So our communication is basically a big party line among all our friends.

I was at a loss when Lary then asked casually, like this would be no big deal if it were true, if Grant and I had ever slept together.

"*Hell no!* Where the *hell* did that come from? *Hell no!* What in *hell* are you asking me that for? Me and Grant? *Hell no!!*"

It turns out Grant had made some comment from Mexico, between singing the praises of "manly Mexican marine meat" and the tastiness of dead scorpions soaked in tequila, that might have been misconstrued (maybe if you had eaten a basket of those marinated scorpions or something) to imply that Grant and I have a history that's more than platonic. And maybe we do. I miss him so much that sometimes I sit around and just wail like a sick sea cow. I can't tell you how many times during our friendship that Grant and I have laughed so hard it felt like we could cough up our shoes. We've cried together too, and faced the terror of the truth together, but we have never slept together. I love him, but who doesn't? He's so awful in the most irresistible way.

But he's been on that island so long that he's getting his memories mixed up. Either that or he's taking his inner evil out for a little exercise again. "You mean that wasn't you? I could have sworn it was you," Grant tells Lary to tell me. So I tell Lary to tell Grant to come here and tell me that to my face.

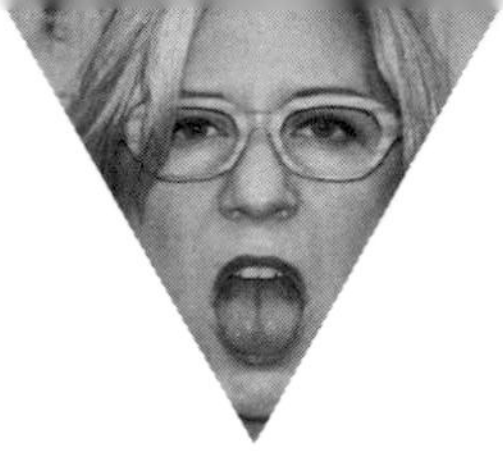

Welcome to Heaven

I decided to go to Isla Mujeres myself, especially since Grant called recently and said he'd found God, which is funny because I had always thought *he* was God. But Grant's version of God is a nineteen-year-old Mexican sailor boy named Jesus, and to pronounce his name correctly you have to bark out the first syllable like you're trying to stop a purse snatcher: "Hey!" And then directly following that you say "Zeus," which is a different God altogether. But "Hey Zeus" is how you say "Jesus" in Spanish. "I have seen the coming of the Lord," Grant proclaims.

So there I was, on my way to Isla Mujeres so Grant could introduce me to Jesus. I begged Daniel to come with me, and I couldn't believe he turned me down, because I felt it was pretty essential that the three of us got together again. I worried that our bond was fading. We used to sit together on top of the Telephone Factory lofts in Poncey Highlands and belt back wine. It was the perfect

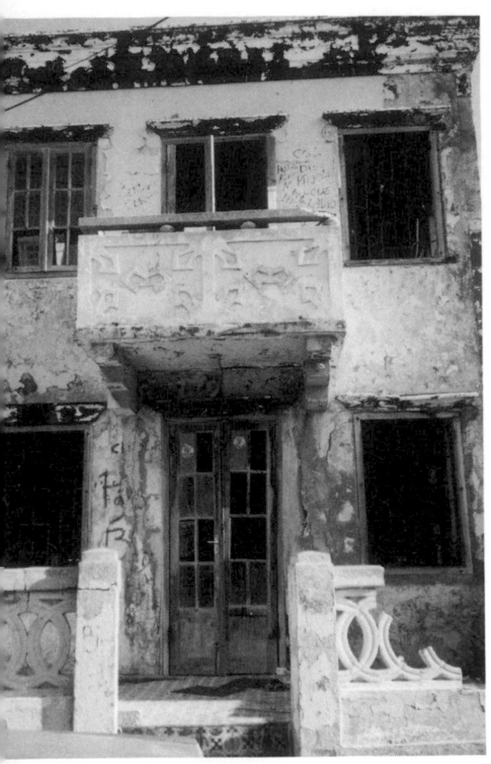

Isla Mujeres

place to watch the sunset, and we'd toast the mirrored buildings of downtown, which reflected the light and looked like big, beaded evening gowns in the distance. "It is our duty," Grant would say solemnly, "to catapult each other into greatness." Now Grant is gone, and Daniel and I aren't great yet. Daniel is getting there, though, now that his art is selling at a hearty pace. "Daniel's got a new car," I e-mailed Grant, "and this morning he bought my breakfast! You've got to see this!"

But Grant stayed put in paradise. He'd been saying he was going since I had met him, not to Mexico exactly, but simply said that one day he was going to take off his shoes and "just walk." Daniel and I knew that meant Grant was leaving. We should have known it would be the day after his daughter graduated from high school. That day, Grant boarded a plane with nothing but a backpack containing little more than eight pairs of prescription sunglasses and a mysterious small fortune accessible by an international ATM card.

It had been four months since he left, but it felt like an eternity to me. I'd seen pictures of him in the meantime. Daniel had taken some when he visited him and they sailed toward Cuba on a catamaran, an adventure that was supposed to include me, but I had to work.

They never made it to Cuba; instead, they were sidelined by a storm, and I have to laugh now that I know they survived. I can just see their sissy asses clinging to the yardarm, completely useless if the captain had clung to the ludicrous hope these two could help keep the boat afloat. If that had been the case—if Daniel and Grant had been expected to help pilot the boat as if they were on one of those "barefoot" cruises—I would have flown straight to Miami and waited for them to wash ashore. But, thank God, the crew was competent, and all Grant suffered was a badly sunburned chest, or at least it looked that way in the picture. "In the future," I e-mailed him, "please try not to die." He told me he couldn't make any promises.

"Come with me," I implored Daniel. "The three of us need to be together again." But for Daniel, it was not the time. He said the following spring would be better, when the three of us could go to Peru and climb a mountain. I have never climbed a mountain before. People say you can find God at the top. But for now, I have to go to a tiny island off the coast of Cancún to find God. He'll be as brown as an overroasted peanut, with a new tattoo on his arm and hibiscus behind his ear. He'll throw his big head back and laugh. "Welcome to heaven," he'll say.

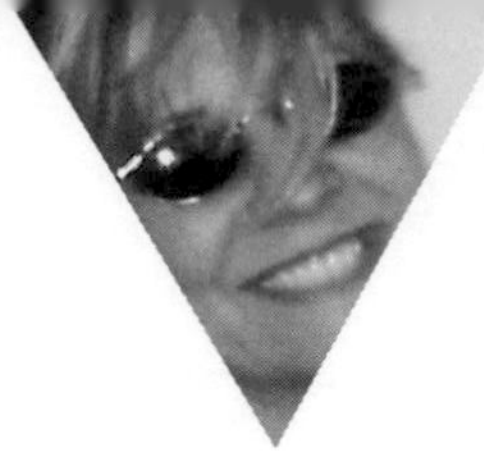

I Don't Swallow

I'd been in Isla Mujeres for five days, and I was starting to turn into one of those human barnacles whose only goal is to make my own hats and go barefoot year round. I wanted to lie on the beach with a bottomless margarita in my hand, communicating only by scratching into the sand important messages like "Extra pineapple, please," with no concern more dire than my diminishing supply of ointment.

I've worked hard to acquire this ability to blow off responsibility. I was really bad at it in the beginning: bringing my laptop along and spending four bucks a minute to return phone calls. But eventually I came around to sleeping until noon like Grant and the rest of the island expatriates, and converging at sunset for tropical cocktails at the tiki bar, with my body the color of old boat planks and wearing whatever had stuck to me from the floor when I rolled out of bed that day. And I would think to myself, *God! Life isn't passing me by! This is the life! Why work? Why suffocate yourself with your safety net?*

Why bear the flapping big albatross of petty obligations? Why freak out over a bunch of crap you can't help? "Bartender, another margarita, please!"

It was a bummer that they expected you to pay for those drinks—with money, not the fistful of soggy flotsam you pulled out of your pocket. I suppose I could formalize this life by moving to Isla Mujeres and getting a job, but my only island-type talent is sitting at the bar and begging for scraps at the bottom of the blender every time the bartender mixed a pitcher of piña coladas.

At Isla Mujeres

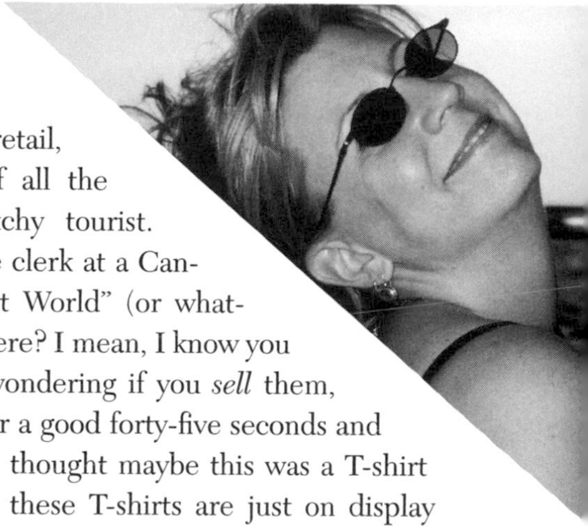

I couldn't go into island retail, because I'd already pissed off all the shop owners by being a bitchy tourist. "Excuse me," I once said to the clerk at a Cancún T-shirt shop called "T-shirt World" (or whatever), "but do you sell T-shirts here? I mean, I know you *have* T-shirts here, but I was wondering if you *sell* them, since I've been standing here for a good forty-five seconds and you haven't waited on me. So I thought maybe this was a T-shirt museum or something, and all these T-shirts are just on display rather than actually for sale. Am I wrong?" So you see how I can't exactly go back to these places and beg for work.

But I did catch what passed as a performance at one of the island's finer hotels. It was a fire-eating guy in a loincloth. Well, he didn't actually *eat* fire, he just spit it out. Well, he didn't actually spit it out, he just sort of held a torch to his lips and spit lighter fluid into it, which caused a cloud of flames to seemingly burst forth from his face.

The important part is not his technique, but the fact that I was certain I could master it. *This* could be my ticket to a lifetime of island bliss. Imagine, I don't have to swallow the fire, just spit it out. I can do that! Spitting, rather than swallowing, has always been my forte. The downside to life as a fire eater is not insurmountable. For example, I've never been that attached to my eyebrows, and eyelashes are replaceable (heard of Max Factor?). And I'm already so sunburned my face looks like an old car seat, so what further harm could occur by immersing it in flames every Friday night? And with all the booze I've been swilling lately, a mouthful of lighter fluid would feel downright familiar! I can leave Atlanta, stop frying my soul, and move to the Caribbean and start frying my flesh. Who said happiness comes at a high price?

That was my mind-set when my plane landed back at Hartsfield after my trip. My plan was to go home, stuff my cats in a sack, and head straight back to the airport. But then I checked my messages, which included a few from editors with interesting assignments, and before I knew it, I was working again. It's the story of my life: I keep meaning to permanently fall off the face of the earth, but I just can't get around to it.

Isla Mujeres

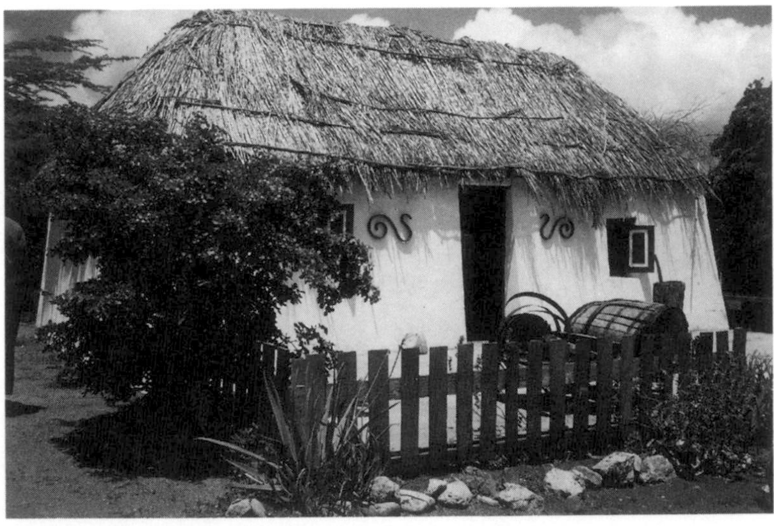

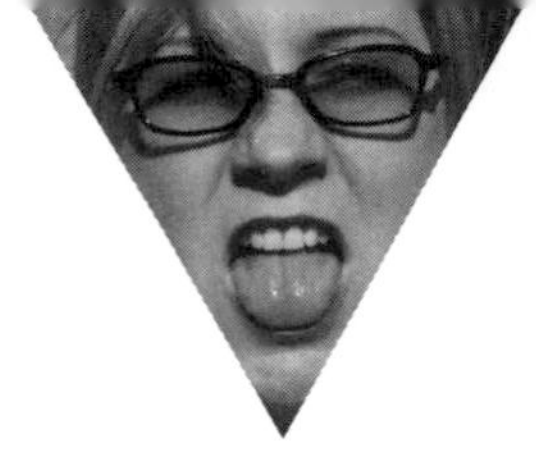

Gay Man Loves Woman

I love big lesbians. I'd be one myself if it weren't for the fact that I'm not gay—not that I don't try to fake it occasionally. I French kissed my incredibly hot friend Mary at a raucous bachelorette party almost two years ago. "Look at me, I'm *gay*!" I gleefully told Grant.

"You are not gay," said Grant, who was also drunk. To illustrate his point he grabbed Mary and planted a passionate kiss on her himself, his big slippery lips flopping over her face like two wet tentacles. "There, I just tongued her whole head, that doesn't make me straight."

"Get your hands off my girlfriend," I slurred, but Mary, who is straight, had already wandered off and was making out with Kevin, himself a hunky morsel whom Grant and I had both agreed would make a nice human chew toy. Watching them I had a wistful thought. *If I were a real lesbian, just think of all the* guys *I could turn on!*

Right there is why fake lesbians like me probably piss the hell out of real ones, because surely the last thing on a real lesbian's list of priorities is to get a *guy* off. But pretending there's some possible chick-on-chick action in the wings has always been a straight girl's reliable standby to get a guy's attention . . . and if that doesn't work then he's probably gay.

I thought Lary was gay when I first met him. His face was a little too chiseled, his hair a little too blond, and his waist a little too thin not to spell f-l-a-m-e-r. As my friend Jim Hackler says, "If his waist is under thirty-four, but he is not, then he's probably gay." But then I visited Lary's home, basically a renovated alleyway boasting little more than a bed and art supplies surrounding a bog of live mosquito larvae, and I determined that a gay man would rather rip out his own eyes with a rusty fondue fork than spend one night in that place. I myself stayed there once while Lary was on vacation, and his mattress felt like it was stuffed with bags of open switchblades. It almost renewed my suspicions that he might be gay, since his furnishings were obviously a ploy to ensure women wouldn't overstay their welcome, but since then he's upgraded the place to the point where it's almost comfortable, and I hear the spiders have all been corralled into one corner.

Now Grant, even though he was an "acting" straight man when I met him, wasn't fooling anybody. I saw a video of the wedding reception that followed his second marriage, shot only a short time before we became friends, and I had to lie down because I was laughing so hard. In the video, he had impeccable curly hair cut in an asymmetrical flip, two-toned shoes, and he breezed through the crowd with his hips swinging like saloon doors, offering appetizers from a plate. "What a fucking *fairy!*" I squealed, pointing at the screen. "I don't know how this is possible, but you were more gay when you were *straight!*"

In the video his daughter twirled in the foyer of the reception area, watching the hem of her velvet dress balloon outward at her knees. She looked like a perfect little buttercup, and she had

Grant's smile—such a big smile for a little girl. But she's not little anymore. She's the reason Grant returned from Mexico.

As I said, Grant had waited until the day after his daughter graduated from high school before he made his early retirement on that island. He had spent the afternoons sleeping on a hammock overlooking the bright blue ocean, which was more like a big turquoise pond, really, with tiny warm waves that lapped at his toes like a litter of liquid puppies. It was perfect, that ocean and that life, and its succession of caramel-colored young Latin lovers. No man on earth could have brought him back here, so the job fell to a young woman.

"I was so naive to think I could leave after she turned eighteen," Grant admitted. So he's back in Atlanta, where his daughter needs him now more than ever, having hooked up with an unsavory boyfriend who is trying to talk her into signing her paychecks over to him. When Grant was fresh off the plane, his tan hadn't faded and his sun-bleached hair was still coiled on his head like bright hay. He was even wearing shorts in the fifty-degree Georgia weather, a testimony to the fact that he'd been torn prematurely from his Caribbean paradise. I beamed with selfish bliss when he came back, and couldn't help myself from taunting him, "Grant loves a woman. Grant loves a woman," in singsong. To shut me up, he would get me in a headlock and rub his lips all over my face.

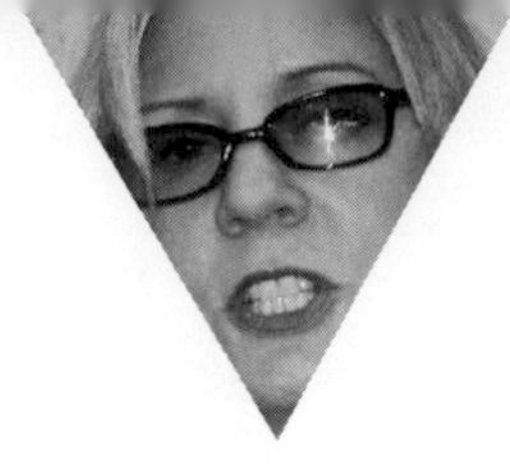

A Jar of Teeth

Grant and Daniel have pissed off God again. They've opened a retro-furniture store and art gallery across from a church on Charles Allen and called it "Sister Louisa's Worldly Possessions in the Church of the Living Room." They are selling porn-theme evangelical paintings created by a fake nun who lives in a beat-up Airstream outside Baton Rouge. The minister from the church across the street keeps coming over and telling them they're going to Hell, but they are fearless. Especially Grant. I, personally, am not fearless, though it's seldom in life that I actually scream—I mean the blood-curdling kind that makes your neighbors think you're getting murdered. Actual screaming is reserved for when spiders land on my face, which has yet to happen, or for times like the one when Grant showed me a crusty jar of tobacco-colored loose human teeth.

"Look what I found in the crack house," laughed Grant as he reached into the backseat of his truck. I don't know what I expected, since the fact that he bought the house in the first place—it's an actual crack house that he swears he can renovate—has taught me never to underestimate his ability to surprise people. "Can you believe this?" said Grant, pulling the jar from a satchel and shaking it near my face. When I registered what was in the jar—thirty or so human teeth, their roots winding upward like calcified worms—out came the scream. It was quite a long, loud scream, and had it been recorded, John Carpenter might have paid handsomely for its use as a sound effect. I knew the bathroom in which the teeth had rested before Grant exhumed them out of the mirrored medicine cabinet. The cabinet had been ripped out of the wall and laid flat to serve as some kind of drug caddy, judging from the razor blades and residual narcotics left on the surface. The bathroom was dark with bloody tissues strewn about, and I'm glad I didn't find the teeth. Grant, on the other hand, always looks in places other people don't. As I said, he is fearless.

Consider this: The first time I walked into Grant Henry's new crack-house home, there was a pile of human shit in the living room. I hadn't noticed it at first, because there were other things demanding my attention, like the feeling that I was harming myself just by breathing the air in there. But

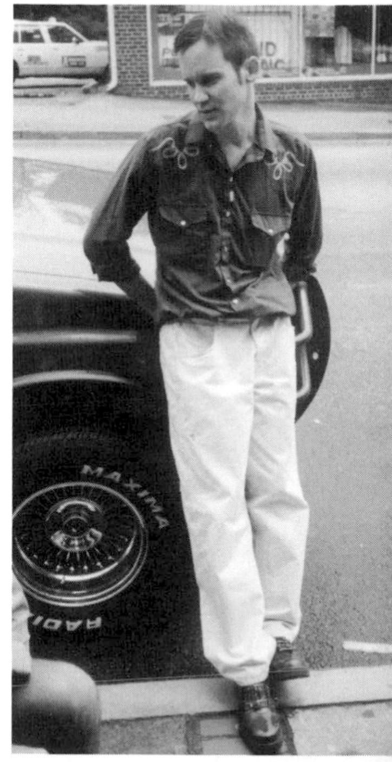

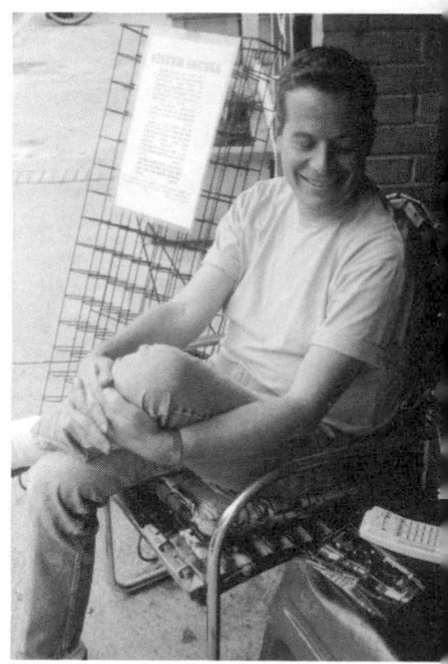

TOP: Daniel outside Sister Louisa's
BOTTOM: Grant outside Sister Louisa's

Grant pointed out the feces to me when he had a free moment in his negotiations with the previous owner, a man who had once tried to donate the house to Habitat for Humanity, who had rejected his offer. The man literally could not *give* this house away, but Grant, notorious Atlanta used-furniture dealer and self-appointed pastor of the Church of the Living Room that he was, was not going to let a little shit get in the way when he saw something worth resurrecting. He bought the place (strewn crack lighters, crap, and all) for ten thousand dollars, three thousand more than the price the man had requested.

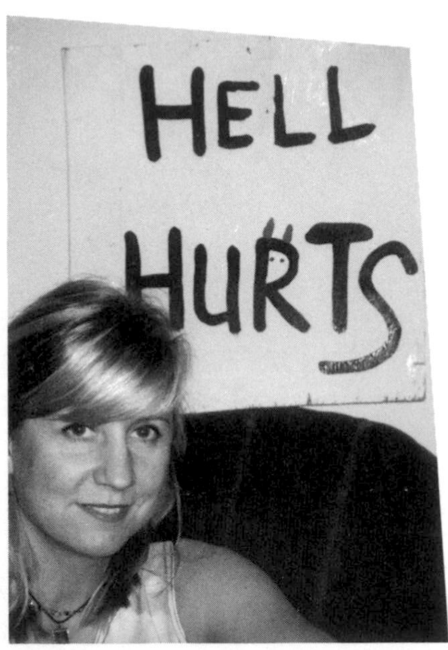

With an original Sister Louisa roadside sign

"Honey, it's *fabulous*," Grant said of his new home in Peoplestown as he drove Daniel and me back to his car. The chef at the Roman Lilly Café had lent us her '59 Ford Fairlane because Grant had forgotten not to drive his nice car to brunch that day, and he didn't want to park a new BMW convertible in front of a crack house (even though, soon afterward, he sold the BMW and re-adopted his truck after having to pass on picking up a discarded pie closet from the side of the road because it wouldn't fit into the BMW's front seat). Fabulous? I wondered. I reminded him that, in addition to the pile of shit, there was bloody toilet paper, rusty razor blades, and what looked to be lice-ridden sleeping bags littered throughout the house. There were holes as big as beds rotted through the wooden floors, every single window was broken, and it looked like homeless people had lit several campfires in what would be the bedroom if the house had had a conventional floor plan. Instead it was a three-room shotgun shack with no hallways, closets, cupboards, or even kitchen-counter space.

"Give me three months," Grant said with certainty. "Three months, honey, and this new place will be *fabulous*."

Daniel rode in the backseat. "Hollis," he assured me, "when Grant bought his last house its condition was as bad, if not worse than this place. There was a dead chicken in a plastic bag nailed to the front door."

"That's right." Grant nodded. He had just sold that house in East Atlanta for a $110,000 profit and had thrown a party to celebrate. He had owned the place for less than two years and had trained the local miscreants to stay off his property by sounding the alarm every time he saw them set foot on his lawn. But at least that place had space. This little crack house he just bought was the size of a single-wide trailer, and it didn't help that Daniel was suggesting Grant throw another party in his new place, with invitations specifying that everybody bring their own Clorox.

Grant shook his head at our consternation and flashed us his smile that's the size of a solar eclipse. "Honey, honey, honey," he admonished us, "you gotta have vision."

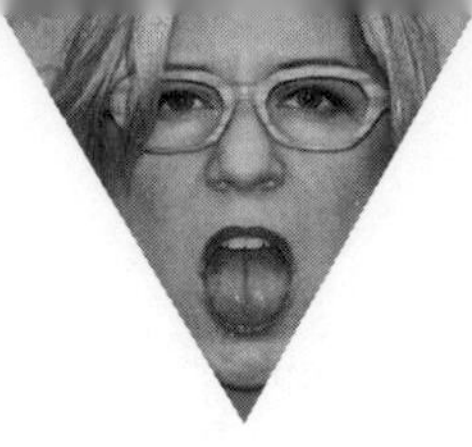

Nothin' Harder Than a Preacher's Dick

Two weeks later, Grant was shaking teeth in my face, again. I screamed, again. Something about a bunch of disembodied old teeth rattling around loose in a jar, making plinking sounds against the glass like a demonic musical instrument, is just *spooky*. What's Grant going to find next? The *rest* of the body boarded up in the windowsill?

"Oh, it's nothing to be afraid of," said Grant, who planned to frame the teeth in a shadowbox and display it in his new home. "When I was four, we had a maid named Flossie who pulled out all her teeth and kept them in a jar." Grant didn't say why Flossie the maid pulled her own teeth out, but some things I guess you don't question. Young Grant used to share a bedroom with Flossie, who slept on the bottom bunk and was too afraid of ghosts (which she called "haints") to leave the room in the middle of the night to go to the bathroom, so she kept a pot by the bed. "I used to wake up and look over the side of my bunk and there'd be big old Flossie peein' in a pot," said Grant. "I think I was traumatized," he finished, laughing in a way that showed he definitely was not.

Now he and Daniel have opened a store that features porno-religious cha-cha. And when I say "porno" I am simply attaching my own personal interpretation to the works, even though I can't imagine what else you would call a crudely painted plywood sign that proclaims "Nothin' Harder Than a Preacher's Dick!"

"You call it *art*," Grant insisted, adding that whatever meaning I chose to attach to it was my own trip. So, in other words, if I see porno when I look at Sister Louisa's art—and let's face it, she doesn't paint *pictures* or anything, just words—then it's only because my own brain is a festering cesspool of tawdry thoughts that I'm projecting onto everything.

"It says 'Preacher's Dick,'" I emphasized, pointing to the sign. "I'm not making that up, it's *right there*."

Grant ignored me and stayed busy covering the interior of his new shop with white paint. "Everything, just *white*," he'd said earlier. "A blank slate. Are you not *loving* this idea?" Of course it's great, why wouldn't it be? Just *white*. If you're going to spend a lot of time projecting meanings onto things, what better surface color is there?

I wonder when it starts, this need for meaning. I can remember when I didn't have that need, when I used to catch blowfish at the end of the pier in Melbourne Beach, Florida. I am almost positive I was damn happy then. I had a rich friend who lived in a riverfront house, and a group of us would go there and play spin-the-bottle. Only we used the plastic baby Jesus from his parents' Christmas nativity display instead of a bottle. It spun really well, and those baby Jesuses are inevitably reaching out with one hand—toward the heavens or whatever, or maybe toward all that gold, frankincense, and myrrh the wise men brought him, who knows—and that little hand made for a perfect pointer. It pointed at me to French kiss a kid named John Carnegie, a kiss we accomplished with lots of slobbering and lethargic pawing of each other, in perfect imitation of two groaning zombies from *Night of the Living Dead.*

Another school friend fancied herself something of a psychic, and one day at recess she told me about her vision—a vision of an angry river of blood. Among the flotsam and roiling debris was my favorite shirt, the shirt I happened to be wearing right then. "I saw that," she said, pointing to the little embroidered sailboat on the front of my tank top, "I saw that shirt in the . . . in the *blood.*"

I realize now that display was meant to frighten me, but nothing frightens you when you are someone who has no need for meaning. My brain didn't even go there. "River of blood?" I responded cheerily. "How cool is *that?*" I bounded happily away, leaving her with her little key chain pentagram charm jingling.

It was sometime around then, though, sometime between fish-

Wares from the Sister Louisa store

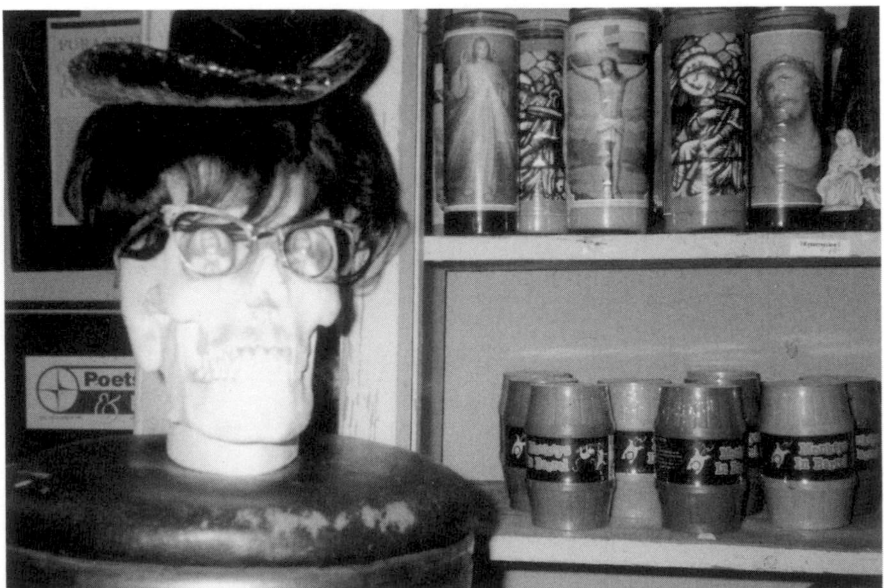

ing barefoot off the pier and being busted for smoking some very poor-quality pot in the restroom at the skating rink that I became more attuned to a need for meaning. Something turned when I was twelve. I can date it to the time when my friends and I were in the midst of our ritual routine to terrorize the insane old lady who lived in our neighborhood. She used to walk out in her underwear and knock us off our bikes, and holler about how we were such Satan spawn. When she got in those moods, her husband would have to come and fetch her, and when he did we would flee, chanting "crazy lady" as we receded into the distance.

He was always quiet when he came to get her, murmuring "Now, now, Mabel" in her ear as she shrieked at the kids who buzzed around her like fruit bats. One day I was about to join the melee when I saw him take her arm and gently place his hand on the side of her face. She looked at him, and her anger immediately melted. Her eyes became lucid and knowing. "George," she said, smiling. "It's so good to see you." And then he hugged her.

What is this? I thought. *Old people don't hug.* But there they were, clinging to each other like lost children. Something happened to me then. Something inside me changed at that moment, and from that moment on I began my search for a reason—a reason why an eighty-year-old man would stand on the street in a small town in Florida embracing his wife of fifty-five years, burying his face in her hair so we wouldn't see his tears.

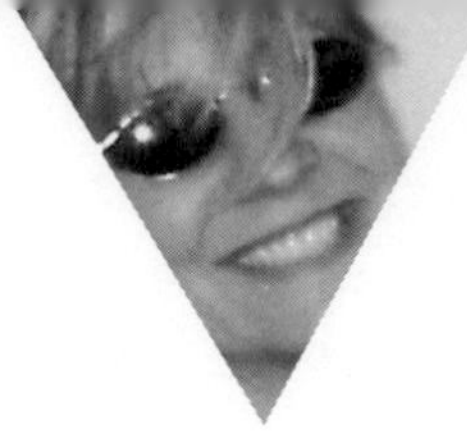

Bad Vision

I'm sure I'm like most people when it comes to my friends, which is to say I love them dearly but sometimes I wonder how they got this far in life without someone driving a spike through their skull. Take Grant. And before I say what I'm going to say, you should know I'm only saying it out of jealousy. And before I even say that, I want to say this: Here's a guy who one day decides he's tired of being fat (and he wasn't even fat—teddybearish would be more accurate), so he goes on the Body Ecology Diet, which has so many rules about mixing and matching foods you have to be an alchemist to understand it, and he drops sixty pounds faster than a sack of maggots. But here's the thing: He didn't even *really* follow the rules. He just used them as guidelines from which he made up his own rules, which worked better for him than the original ones. If you or I tried that . . . wait, I *did* try that. I went on that Body Ecology Diet for two weeks, and it worked fine for me until I fainted flat out at the Frankfurt airport and woke up in a wheelchair with no color in my lips and my carry-on luggage in my lap.

So there you go. Grant makes up his own rules, only you can't copy him with any success. He plays with the world like a drunk kitten would play with a geriatric parakeet: He pounces on it and doesn't care where the feathers fly, but none of them seem to land on him. As far as anyone can tell, he doesn't even have a *job,* but he makes more money than I do. "I got no dreams, no goals, no aspirations," he says, and there's that grin again. "I'm the happiest man alive."

It wouldn't be so bad if Grant were at least sympathetic to the lost lemmings like me out there, but he's not. Take, for example, my longing for a home of my own. As I've said, I'm not like those women who yearn to spawn, moving through life with their uterus on their sleeve hoping someone will inseminate them before cobwebs cover their ovaries. I don't have a biological clock. What I have instead is that "property clock," and I've begun the ritualistic preparation for the inevitable home-loan process. For example, I just replaced my cushy new Honda with a vintage 1974 International Scout, so I won't have a car payment clouding my loan qualification. I love my Scout, I think it is quite possibly the coolest car outside of the original *Apollo* moon buggy, and I don't want to hear anything bad about it or about my decision to make it my primary mode of transportation, period. Yet Grant, my dear friend, sat in the backseat while I drove around house hunting the other day and, like a big Buddha of bad Karma, let fly a constant stream of ill portents:

"I smell a new transmission in your future."

"Is that the sound of metal against metal?"

"I estimate those u-joints will last another month, max."

"Is that a toddler on a tricycle stuck in your car grille?"

When he's not torturing me he pretends to feel my pain. Just how empathetic he really is is suspect, however. It was five months ago that he bought the crack house in Peoplestown with a pile of dehydrated human crap in the living room. He has since renovated it into an impressive home-decor folk-art enclave that people from all over the state come to see. He gives *tours*. He makes art out of the crack lighters that people in the neighborhood bring him by the bagload. Already three newcomers have bought homes in this neighborhood just to be near him, which means that he is almost single-handedly increasing the property values in Peoplestown. Sometimes he takes me on tours through the neighborhood and points out a few crumbling nailed-shut shacks that I swear must have a few bodies boarded up under the floors, and he says, in all seriousness, "Look at that! Move-in condition!"

My response is lackluster, because I know there's no way I can do what he did. He shakes his head and says what he always says, "Honey, you gotta have vision." I take another look at the shack he's pointing at, but the only vision I have is of myself being eaten alive by black widow spiders.

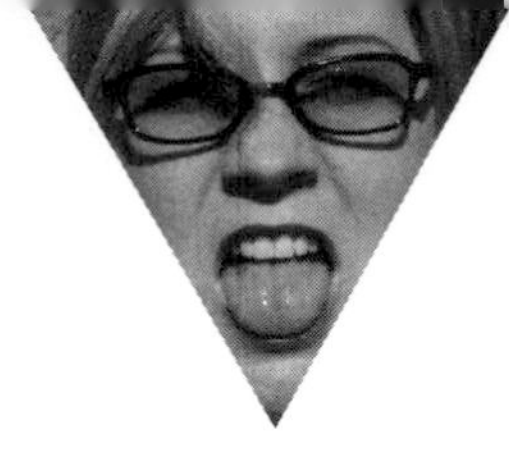

One of Those Nights

Did you ever have one of those nights when you thought you were going to check out a new Mexican restaurant with your neighbors but they took too long getting ready so you figured you'd duck back into your place real fast in case someone left a phone message? Not that I was expecting anything special, what with how my life, one day about two years ago, suddenly became a social wasteland—I never thought it would *stay* that way, but there it is. Even so, by some stupid Pavlovian pull, I still check my messages thinking I might catch a cosmic break and the light will be blinking, and there'll be a message other than the one I left myself the last time I checked my messages.

So anyway, all I've got on my mind is the hope that this new restaurant I'm about to visit will break the curse of crappy margaritas Atlanta seems to be suffering from. Maybe they'll be able to mix one that doesn't taste like battery acid, and since I once lived in a trailer two miles north of Tijuana, I consider myself an expert on all things Mexican, right? Anyway, I walk into my home and I see that, hey, looky there, the little light is blinking, but I still don't think anything of it because I figure it's probably that "editor" I met at a writers' junket who turned out to be a closet Amway rep.

So I push the button on my answering machine and I hear the voice of my little sister's husband calling from Arizona, the person I used to unkindly refer to as "the drunk walrus," and I think to myself, Why is he leaving me a message again so soon after the last message he left thanking me for those fashionable pretzel-printed Bermuda shorts I sent him for Christmas?

And then I hear him say, ". . . little Monica has been in an accident . . ."

And I just stop. I stop everything—breathing, thinking, living—everything. Little Monica, who just three years ago peeked up at me like a little blood-smudged kitten as I held her minutes after being pushed out of my little sister's loins, and who, just by waving her tiny wrinkled fists and blinking her dark, almost cartoonishly huge eyes, elicited from me in that instant a lifelong slavish devotion, has been in an accident.

And so I'm stopped, but my bother-in-law's message isn't. It goes on. He's saying stuff like "car door," "crushed," "medical helicopter," "intensive care," "spine," "liver," and "lacerated."

The words actually seem to fly like evil bats out of the answering machine and down my throat. *Jesus God*, I think to myself, *lacerated liver?* She's three years old, so her liver must be like, what, the size of a silver dollar? Right then I would fall to my knees if I could, but I'm stopped, and then Daniel comes through the door, laughing.

"What's taking you so long?" he asks, and then he sees my face.

"My niece," I say, and I really don't have to say much more, because he sees my face.

And so, exactly one hour and forty minutes later, instead of spending the evening being overly critical of Mexican food with my friends, I'm on a plane to Phoenix saying "no" to the flight attendant every time she offers me something from the bar, wasting the first-class upgrade the gate agent was kind enough to give me after hearing my circumstances. And then I'm in a rental car on the way to St. Joseph's Hospital, and for a second I'm amazed at how efficiently I'm accomplishing things, considering that I'm stopped.

Then I remember: After Sunday school, little Monica, in the church parking lot, got stuck between the door of a roll-away car and another car, and the word "crushed" was used when I later talked on the phone with my sister, my little sister, Kimberly, who used to make mud pizza and whose fingers used to be too short to reach the last morsels at the bottom of the bag of M&Ms.

"Can you come be with me?" Kimberly had asked me over the phone, and since then I've been on autopilot to close the distance.

And suddenly I'm there, and my sister and I are clinging to each other. And I'm crying, but not because the news is bad. The news, so far, is good. There was no spinal damage, no oxygen loss to the brain, not even any broken bones ("A three-year-old's bones are like rubber," the doctor told us. "If she were a few years older her entire chest cavity would have been crushed"). There's just those nasty internal lacerations caused when Monica's ribs poked into her liver, and there's a chance those will heal themselves without surgery. Kimberly leads me to the crib in intensive care where Monica lay sleeping with so many tubes sprouting out of her it looks like her little body is resting in a nest of giant albino spiders, and I reach down to smooth a strand of hair away from her beautiful little forehead. Suddenly she opens her eyes, looks at me, and smiles. With that, I am started again.

Ever had a night like that? Me too.

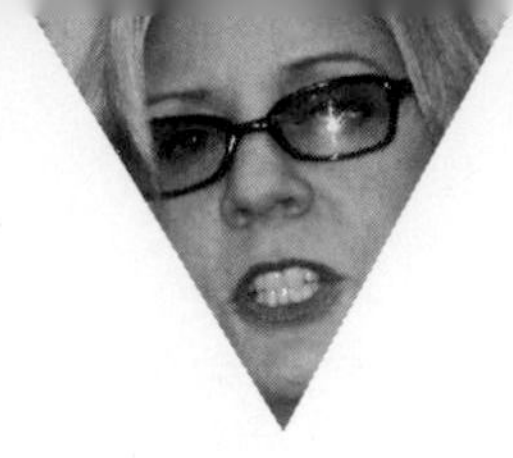

Grant Makes It

Grant—in a move no one could have predicted—has become a professional bartender at an actual bar on Ponce de Leon Avenue called the Local. How the hell this all happened I have no idea. In all the years I've known Grant the only interest I've seen him take in cocktails was his penchant for demanding, like a petulant emperor, that they be handed to him. He once made a mean pitcher of Midori margaritas, and when he's on that diet of his he can throw together some pungent cups of vodka and unsweetened, unfiltered, unflavorful cranberry juice that he always tries to push off on us but, really, it's about as easy to swallow as a big bowl of sperm. But let's face it, bartending involves, like, *ingredients* and stuff, some of them probably perishable.

Until recently Grant didn't even own a refrigerator. Or an oven, come to think of it, and at parties he simply served loaves of bread. You would think that if there was a bartender hiding under his freckled hide somewhere, there would have been maybe a cabinet in his kitchen with liquor in it other than the signature big bottle of vodka that he probably gargles with before going to bed. The making of drinks was not a talent I ever suspected he possessed.

In fact, I'm suspicious of his ability to *make* anything. Like I personally *made* curtains to cover my windows. I finally had to after I woke up one morning with perverted workmen leering down at me through my bedroom's clerestory windows as I slept topless in tatty underwear. So I bought reams of cheap muslin, and damn if I didn't fashion some stylish window treatments that only occasionally resembled the cast-off grave garments of mummies. Grant, on the other hand, draped lacy kitchen aprons across his windows. Of course it looked fabulous, but it's not like he *made* them. I mean he just *put* them there, so why should he get credit for that?

Once we had to construct a vendor tent so Daniel could showcase his work at a folk-art festival (right before Daniel discovered he hates folk-art festivals because they're too much like carnivals). So there we were—or I should say there *I* was—trying to construct the booth while Grant and Daniel spent their time twirling the tent poles like batons.

So Grant didn't make that booth, I did. All Grant made was a crude bullhorn from a rolled-up piece of poster board so he could blare like a sideshow barker, "Come see the artist formerly known as Daniel, now known as the 'Festival Whore'!!" And, Jesus God!, Daniel soon discovered he *hated* being there and having to sell his art like flea-market flotsam. Grant just laughed. *"Festival Whore!!"* he barked over and over through the bullhorn.

That day, after the festival whore fiasco, we toasted the sunset from the top of the Telephone Factory, where Daniel and I live. That was the first time Grant told us it was our duty to catapult one another into greatness. "Dare to leap," he said, and he acted like he was going to leap off the top of the building. Daniel and I did nothing to stop him; we knew there were bushes below that would probably break his fall.

"Clarity" is ironically Grant's mantra, and he uses it when he's making us be clear about what we want to accomplish in life. He's not so perfect, what with his twelve different careers in the past six months, and his retirement that lasted, like, five minutes. Now he's into this bartending thing, which is a complete comet out of nowhere.

But Grant thinks it all makes sense. "It's all coming together," he says excitedly. Bartending, he argues, combines all his passions—people, conversation, creativity, sex, and *booze*—all essential ingredients of the cosmic cocktail that is his life. It is all coming together to create the momentum that will catapult him to heights heretofore unknown. And I guess I can't say Grant never *made* anything after all. Looking back to the Telephone Factory rooftop that night, Grant made us beholden to one another. "Our duty," he said, "is to catapult each other into greatness!"

We are not great yet, but at least we sometimes experience moments of immeasurable glee. At least we are not wholly miserable every minute of the day, and we know we have made one another into what we are today.

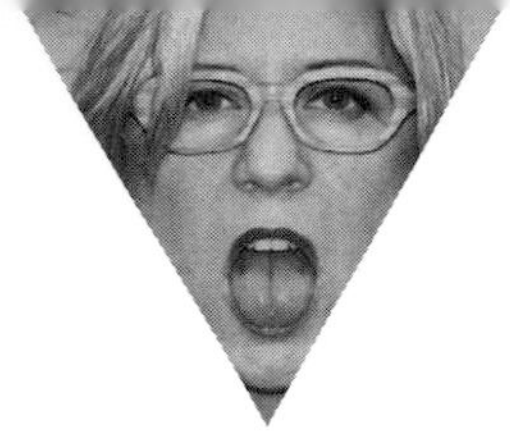

Putting Out

I swear, I had no idea it was bad practice to stand on top of your toilet tank. But even Grant says he knew this, which is humbling because if you ask me he is always on top of something scary. Let's not forget that his living room had once actually been *used* as a toilet, with mummified curls of human crap right there on the carpet—and Grant stood there in the middle of it all and handed the owner a check for less than what you'd spend on a used truck. He fixed it up very nice too, but in all the work he did on that place, and especially in the bathroom, all the cleaning and scraping and painting and decontaminating, he never stood on the top of the toilet tank in order to reach places to get it done.

"Hell no," he says, "you could bust a bolt and be knee-deep in sewage in no time."

Actually, it takes about a month to get knee-deep in sewage. Today my place smells like a stadium urinal, all because I thought

I'd been clever to paint my whole powder room without needing to drag in a step stool, because to me, that toilet tank was *begging* to be stood on. I've been standing on toilet tanks my whole life. The first time was after I hit my cousin Kelly across the head with my shoe.

When I was five and she was about seven, my cousin Kelly used to be trusted to look after me, but all she ever did was dress up in her mother's underwear in the name of the Lord and strangle me unconscious. "Holly, it's Jesus, I command that you bow before me," she would call from under the flapping laundry line behind her house. She wore my aunt's white slip pulled over her T-shirt and dungarees. It billowed around her ankles like a delicate nylon shroud.

"No!" I'd yell from my hiding place in the small vineyard my aunt and uncle cultivated farther back on their California property. "You're gonna choke me again!"

"I won't! I'm Jesus!" she responded incredulously. "Now get over here!" So, as always, I went. I was afraid not to. I had seen Kelly shit in the woods and wipe her ass with an oak leaf. A girl capable of that was capable of anything. I knew she would strangle me, but the evil you know is less terrifying than the evil you don't, and I didn't know what she would do if I made her chase me down. So I went, knelt before her, and waited to feel her bony fingers around my neck. Later I'd regain consciousness and see her face hovering over me, feigning concern. The slip was off, the evil Jesus gone, and she was Kelly again.

I remember Kelly's father kept a "game room" in their house, which had lamps with leather shades and bases made of clustered deer antlers. There were mounted animal heads on the walls and a real bear-skin rug in front of the fireplace. I used to lie down and stare into the bear's marble eyes, touch the necrofied flesh on its forehead, and wonder how such a majestic creature ended up a lowly footpad for this freaky family. "Please wake up and eat the evil Jesus," I silently implored it, but even at the age of five I knew revenge would have to come at my own hands.

So I plotted and decided that the best method of attack would come at a moment of complete repose, when Kelly was in her "Kelly" phase, her mother's underwear folded neatly in a drawer and not accessible as a shroud. That moment came when she was in the game room, her back to me, talking to a friend on the phone. I had planned to clout her on the head with one of the antler lamps, but at the last second decided that my own shoe would work fine.

"STOP CHOKING ME!" I shrieked, and swung the shoe in my hand with all my might. Startled, Kelly turned to look at me just in time for the thick rubber sole to make a satisfying *thwack* against the side of her skull. Her ensuing scream was shrill enough, I'm sure, to make her friend's ear hemorrhage on the other line. I darted away and locked myself in the bathroom.

But the lock was one of those flimsy kinds you can pop from the other side as easily as a pushpin, so I ended up having to barricade the door with my own body—bracing my feet against the toilet tank—while my cousin shoved from the other side. I can't believe I kept her at bay until my mother intervened, at which point my aunt asked her to never leave me there again.

"Kid," my mother said in the car on the way home after I told her what happened, "I'm glad you locked yourself in the bathroom."

Because of that experience, I always thought toilet tanks were as sturdy as tree trunks, and stood on them almost every chance I got, especially since my mother kept a coin bank on the top shelf of our bathroom towel rack, which was accessible to any adolescent by simple toilet-tank ascent.

The bank was in the shape of a little wooden beer keg, with a slot on top to receive the coins but no other opening to retrieve them once they were inside. My mother said that's what she liked about it, the inability to put out what she'd put in. But with tweezers and a light touch, I became quite deft at putting out what my mother had put in.

I used to take the money to the liquor store where the proprietor used to masturbate behind the counter when kids came in to buy penny candy. But it's not like I knew what he was doing back there, not at first anyway. I just thought he was just taking a really long time to tuck in his shirt. Then the day came when he showed me the picture of two people copulating, and tried to get me to agree that it was a good idea.

It was a hot day, and I was wearing a bathing suit with a big buckle on the front, a mini version of Ursula Andress's famous Bond-girl getup, and damn if he didn't reach out and grab ahold of that buckle and start pulling me back behind the counter with him! Jesus God, there I was about to be molested by the man who sold me my mother's menthol cigarettes, and I couldn't think of what to do except get to the bathroom and lock the door. I knew where it was because, junior klepto that I was, I used to steal candy from this very place by packing my pockets, walking into the restroom, and pitching the candy through the window to the alley on the other side. Either a friend was waiting there, or I'd simply retrieve the contraband later at my leisure. So after I extricated my bathing-suit buckle from this man's bony claw, I ran straight to the bathroom, where I locked the door, climbed the toilet tank, and this time pitched *myself* out the window. That is how I escaped from Horny Pete.

I have my mother to thank for it, I think, because if she had not stood up for me at my cousin's house like she had, I don't know if I'd have had the mettle to do what I did at the liquor store. She instilled that grit in me, and over time I've started to feel better about things, even about taking the coins from my mother's bank, because no matter how hard some will try, for good or for bad, in the end no one—I mean *no one*, not even you—can put out what your mother has put in.

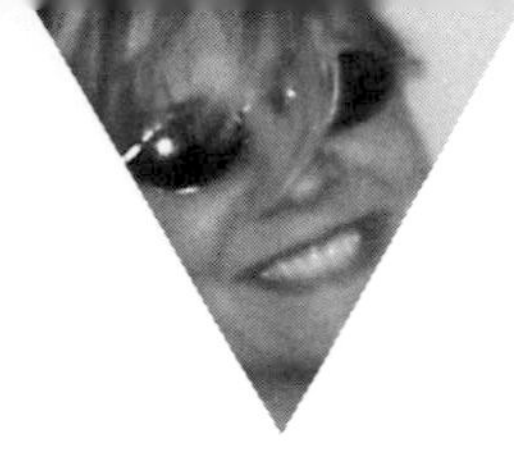

Fugitives from Bad Credit

As I looked for houses to buy, I underwent pre–separation anxiety from the place I rent at the Telephone Factory, a beautiful loft in Poncey Highlands that I could never afford to buy even if I sat ass up in stirrups every day producing Aryan eggs to sell on the black market. The only reason I could afford to rent it was because the developer received funds to renovate via a bond referendum, a condition of which was that eleven of the loft apartments be made available to "moderate income" tenants. He allocated those units to ten struggling artists and me, a writer. So Daniel and I lucked out and got fabulous lofts. He lives across the hall from me and has a huge patio courtyard, while mine has a view of the city and is so big I can ride my bike around in the living room. The rent is only $475 a month, and all we have had to do to stay there is keep our income under $22,000 a year. Clermont Lounge is right up the street too, and we go there about once a week. On one visit, Grant caused the big stripper we call "Butterball" to fall off the stage by making her reach too far for her dollar tip. She hit the ground like a sack of cement.

Grant, of course, has his nice new crack house to call home, and doesn't live here, and Lary has the pile of cinder block and bent steel that used to be a candy factory to call home. Lary owns his house, but even so, Daniel and I used to consider ourselves to be the lucky ones. We thought we caught a cosmic break with our loft spaces, since all we had to do to maintain the status quo was to stay failures.

That has been harder than you might think. When we moved there, Daniel and I both joked about how we were going to be eighty years old and still living there with no money. I would be on stage at the Clermont, with my walker, shaking my ancient tits like two sacks of taffy to make a buck. That sounded fine to me at the time. But then we met Grant, and he kept buying houses, fixing them up and selling them, and making truckloads of money—and he made it look *so easy*. He told Daniel that he could buy a house with a credit card, and that he even had the house picked out for him right across the street from his own, a little shotgun shack that had been foreclosed on. Daniel tried too, and made an offer, but it went to another guy, some artist who moved into the neighborhood to be near Grant. The house sold for fifteen thousand dollars.

I admire Daniel for making that effort, because we were both fugitives from our bad credit reports. His stemmed from a defaulted student loan and accompanying fees that had multiplied over the years like tribbles on the starship *Enterprise.* My own credit problems stemmed from a post-college period during which I lived like a soap-opera actress on the income of a part-time receptionist. But at least Daniel still *has* credit cards. At that point, I didn't even have that anymore. Here's what a crawling piece of wasted space I am: First, I got turned down for credit at one of those big, blow-ass department stores that goes out and recruits future credit card holders by having salespeople shove applications through your car window as you're driving past the mall. I was curious why they had turned me down, seeing as how they're not that picky, this department store, having extended a huge reservoir of credit to my crusty friend Lary, who basically lives in an alley. So I wondered, what's with the rejection? I popped Equifax a request for my credit report.

Upon inspection of said credit report I discovered a mysterious lien filed against me in the state court of my hometown of San Diego. Somebody had sued me, won, and I'd never known anything about it. Because of my fugue-like fear of bureaucracy, I wanted to move to the hills and live under a lean-to fashioned from sticks and a pair of piss-stained homeless man's pants. "They'll never find me here," I'd cackle, while spearing rodents with my foot-long, tobacco-colored toenails. My own mother once got a notice saying she owed the IRS $1,500, but rather than pay it, she, like, *went underground.* Within a few years, that debt had increased to $150,000. Stuff like this scares me to death. It's terrifying that everything can be taken from you just because of a blip on some government computer that could be wrong, but you can't fight it because you don't know where to start. But my mother didn't have everything taken from her. She made sure to divest herself of everything before that could happen, and she never let herself get too attached to *things.* Even on the day my little sister almost drowned, my mother's gratitude over a tragedy diverted could only be shown by taking Kimberly by the shoulders and shaking her briskly.

Then some molecular piece of me that rebels against the dominant walking-apology part of my personality stopped and said, *Hey, maybe the lien is a mistake, so before you tunnel underground at least attempt to rectify it.*

So after letters to both Equifax and the San Diego court system resulted in a big, huge cavernous basket of *nothing* (I mean, at least they could have sent me a swastika lapel pin), I actually *flew* to San Diego, rented a car, and spent a day doing a fire drill of every municipal building in the city until I tracked down the demon lien. It had been awarded to the franchise tax board of California, which issued the case because, so partial were they to my presence in their territory, they had mistakenly continued to assess California taxes against me after I became a resident of Georgia. The sum total—with fees, penalties, and various other drippings the bureaucratic quagmire loves to attach to crap like this—was more than I could afford even if I spent the rest of my life giving bionic blow jobs for cash.

So I swallowed my fear and went straight to the state tax office. I was sure they'd slap the cuffs on me the second I came through the door, but instead a tax technician graciously decided to help me. I know she was gracious because she told me so.

"I like to help people, so you're lucky you got me," she said as she set about eradicating the false tax assessments. Now here's where I'm the crawling piece of wasted space: After having my credit fucked up and having to interrupt my life and fly across the country because of a falsehood her office generated, I, like, *believed* her. Boy, am I lucky, I thought, and genuflected as I backed out of the door.

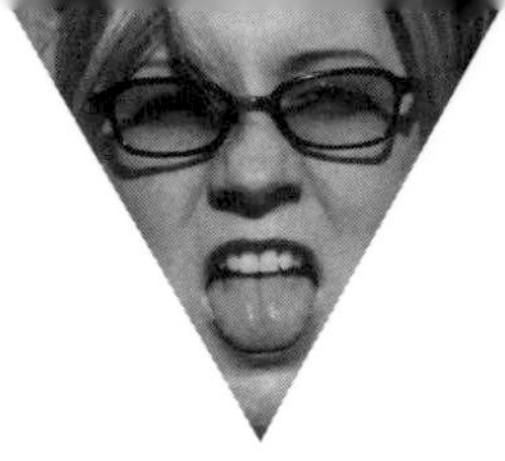

A Strange Man

My father used to say I had him to thank for being alive, and I guess that's technically true, though secretly I always thought I owed my life to a strange man who once held my mother's hand. Maybe she shouldn't have told me about him, maybe she should have kept him hidden along with the rest of her secrets she had locked under the chastity belt around her chest most of the time, but she let it crack one day when I was seven, and out came the story. After that I thought about him a lot, the strange man, in a way opposite of a nightmare but somewhat frightening nonetheless.

"What did he look like?" I'd ask my mother.

"He was very nice," was all she'd say, "and tall."

It wasn't any use trying to imagine what I'd be like if my father were not my father, because my mother was already married to him when the strange man saved her life, so it's not as if she could have taken a cosmic side turn to rescue me from my present self at that point. No. She was already two kids into a bad marriage and was pregnant with her third. Seven months later she popped me out as easily as an olive pit, and named me after a female character in a newspaper comic strip titled "Smilin' Jack," or that's what she said anyway. She told me many times that she named me after a character in this comic strip, which is about a pilot, and evidently in that strip, Smilin' Jack had a girlfriend named Holly. I have no idea whether Smilin' Jack really had a girlfriend named Holly, just that that's what my mother told me. I don't see why this matters, anyway. My name is Hollis. The character's name was "Holly," which is similar to my name but not my name. I ended up with a man's name for some reason. A *strange man's* name.

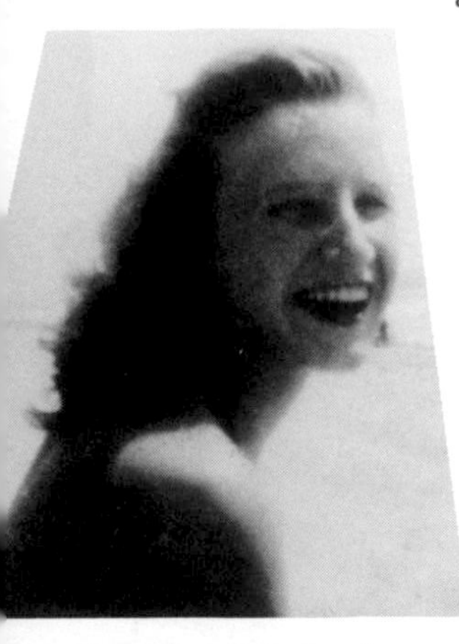

My mother at the beach

"What the hell are you talking about?" my mother would say, waving the smoke of her Salem menthol away from her face to eye me sternly. "I told you, your name came from a comic strip."

At this point she would bustle me off before I asked any more questions, maybe send me to the liquor store down the street to buy another carton of cigarettes. At that time she didn't know the store had been bought by that pervert who sat with his pants unzipped behind the counter. She was under the impression it was still owned by the nice man missing the two middle fingers on his right hand. That man once sold me a bongo drum for seventy cents after I'd misread the price tag. The real cost was seven dollars, not seven dimes, but he'd sold it to me anyway, holding out his chopped-up hand to take my change. But then one day he was gone and the pervert had taken his place. When he showed me that picture from the magazine of two people copulating, the girl in the photo didn't look like she was having all that much fun. She looked like she was being stabbed to death, and maybe she was.

"Someone should save her," I remember thinking as I rushed home.

And being saved brought my thoughts back to the strange man who actually did save my mother, who even afterward never bothered to learn how to swim. I don't know what she was doing in the ocean that day, anyway, pregnant like she was, in a tatty bathing suit even she admits would have been an embarrassment to her corpse. She always emphasized that point too, because if she had been out there as part of a plan or anything—if she had *meant* to get swept under by a strong wave—she would have worn the blue bathing suit with the ruffle and underwire, not the faded red-and-white polka-dot number that practically hung on her like a hospital gown.

But at least the red suit made her stand out from the rest of the crowd, which is why my father, drinking beer with his work buddies in the parking lot, noticed her heading toward the surf in the distance. It was during one of his rare periods of gainful employment selling trailers for a company based in northern California, and they were at the beach for a corporate-sponsored picnic. "What is she doing?" my father mused to his coworkers as he watched his wife wade into the water. "She can't swim."

And then my father laughed, because he didn't know what else to do. It was his coworker who walked across the sand, out into the ocean, and took my mother's hand. He was tall, like she remembered, and when the big wave crashed and the water tried to take her he wouldn't let it. She remembered the powerful pull, she said, of both the sea and the strange man. She remembered she was already chiding herself for not having the foresight to die in the better bathing suit, and she remembered she had already let go, but he hadn't.

After pulling her out of danger, he silently walked her back to her beach towel. Seven months after that I was born, and seven years after that I learned I had a strange man to thank for it. I would dream about him then, and in my dreams I had a happier mother, one who wouldn't let go so easily. And I still think about the strange man a lot to this day, especially on those occasions when the world weighs on me like a lead sea. He is nice and tall, and his hand is outstretched. I take it and he pulls me through.

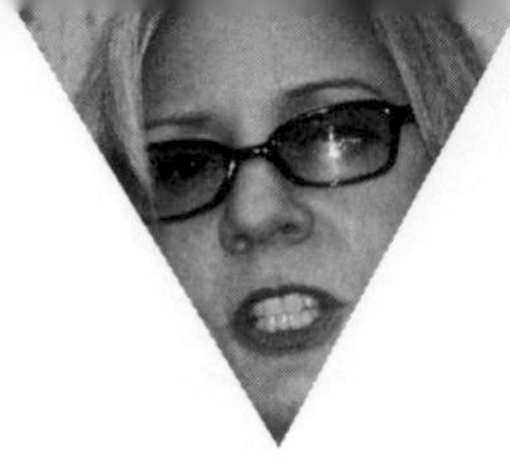

Bleachy-Haired Honky Bitch

It was on one of my house-hunting excursions that I came close to killing a guy. Or maybe he might have survived, but I bet it would've hurt, getting hit by my car. The crack dealers standing by would've been really mad at me too, probably, for murdering or maiming their customer. For show I'm sure they would have dragged me out of my car and fractured my elbows at least because, you know, I would have *stopped* and all, after hitting the guy. It's not like I could have *escaped*. So I would have pulled over and offered my arms obligingly, as if to convey, "Sorry I killed your friend, go ahead and break these."

The guy I almost hit was doing one of those "asshole strolls," which is to say he picked the middle of the street as a starting point to walk into traffic, strolling at the speed of a diseased bovine, and in this situation my job was to slam on the brakes and sit there stewing until he was damn good and finished being in front of my car, because the only other choice I had was to run his ass down.

Or try to . . . but it's not like I *tried*. I would have stopped if I had been paying attention. "Bleachy-haired honky bitch!" is what he hollered at me as my car barely missed him. He probably wasn't sure which he was more pissed about—the fact that I almost killed him, or the fact that I hadn't been noticing his nonchalance as he did the asshole stroll into ongoing traffic. This near miss occurred in Capitol View, on the West End, where the crack dealers have the privilege of not paying attention and where bleachy-haired honky bitches like me are supposed to be, well, *scared*.

At least, that is normally the correct order of things in Capitol View. And it was, at first. When I first started looking for houses there I was plenty scared, because a whore had been shot dead while running down the street naked. Usually I obligingly rolled to a stop in reverence of the asshole stroll every time, and I tried to appear appropriately frightened so as to show that their effort wasn't wasted on me, because who knew whether that was a retractable hacksaw in their back pocket?

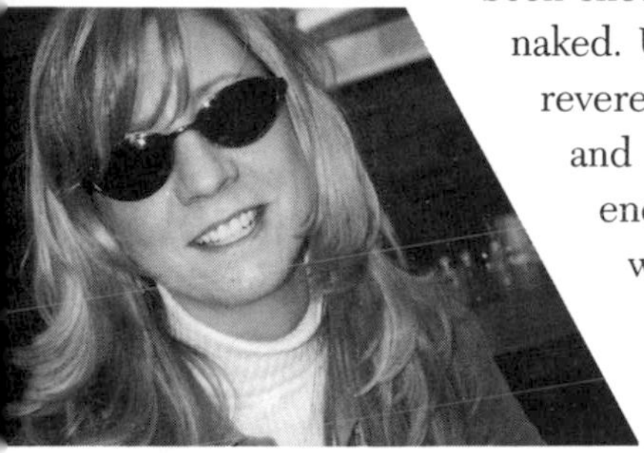

Bleachy-haired honky bitch

But crack dealers and dead whores don't daunt those who have "vision." I'm not one of them, mind you, but Grant, who has "vision," told me that other people with "vision" would be buying houses there, and that it was best to get in on it while I could still buy a house with a monthly note less than what I paid to spay my cat. So I looked for a house, and even though I was plenty scared by my potential new neighbors, what *really* scared me was the fear I'd make a bad investment.

"Just wait," said my friend with "vision." Creative poor people can't afford Kirkwood and East Atlanta anymore, so the West End is the next wave. It looks like he's right. Creative poor people are snatching up houses there like pigeons attacking an abandoned picnic. Caravans full of poor arty types come through every weekend, and off they scatter into the Land of Affordable Houses, with their body piercings and cargo pants, retro furniture and upscale-burrito breath. They hardly pay any mind to the crack dealers, who shake their heads dejectedly, knowing it's a bad day for the neighborhood when bleachy-haired honky bitches can't brake to accommodate a good asshole stroll.

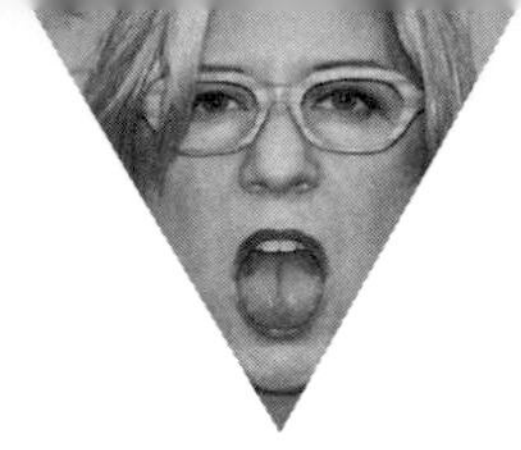

A White Father

My father was the worst kind of bigot—not that he lynched people or anything like that. Not that I know of anyway. In fact, there is not much I know of my father's past, except that he grew up fatherless in Alabama, and his mother died unexpectedly one night while he was still in college. Though my father was always rumored to be very charming and well liked by all except surly service personnel (such as the local grocery clerk who refused to cash any more of his rubber checks), as a preteen I always wondered what people saw in him.

For starters, his favorite daily ensemble consisted of a Hawaiian shirt and a pair of cutoff shorts made of printed material featuring big cartoon pretzels, and that hat fashioned from flattened Budweiser cans and blue yarn. I have solid evidence of this in an old picture of him taken in front of a monument in Washington, D.C., during one of our road treks across the country. His head crowned in beer cans, and his shirt loud and busy enough to be seen with the naked eye from other planets, my father is grinning like he had no idea his daughter was dying of embarrassment. In the next frame on the same role of film is a picture of my sisters and me, the two of them smiling sweetly while my face is caught in the perpetual eye roll that became my signature expression that summer. I am swathed in what amounted to be a basket of rags, with the ass of my denim shorts an explosion of fabric patches. A few days prior to these photos, my father had kicked my denim-clad ass all over the city, all because a black man in Arlington Cemetery had asked me for a piece of candy, and I had given it to him. That's what I mean when I say my father was the worst kind of bigot.

To make it worse, my father never said flat out that we were not allowed to be nice to black people, though you'd think the beatings would have been an effective Pavlovian method of molding our behavior. On the trip to Washington, D.C., my father fumed until we left Arlington Cemetery, barely able to hold back a butt-kicking until an acceptable excuse availed itself. Then an activist handed me a *Roe vs. Wade* pamphlet. At that, my father saw his opening, because I guess in his head people would be more accepting of a father smacking his kid around because of her interest in legalized abortions as opposed to smacking her around for having been nice to a negro. He snatched the pamphlet from my hand and began whacking me upside the head.

This tirade lasted into the evening, and finally I was given a reprieve when my sister befriended the black motel receptionist's young son, who spent every afternoon waiting in the game room for his mother to finish work and walk him home. My sister brought the boy to our room, where my mother was cooking hamburgers on a hot plate in the bathroom, and asked if he could stay for dinner. With that, I felt my father's fury lift off me like an escaping toxin, and there it lingered, waiting to be redirected.

On that particular trip we were on our way back to California, where my mother had procured another job designing defense missiles with a computer company that had recently won a large government contract. We settled on a house south of L.A., on a hill in the Hollywood Riviera overlooking the ocean. Across the street lived a gaggle of rambunctious foster children cared for by a religious couple, and among them was a black girl named Sonya, who was my age. She was the first friend I made there. The ass-kickings lessened in intensity over time, as my father reconciled himself to the permanency of my friendship with this girl. Often he drove us both home from school. He'd heard Sonya had a white father, and while I knew this was not true, I didn't correct him.

Sonya liked to spout lies like a carnival barker, but I usually enjoyed her stories. One day I discovered she had told our entire middle school that we were half sisters, sharing the same father. To my surprise, even the teachers believed her. This rumor thrived like a seabed, so well that, much later, when my father came to school to sign a permission slip, his identity was actually challenged by the school secretary.

"I happen to know she has a black father," she said, pointing to me as I stood beside Sonya, "same as Sonya's father."

I cringed, feeling my father's fury begin to grow like the foam in a bottle of shaken champagne. I think Sonya felt it too. I waited for the ass-kicking to commence, but instead my father simply glared at the secretary. "She has a white father," he hissed, pointing to me, "same as Sonya's father."

With that, the secretary's eyes brightened with realization. Apologizing for the gaffe, she handed my father Sonya's permission slip to sign as well. Taken aback, his anger abruptly extinguished in midflare, my father signed the slip. The secretary seemed charmed by him after that, and as a preteen I wondered what she saw in him. "Let's go, girls," my father said, and with that, the secretary saw two girls follow their father out the door.

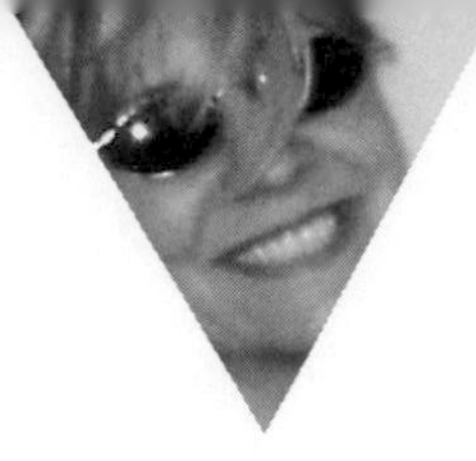

You Can't Get Away

There are billions of spiders on my ceiling, way up there where I can't reach them with a broom, and I'm afraid one of them will swoop down and bite me on my brain. They must be at war with the roaches in my kitchen, because I notice those have taken to skirmishing in battalions lately. My exterminator even stood me up for my second follow-up appointment, probably because she's petrified. I don't blame her. I myself am constantly shrieking, "Is that a *roach*? What is this place, a *peat bog*?!?!? Do I live atop a *mass grave* or something?!?!?"

Daniel ignores me. He's not that chivalrous when it comes to killing bugs anymore, not since my place turned into Amityville Horror for insects. If he had to kill bugs for me it would take up his entire day, so he does his share by coming over occasionally to slaughter some that cross his path, and I'm expected to do mine. But roaches don't bother him as much as they do me, which is odd because he grew up in a house with a mother who could clean. My own parents were wholly housework-impaired. Growing up, I remember at one point our bug infestation was so bad that roaches were actually falling off the ceiling *into our hair*.

"Kids," my mother finally said, "I think we have a roach problem."

"Really?" I smirked. "You mean the kitchen floor isn't *supposed* to be crunchy like that?"

Our family's solution was to move. We moved three times in one year, but not just to escape roaches. We were escaping other things, I suppose, but it coincidentally solved our bug problem. But only until the ones that followed us found each other and commenced copulating and created a new swarm of their own. You can't get away. It was like being chased by little demons. Finally, we moved to Florida, where the roaches are giant and resemble big black tanks with antennae.

"Get comfortable with it," my mother told us. She herself was still getting comfortable with the reason we moved there. She'd given up her nighttime cosmetology courses she'd so enjoyed in order to work on the space program at NASA, and to this day I believe my sisters and I were the only kids in class being raised by a rocket scientist who dreamed of one day working at a beauty parlor, but I could be wrong.

And the roaches—well, I never got comfortable with them. In my loft, it's like an eco-experiment gone awry. On a trip to Mexico City, where I stayed at the Hotel Nikko, I spotted one in my bathroom, and I *recognized* him. That's one of *mine!* Jesus God, how do they *find* me?

You'd think you could get away, but no. I remember once in second grade I had a baby molar that was rotting right out of my head, probably because of my mother's penchant for leaving out bowls of Halloween candy for breakfast. The tooth had to be pulled, which necessitated a dental appointment, so my mother told me she'd pick me up at school after lunch. "Just wait for me in class," she said.

I hated that dentist, so God, did I want to get away! I thought I could escape the whole ordeal by making a break for it at recess and running home. Once there, I sequestered myself on the top shelf of the hall closet behind a box of notes my sisters and I had written, ironically, to the tooth fairy. My mother had kept them ever since our baby teeth began dropping from our puckers like pomegranate seeds. The teeth were in there too, along with the letters. *Ha!* I thought. *She'll never find me here.*

It had always been my foolproof hideaway. I used to sit up there and listen to everyone look for me. "Anyone seen your sister?" my mother would ask. Sometimes I even detected concern. I'd smile and eventually come out as long as I was sure there wasn't an ass-beating on the agenda.

So imagine my surprise when she came through the door that day and barreled straight toward my hiding place like a magnet drawn to a big tool. There I was, all quiet because I thought maybe I was still invisible, but she swiftly moved the box aside and reached for me. "Come," she said simply. "You can't get away." I whimpered all the way to the office park. "How did you find me?" I asked. "You'll feel better after it's all over," was all she said.

Of course I know now that I'd always been "found"—until then, she'd simply let me believe I had a hiding place. I think about that a lot these days, because I'm old enough to have a box of broken dreams all my own. Because she's right, you know, you can't get away. You need to look inside that box sometimes and see what isn't beyond mending. You need to face your demons, and then feel better after it's all over.

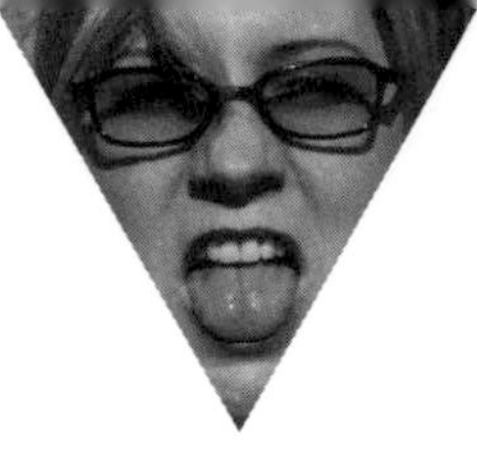

A Sign

God, I miss drinking during the day. I used to like to get it all over with early, you know: get drunk, pass out, wake up, and be hungover before the channel 3 news team started staring down at me like high school librarians. To this day, on those rare occasions when the sun shines brilliantly in the winter, I still feel that tug toward a restaurant patio, still hear that pitcher of margaritas cooing like a lover in my ear.

But my first real job after college sucked all the fun out of it for me. I worked for a publications company in La Jolla, in an office only two blocks from the beach and near this awful but insanely popular Mexican restaurant, Jose's. I used to talk my friend Tom from the graphics department into joining me there for tequila-soaked lunches. Then we'd wobble to the cove and throw Frisbees at each other until we remembered we had jobs.

I loved Tom, his presence made my pointless job infinitely more tolerable. He made me a big sign once, of a mime with his thumbs proudly tucked under his suspenders. It was dumb, made even more so by the caption "Never Mime," but it harkened back to an inside joke of had-to-be-there hilarity surrounding an incident at the cove that involved a street performer, a copious amount of tequila, and pornographic balloon animals.

Tom and I had a great time working together until our company's owner came back from prison. I had yet to meet our boss, Richard, because I was hired in the middle of his eighteen-month term at a minimum-security prison for embezzling hundreds of thousands of dollars from a young man's trust fund, for which Richard had been the (very bad) executor. I considered his incarceration a perk when I applied for the job, because the fact is that even today, with the wizardry of modern communication, it's still hard to harass your employees all the way from the hoosegow.

Then one day I walked into the office, and there were signs everywhere—not overt signs, like the kind Tom was good at making—but subtle, maddening signs that things were different. My coworkers were guarded, well dressed, and, worst of all, *working*. Tom hissed a warning before I could shriek out my usual obscene salutations. *"Richard's back,"* he hissed. So I finally got to meet Richard, and immediately afterward he handed me an assignment that would take actual effort to complete.

God! *This sucks,* I thought. That day I could hardly get anyone to come to lunch with me, even after offering to pick up the tab on a round of shots. Only Tom took me up on it. In a spree of hooch-generated defiance, we spent the rest of the afternoon on a terrace overlooking the ocean at a restaurant we could afford only because of promotional coupons. Tom told me how he had lost his former job as a chauffeur in Atlantic City because he stopped the limo on the freeway to save a dog struck by a car, stuffing the injured animal into the front seat and ignoring the irate complaints of the paying passenger in back as he detoured to the animal hospital. "He was just lying there on the emergency lane with his legs broken but sitting up, you know, watching the cars pass," Tom recalled of the dog. "Every time a car went by it would ruffle the fur on his coat."

As we belted more margaritas he kept talking about the dog. Stupidly, I thought he regretted losing his job as a driver. But I should have seen the signs. I should have seen Tom's eyes—big, spaniel eyes rounded in regret—and his hands, cupping and uncupping his margarita glass in painful reminiscence. "Hey," I said nervously when I saw the tears start to well up in his eyes. "Hey, Tom. So you lost your crappy job carting people around, so what?"

Then he told me the truth. He hadn't saved the dog after all. As his limo passed the animal on the road, the wind ruffled the fur on its coat. He'd hated himself ever since, hated himself for not even slowing down as the dog looked up hopefully. Sometimes, though, Tom would rewrite history and see himself stopping the car and laying the injured animal in the front seat, oblivious to the bitching from the passenger in back. But Tom was incapable of maintaining this fake recollection, and after enough margaritas the truth would return. "I should have stopped," he said softly, then his big eyes began to leak.

After we returned to work, Tom was canned but not me, so I quit out of sympathy. It was the least I could do for my kind friend, the guy who made me signs and supported my boozy ravings against the establishment, my Frisbee buddy with the sad eyes of a spaniel who is forever haunted by the ruffled fur of a dying dog he did nothing to save. Yes, I quit right on the spot.

Or I wish I had. Christ, I really wish I had. Instead, I just took it as a sign to stop drinking during the day.

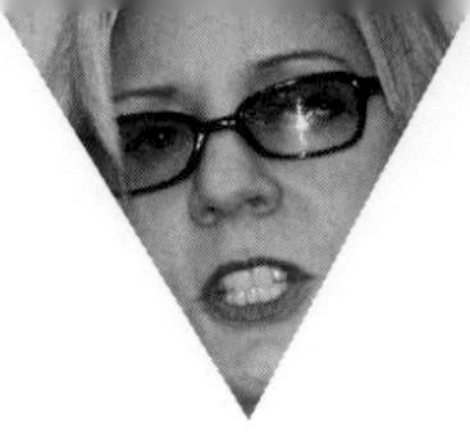

A Reason to Live

I was driving along that butt smear of a freeway section south of Freedom Parkway, the part where the badly planned number of lanes swell and contract like a big constipated boa constrictor, and I was thinking about life in general, and how it would be nice not to die that day in particular. I've had days, of course, when I felt differently. Nothing major, it's just that there were times when I got out of bed completely burdened with the fact that I was still breathing, having missed a perfectly good opportunity to croak in my sleep. On those days I'd call Lary. "I'm on the ledge," I'd bleat. "I'm gonna jump."

"Well," he always says, "what's *stopping* ya?"

"I meant *figuratively*, you fuck!" I'd shriek, and shrieking at Lary always provides me with a reason to live. Soon I'd be chirping into the phone, "Why do you keep bags of cat litter in your dishwasher? I mean, what's the *reason* for that?" But Lary's redeeming quality is his complete comfort with lack of reason. A few years ago the four of us, Daniel, Grant, Lary, and I, traveled to Prague, and I thought I'd be the tour guide, considering that I am, after all, an official foreign-language interpreter. I don't speak Czech specifically, but on the average I'd traveled to Europe more times in one month than these three plebeians had in their lifetimes, so I assumed they would all sit at my knee enthralled with my knowledge the whole time, letting me explain the reasons for things.

"Wanna know why you should keep your head at armrest level when evacuating a smoke-filled aircraft?" I'd tweet smugly during the safety demonstration. "It's because smoke rises while noxious chemical fumes sink, so the safest air is in between."

Out of the perfect pureness of friendship, Daniel and Grant were prepared to ruin their vacation and provide me with a constant audience, but once in Prague, Lary kept ditching us only to reappear later with absorbing stories of peg-legged whores and, like, bald cab drivers with boils on their heads and stuff.

Soon even I had to admit—after a spitting fit of jealousy in

With Grant and Lary at a subway station in Prague

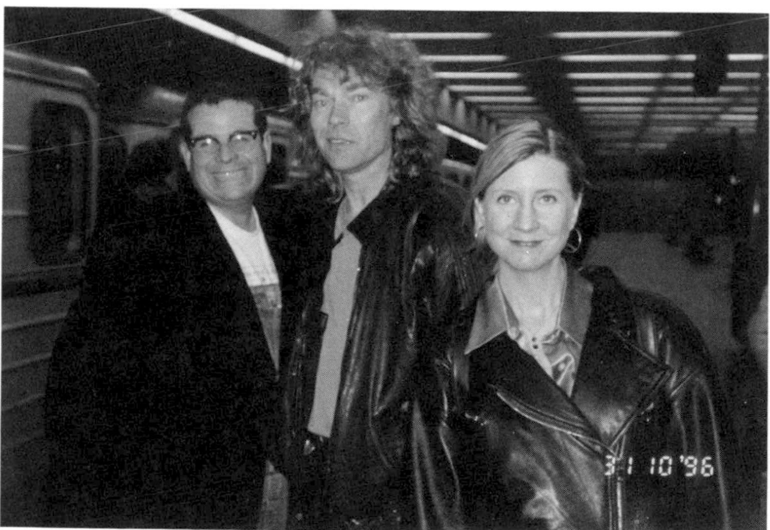

which I hit Lary with a plastic jar of Vaseline—that we'd have more fun if we just followed Lary around. After that we stuck to him like putty and, as a reward, were given a fascinating tour through the human sewage pipe of Prague. At one point we found ourselves in a sweaty underground gay bar belting shots of ouzo. Grant, who at that time was still an acting straight man (it was a bad act, but still), noticed that the walls along the dance floor were outfitted with rows of toilet-paper dispensers.

"What's the *reason* for that?" he asked.

But Grant is another who feels no need to search for reason, so he simply resumed his practice of allowing the world to unfurl its surprises. The fact that he's gay isn't one of them. We all knew that before he did, or before he chose to tell us since on some level he always knew. Since then he has lived completely unfettered by expectations. "I feel so much better," he likes to say, "since I gave up hope."

A Jewish cemetery in Prague

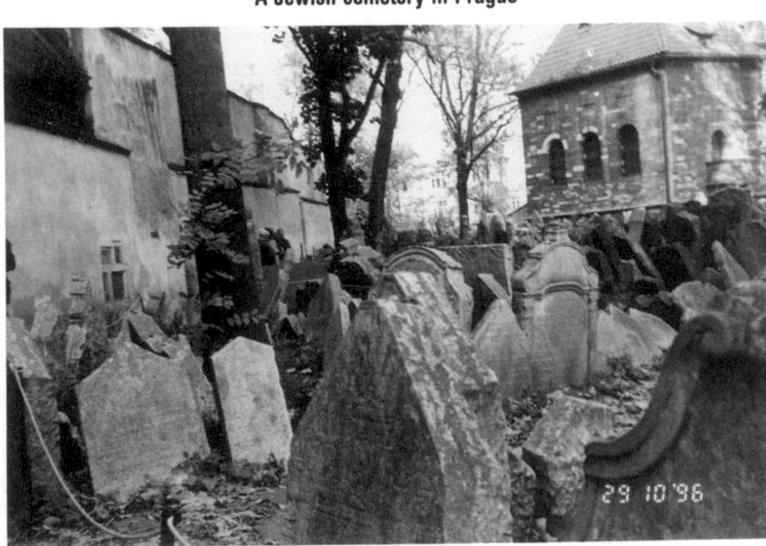

Daniel and I wish we could be that way. In contrast we are always searching, and we don't even know for what. "Why do I do this?" Daniel says sometimes, referring to his art. Usually it's after a bad newspaper review or an unsuccessful meeting with a New York gallery. Once we both found ourselves in a slough of despond at his place, drinking wine while he colored in lips on the faces of his hand-drawn exhibit announcements. That was back when he did faces. "What's the point?" he grieved while methodically brushing each envelope with a red crayon. There were hundreds of envelopes. "I should just give up."

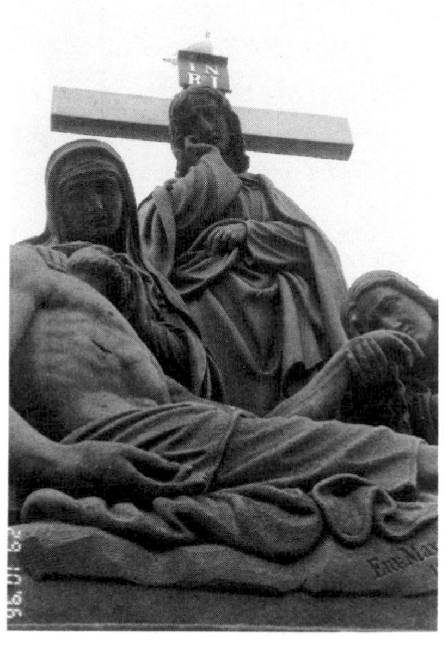

Prague

"Right," I slobbered. I was there seeking solace myself because the editor who'd accepted my article at *Esquire* had just been fired, pulling the chair out from under the biggest milestone of my career. So I wasn't jolly full of fun either, but still I perked up slightly when I saw that Daniel had accidentally skipped an envelope. "You missed one," I said, handing him the culprit that escaped his crayon.

"Well," Daniel said, stopping to correct the error, "there's no reason for leaving the house without lips, now is there?" Then I helped him resume his task, because right then I realized there's no time for seeking reasons to live when there are stacks of envelopes to be colored.

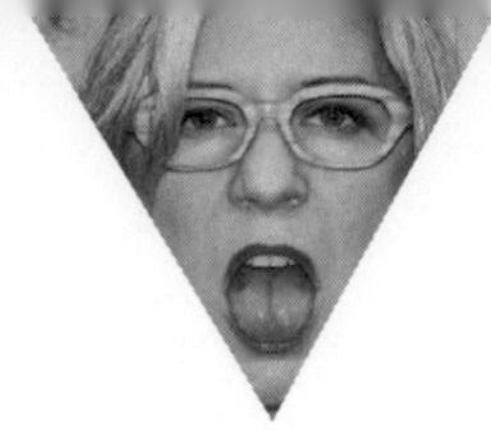

Left Behind

Lary started selling autographed pictures of Jesus, in case anyone's interested. He got the idea after working the TV camera at a Benny Hinn religious revival conference years ago. He found himself surrounded by "thousands of these fucked-up Bible freaks" and it actually scared him, which says a lot, because almost nothing scares Lary. For example, one Halloween he showed up in white flowing robes with the words "I'm Jesus, Your Fucking Savior" scrawled across his back in black marker. "I'm tempting the gods," he laughed, "like there are any."

But the religious freak show at the old Georgia Dome scared Lary. "Why?" I asked him. "I mean, did you feel yourself start to convert? Was a tiny piece of your condemned soul tugging at the rest of you, threatening to draw you into the writhing throng? Threatening to chisel a crack in that crab shell you keep around your heart?"

"Hell, no," he said, irritated that I implied he had a heart. "These people were insane, possessed. Shaking and twitching and foaming at the mouth and falling over one another. *Thousands* of them, surrounding me, screaming and moaning and chanting." He shivered, as if the memory was too much for him.

And I get it. It's like that Left Behind series of books in which all the good Christian folk get sucked into heaven and leave people like Lary to deal with the ensuing Hell on earth. "Rapture," it's called, and I'd probably fear it more if I'd been allowed to go to church as a kid. But my mother was an atheist and my father was too busy nursing his hangovers on Sunday mornings to drive us—both very viable reasons if you ask me.

"What bigger Hell is there," my mother used to say, pointing her cigarette at a passing church bus, "than a heaven full of people like that?"

So I figure that explains why Lary was scared at the Benny Hinn conference. He must have looked around and found himself in pretty much a pit, packed with undulating, screaming, sweaty possessed people, heads flailing, voices modulating, arms reaching, fingers grasping. And the crying. God, the crying. "Wailing and wailing." Lary shuddered, remembering that they sounded like sick sea elephants.

Lary realized he was alone in that pit, having been left behind by any sign of reason or civil decorum, and his whole personal philosophy was tested at that point. He believed it was foolish to go through life frightened by the prospect of Hell, because up until then he'd been so certain there was no Hell. But when he found himself in that pit with those people, penned in by an ocean of sobbing fanatics, the realization hit him that there certainly is a Hell after all, and that he was certainly in it. "Get me out of here," he inwardly screamed.

I've felt that way before. In high school I once went to church with a fragile girl who had latched on to my inability to gracefully decline her efforts to salvage my endangered soul, and I decided to take it as an opportunity to rebel against my irreligious upbringing. The church was not really a church but a cinder-block building that had all the beauty of a big public toilet. The service was a barely tolerable torrent of promised eternal agony for those who didn't adhere to every letter of their particular sect, and when it was over, I felt a soaring relief interrupted by the distressing realization that it really wasn't over after all. The worst was yet to come.

"Now we will speak in tongues," the girl told me, her translucent skin glowing with an inner awfulness visible only to me. Speaking in tongues entailed, as far as I could tell, basically flopping around at the foot of an icon and babbling. I was a shy kid at fourteen, and tough, already having grown an emotional crust not easily penetrated by fervor of any kind, so my enthusiasm for flopping and babbling was found to be insufficient by this crowd. They tried to correct it by literally pushing me around. So there I was, the daughter of an atheist and a drunk, bobbing around in a little sea of gibbering religious freaks, bouncing from fist to fist like some infidel hot potato. In all, it failed to knock me free from my ingrained paganism. I did gibber a little though. "Get me out of here," I gibbered again and again, drowned out by the bigger babbling around me.

Lary and I laugh because we have this in common: Both of us, at one point in our past, walked right into Hell and were left there alone for a while, begging to be freed until finally, graciously, we were. "Get me out of here," we'd each pleaded inwardly. Yes, we'd pleaded, but to this day I'm still wondering to whom those pleas were made, and wondering who answered them.

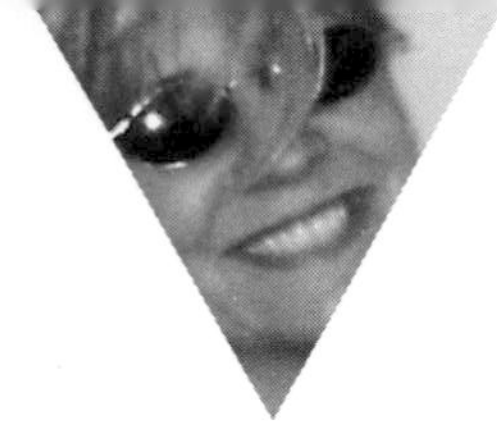

On My Knees

I have my father to thank for my unsaved soul, because my brother, for one, had tried for years to reserve me a window seat in heaven. This is before he became the embittered, godless Starbucks manager that he is today, back when he still had hope and would return from college for the holidays and lecture us on the flammability of our afterlives. He'd have to whisper all the eternal torments in store for my heathen sisters and me because if my father heard him he'd risk a beating with the top of that tin flour bin in the kitchen.

"Hell? I'll give you *hell,*" my father once roared at my brother when he spied my sisters and me on our knees in the living room about to accept Jesus into our hearts. My father got in a few noisy *thwaks* with the flour bin cover before my brother bounded out the side door, shielding his head with his Bible like he was protecting his hairdo from wet weather.

I thought I could go back to finding solace in TV reruns and fantasizing about being one of the five hundred dead fiancées of the Cartwright brothers, but no such luck. There we were, my sisters and me, on our knees, pretty far down the road to redemption, when my father figured he had to debrief us by breaking out the big illustrated children's Bible, the one in which Satan was permanently sunburned and Jesus looked like a honey-haired underwear model. Regardless of the beatings and the bellowing and the downright banishment of my brother's beliefs, my father didn't generally disapprove of Bible thumping, he disapproved of my brother's Bible thumping because he didn't want his grade-school daughters getting a God habit that would require him to drive us places, like church and whatnot, which would've cut into his bar time at the local tavern.

"You got all the God you need right here in this book," my father told us, tapping the children's Bible with the same thick finger he always used to flick us in the head when we bothered him. So there we had to stay, on our knees, while my father read random passages in his imitation James Earl Jones voice until my mother, the one true atheist in the family, saved us by handing him an opened Budweiser.

I was grateful. I don't like being on my knees. I remember accidentally ending up at some marathon mass in England once, lured there by my best friend, Laura, who was studying with me in the same Oxford college program that year. She told me we were just going to look at the interior of the cathedral because she was shocked I'd never seen one. I followed her inside like a bovine and suddenly we were filed into a pew and hemmed in all around by worshipers. Then the priest glided in, all cloaked in sparkly curtains like a parade float, with a pointy hat, and before I knew it we were spending the next five thousand years doing knee bends while the priest bellowed in some language only Beowulf could understand. "Fuck the hell out of you," I hissed at Laura as we herded ourselves out of the cathedral afterward. She laughed in response. "Don't you feel redeemed?"

Not really. It was a spring day in England, uncharacteristically warm, and the afternoon had been wasted while I'd been trapped under a dome of stained glass. This made me late meeting other friends at a pub, so I took a shortcut through a meadow that, I swear, the week before had been little more than a field of mud. In that time, though, it had bloomed to a level of luster that rivaled paradise. And I didn't even see it at first. I was too busy blindly hurrying, as if there was actually a point to my arrival at wherever I was expected, when something caught my eye.

Is that a damn pony? I asked myself, chuckling. Oh, my God, there was a pony grazing not ten yards away. The sight was simultaneously so puerile and so beautiful that I geared up myself to laugh again, but when I opened my mouth, a sob came out instead. A sob so deep it must have started somewhere in the back of my unsaved soul and gathered momentum over the years until it finally burst free, bringing every filament that made up the cynical mess of my life together right then, just for a second, to reveal the unfathomable beauty of the world. And for that second I knew I was young, and I knew neither would last—not the beauty before me nor the beauty within me. Suddenly I felt so fraught with longing, so overwhelmed at having survived the complete car wreck of my life in order to be there, in that meadow, in the middle of Oxford, where ponies roamed in the glow of a rare British sunset. It utterly defeated me, or it redeemed me . . . it doesn't matter, as both occasions are marked by falling to your knees.

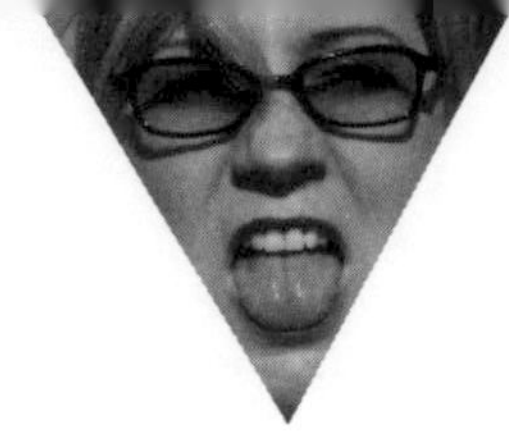

Killer Turkey

Thinking back to our family Thanksgivings, it's a wonder I survived my childhood. My mother knew she couldn't cook, so she compensated with what she considered her own flair. I remember more than one family dinner in which she simply slapped a bunch of Slim Jims on the table and told us to chow down. For fancy occasions she'd take the wrappers off before serving them. So if an entrée didn't come in a can or a box loaded with enough chemicals to kill all lesser life forms, she didn't dawdle with it. That was fine with me, because what kid likes fresh figs in their turkey stuffing anyway?

My father was worse in a way, because he occasionally fancied himself a cook, and would therefore experiment, as he did during his bread-baking binge, when the loaves came out dense as boulders and tasting like beer. The week he got his first food processor he made us a different type of homemade relish every night. That was it though—just a bowl of relish every night for dinner. "Shouldn't we be putting this *on* something?" we asked after a few spoonfuls.

"It's *gourmet* cuisine, goddammit," he shouted from his corner in the kitchen. For some reason he never joined us at the table but stood in the corner where the counters met, with a beer in one hand and a cigarette in the other, occasionally roaring at us for not appreciating the finer arts of food preparation. "Worthless, ungrateful brats," he'd grumble as he watched us pick shredded rind of some kind from our teeth.

So just imagine Thanksgiving in this household. To start the day, we put out platters of fudge. Yes, fudge. The reckoning of fudge as an appetizer is lost on me now, but at the time it was my favorite Thanksgiving Day treat. We made it by melting marshmallow creme and Hershey's chocolate chips together in a big pot. By the time dinner rolled around, we were all shaking from a sugar buzz big enough to set off car alarms across the street. Every year my father insisted the meal include cranberry sauce, which nobody ate. It was the kind that keeps the shape of a can—all grooved like it's wrapped in a ribbed condom—and it sat there through dinner quivering like a kidney waiting for a transplant, totally untouched. Sometimes I'd find it in the refrigerator weeks later, all dried up and looking like a tongue.

It fell to my mother to cook the turkey after the famous barbecue fiasco of the late seventies, which was the result of another of my father's experiments. That one ended with a cluster of his bar buddies passed out on our patio one Thanksgiving, a result of foodless boozing throughout the night because the Thanksgiving turkey my father had promised them was still nearly raw after rotating on a spit over coals for eleven hours. We had to wake them all the next morning, not to send them on their way but because dinner was ready, and that was only because my mother finally took the bird off the spit with her bare hands and threw it into the oven.

After that year my mother always cooked the turkey herself, a task she figured she could handle, because how many ingredients does a turkey have after all? Just one, and that's even if you count the gizzards, which I never really understood. For example, why do the entrails come in a little separate sack? The gizzards were always treated like a big biohazard, sitting in a bowl far away from everything. "Guts!" I squealed happily one year, preparing to plunder them for the sake of some really great practical jokes I had planned.

"Don't touch the gizzards!" my mother shrieked. The gizzards, I vaguely remember her explaining, had to stay far away from the turkey as it cooks, otherwise there'd be food poisoning. Upon hearing that, I was certain the turkey was deadly. This was my mother after all, and the only recipes I trusted her to follow were the ones on the backs of boxes that required you to add water and let the chemicals do the cooking. Our kitchen cupboards were stocked with food like Kraft macaroni and cheese, which sold four boxes to the buck at Pic 'n' Save, a local surplus store that offered old dry goods on the same shelf as motor oil. The directions called for butter as well as milk, but you could do without the butter in a pinch. The finished product was a bowl of noodles so bright orange you could use it to flag down passing aircraft.

It goes without saying that my family was not a family of chefs. Other holiday meals suffered as well: Take our traditional Fourth of July family barbecue, for instance, where my father used everything from paint thinner to hair spray to fuel a grill fire so huge it could cause traffic copters to fall smoldering from the sky. There's still a patch on my brother's scalp where the hair won't grow back, thanks to my father's infamous homemade "honey glaze" sauce that contained melted pure-cane sugar. It might as well have been a big bowl of boiling magma. It melted my father's favorite rubber spatula, but not before a drop flicked onto my brother's head. Screaming and clawing at his skull, my brother zigzagged all over the backyard before my mother was able to tackle him and pour beer on his head to keep my father's lava from boring into his brain.

Though she was deft and quick thinking in that situation, I still didn't trust my mother to follow directions closely enough to keep the turkey from turning into a big teeming ball of Ebola bacteria. They say a diet of chemicals and preservatives can kill you—and it can, because lots of my family members croaked because of the life-load of crappy food they ate—but it took *decades* for that poison to work.

A turkey gizzard is a totally different story. One wrong bite of a turkey gizzard and you're dead before your face hits the plate. It got so I had a gizzard phobia, and every year I begged my mother to banish them from the house. "All right, all *right,*" she finally agreed one year, dropping the little gizzard sack into the trash. "I don't want to poison my family," she finished. Satisfied, I bounded away, clutching a cupcake topped with enough red-tinted frosting to kill a cage of laboratory rats.

But back to the Thanksgiving barbecue calamity. That year, the resulting turkey had blackened skin and a pink interior, and anyone approaching it should have been waved away with lit flares. Among our guests that night was Rosie, my father's skinny-legged alcoholic friend who was known to ball any man who happened to still be standing after the bars closed. She had a teased beehive and a tobacco-shredded laugh, and she kept cupping all the men's crotches that night. This was less appreciated than you might expect. In the end, though, they all dissolved into the customary blubberings of drunk people. "I'm *thankful* for you, you know that?"

And I'm thankful that Rosie, who, swatted away by all the other guests, took to petting my adolescent head instead. Sitting there with this tearful woman was the first time I recall soaking up a sense of true desperation borne of loneliness. "You're beautiful, and you're smart too. I can tell," she'd blubber, stroking my hair. "Beautiful and smart, don't let anyone tell you different." Since people had been telling me different all my life, I endured her attention. She passed out on our Herculon couch with a lit cigarette in her hand, a fire hazard if ever there was one, since the Herculon fabric of the seventies was, as far as I could tell, nothing more than woven dynamite wicks.

Rather than finish the smoke for her (I'd given up my pack-a-day habit the year before at the age of thirteen), I plucked the cigarette from her fingers and flicked it into our backyard. Inside, the guests continued to recount the things they were thankful for, even though technically it was the day after Thanksgiving. "I'm thankful I'm not Rosie," laughed one. At the sound of her name, Rosie awakened, which prompted more laughter from her friends. "Rosie, what are you thankful for?" asked my father. But Rosie simply sat there, looking into the distance with welled-up eyes. "Rosie?" my father implored. She stared vacantly for a few more moments, then finally shook her head. "I'll tell you what I'd *be* thankful for," she said with her booze-beleaguered voice. "I'd be thankful for my goddamn cigarette. Where the hell is it?"

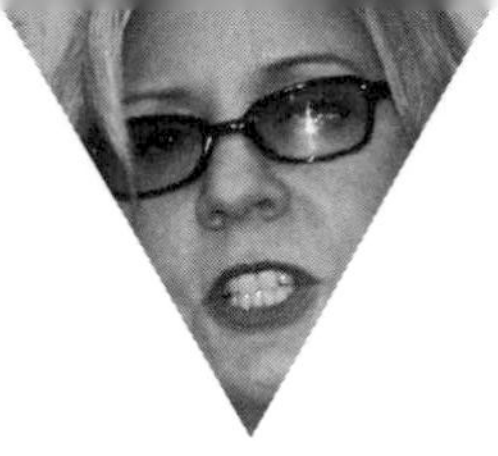

A Land That No Longer Exists

My sister Cheryl called and asked me to visit over the holidays. It was seven in the morning her time, and she was drunk. But I can respect that. She's a cocktail waitress in Las Vegas, her shift ended at 3 A.M., so she was four hours into a hard-ass happy hour, and she missed me. Only it's not the *me* me she misses—not the struggling homeowner-wannabe me, the working Joe with no money me. No, she misses the *old* me.

"Holly, what happened to you?" she slurs. "You used to go to nightclubs half naked, stay up all night dancing. You used to be so wild."

"Cher," I sigh, "I used to shit in my diapers too, and I don't do that anymore either."

Las Vegas holds fond memories for us. Our mother was a "junket" junkie, and she'd take us out of school to accompany her on eight-hour bus rides to Binion's Horseshoe along with fifty or so other booze-addled revelers, each with a fistful of coupons and endless buckets of nickels dancing in their dreams.

Cheryl, in particular, loves the way it was back then, back when she and I were best friends because we moved so much we were unable to get to know anyone else. In grade school we played "Puff, the Magic Dragon" so many times that our father's portable stereo practically imploded under the strain. We thought we knew the words too. "Puff, the magic dragon, lived by the sea, and frolicked in the Ottomiss . . ." we sang.

Later we realized Puff actually frolicked in the "autumn mist," but by then "Ottomiss" had morphed in our minds into an actual place like the Emerald City or Cinderella's palace. To us, in Ottomiss, big luminous castles beckoned in a landscape that looked like a giant unearthed chest of treasure, with sparkling jewels spilling over the side, where you could bound through fields of marigolds as soft as the eyelashes of a million angels with your best friend by your side. It was a place where big dreams came true.

But then I figured out what the song was really saying, especially that whole crappy part where Jackie Paper grows up and dumps poor Puff, who then spends eternity in an empty paradise wailing for his lifelong friend. I hate that part. I mean, how hard would it be for Jackie to go back? Just for a visit, just to press his head against Puff's sweet scaly brow and, for a day, frolic in the Ottomiss again? How hard *is* that? But Jackie never goes back, and Puff remains trapped in a land that no longer exists.

"Fuck *this*," I said, and never played the song again.

Sometime after that, Cheryl and I grew apart. Later, I realized it occurred when my parents separated. Cheryl was eighteen, and she used that opportunity to move in with her boyfriend. My brother had long moved out on his own, leaving my younger sister and me, both minors, to live by ourselves for a while in a beachside apartment that both our parents had temporarily vacated, not that they didn't check in on us occasionally. This kind of left us feeling like we had little to rely on.

Cheryl especially, because she'd always been somewhat of a tortured sentimentalist. She still talks about her beloved cat, Casey, who

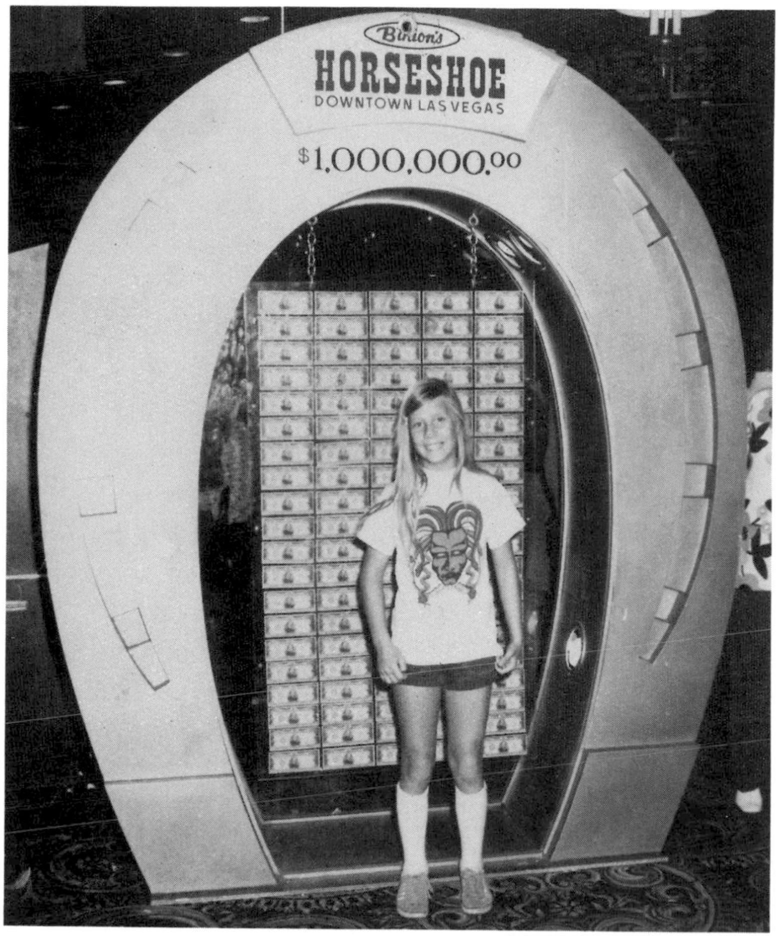

At nine in front of the famous Binion's Horseshoe $1 million display

for years used to meet her at her car door when she parked across the street after returning home late at night. Back then she was known for her beaming beauty fetchingly coupled with her penchant for hard partying. She still talks about Casey because she couldn't rely on much. She couldn't rely on me not to move across the country, she couldn't rely on her parents, she couldn't rely on her boyfriends not to abuse her, she couldn't even rely on herself, really, not to keep making bad decisions in her life. But at least she could rely on her cat to meet her at her car door when she parked across the street. But Casey got old, and one night he was killed by a car right there on the street as he crossed it to meet her.

I wish I could say Cheryl has never been the same since, but she has been exactly the same—the same crazy behavior, the same wild nights, the same fantasy of eternal youth. I know she's simply grasping for some purpose to lend to her passing years, and I know we're alike. I just hide my panic better than she does is all.

"Can't you come visit?" she asked, pausing to puff on her cigarette. "Just for a day?"

I said I'd come because, all around her, even at that early hour, I know the skyline is awash in flashing lights, the Strip is laid out like a magic miniature golf park for massive giants, and there are bright marquees depicting buckets of riches and the promise of dreams granted, and in the middle of it all is my sister, Cheryl, and I don't want her to be trapped in a land that no longer exists.

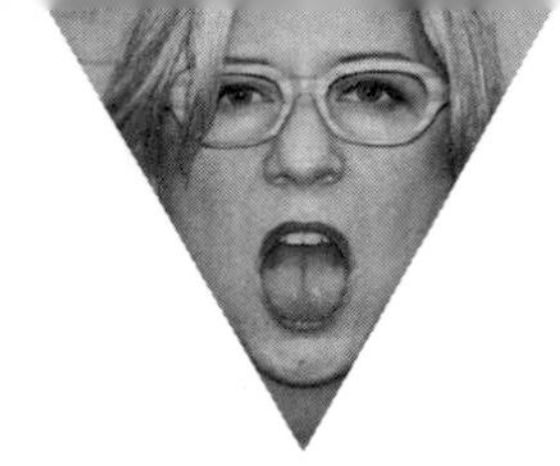

Letting Go in Las Vegas

I'd had two cocktails and it wasn't even 10 A.M., which led me to conclude that I loved Las Vegas. How could anybody not love it? It's so radiantly cheap and impure. Right then I was in the Venetian Hotel on the Strip, a hotel that is the total ass end of tacky, and as much as I would have loved to wallow in the chlorinated canals of the replicated Italian village upstairs, I preferred the casino on the ground floor even better because I liked the noise.

"One more," I told the bartender.

He asked me where I'm from. I told him Atlanta, even though that's not entirely true. I was born in Burbank but haven't been back since, so I've learned not to take the question too literally. People are too attached to hometowns, I think, so I let mine go and just pick a city, and I would pick Las Vegas, only I tend to confine my answers to places I've actually lived.

The bartender, who is from Denver, notices that I'm one-

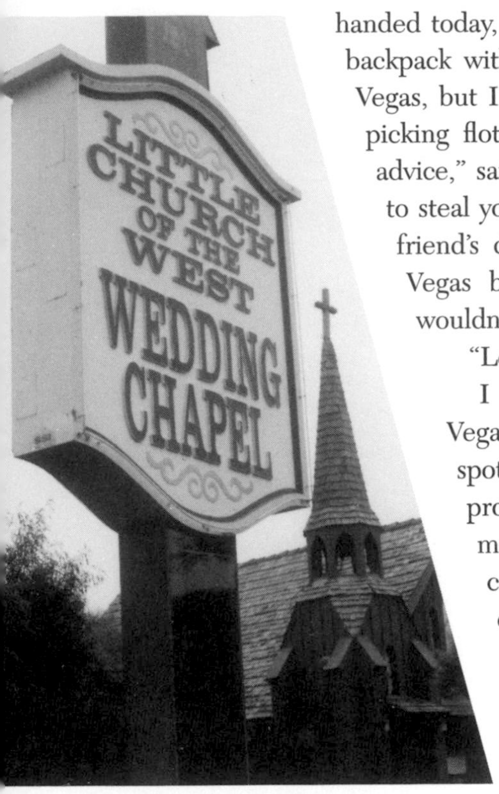

My parents' wedding chapel in Las Vegas, behind the Frontier Hotel

handed today, because the other is clutching my backpack with a lobster-like grip. I might love Vegas, but I still don't trust the crusty pocket-picking flotsam who live here. "Here's some advice," said the bartender. "If someone tries to steal your purse, let go." It turned out his friend's daughter was knifed in downtown Vegas by a purse snatcher because she wouldn't let go.

"Let go," he repeated.

I was eight when I first came to Vegas. For us, it was a family vacation spot before the city figured out it was profitable to bill itself that way. For my mother, who was uncomfortable with conventional displays of parental endearment, gambling became the perfect conduit for family bonding. "Don't get suffocated by your safety net, kid," she'd narrate as she played. "Let go of your chips and go for it."

On one of these family outings, I found a menu of services from the notorious Chicken Ranch whorehouse and learned that in the market of legalized prostitution the going rate for a tongue bath was only $95. *Is that all?* I thought, and to this day I can't think of a harder job than being a whore.

"Give me that!" my mother shrieked, trying to snatch the menu from my hand. "I said *let go!*"

I let go of it, but she didn't. Years later I found the menu again in a box of her possessions, along with her wedding bouquet. The fragile rosebuds were browned and curled like the little fists of a half a dozen mummified babies. It was hardly recognizable from the day my parents got married thirty-seven years earlier at the Little Church of the West behind the Frontier Hotel on the Vegas Strip. Their wedding picture shows my father looking dapper, like Desi Arnaz, and my mother looking like she had no idea what's in store for her. In the picture they were holding hands, but eventually they let go, and I mean that more than in the literal sense.

During the famous MGM Grand Hotel fire twenty-six years later, which killed eighty-four people, heat and smoke had trapped people and pushed others to the outer ledges of the upper floors, where news cameras were trained on them as they clung, dangling, from their useless skytop perches. I hoped the people would hang on, but they didn't. One woman's skirt bellowed above her head as she fell. "No, no, no, *no!*" onlookers cried in anguish. Another group of victims was found in an elevator lobby. They died clutching the suitcases they refused to let go, having wasted valuable time packing them before attempting to evacuate.

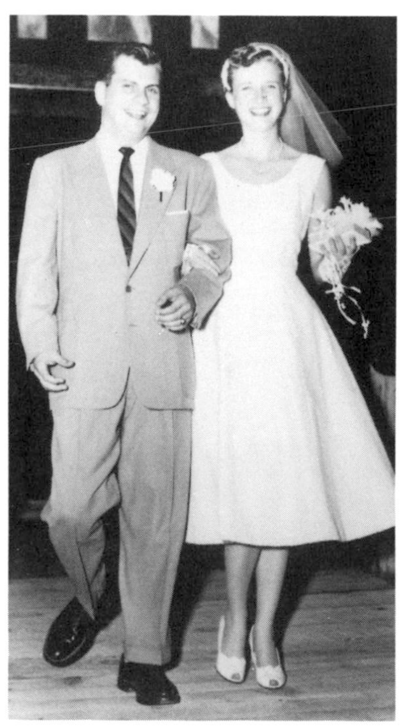

Parents' wedding

Still other victims were found in one of the hotel rooms, five of them holding hands and looking like they were asleep, except for the shadows of soot around their nostrils and mouths. They had let go, but not of each other. My guess is that they ventured as far as they could, then, upon realizing the inevitability of their predicament, decided not to cling to things like frantically packed suitcases or the hotel's unforgiving exterior ridge but instead spent their final moments in the simple comfort of human contact.

So there you have it: perfect

examples of the importance of knowing when to let go, and when not to. It's like gambling, I guess. Back before my mother had gotten good at gambling, she used to play the nickel slot machines at Circus Circus, while trapeze artists performed without a net in the atrium above the casino floor. When she won her first twenty-dollar jackpot, my mother, uncomfortable with most human contact, surprised me by hugging me tightly in her excitement. It's no wonder I love Vegas, because it takes a long time for four hundred nickels to fall out of a slot machine.

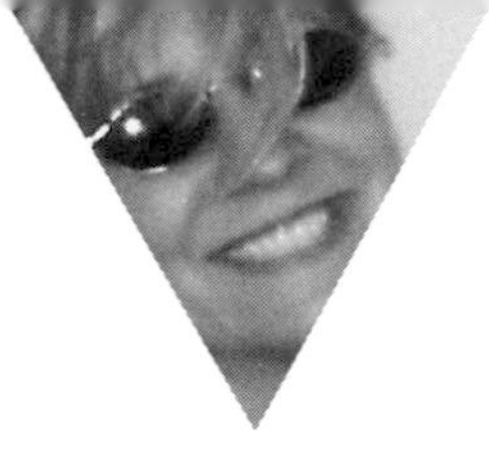

My Mother and the History of Pornography

I'm almost positive not many people have been forced to look at porno with one of their parents, so I consider myself unique in that way. It happened years ago, when my mother and siblings and I got lost in Amsterdam on our way to the Anne Frank House and ended up in the Red Light District instead. It's not that we wouldn't each have ambled there on purpose eventually, just not together as a unit, because Amsterdam's Red Light District is probably the worst place on the planet for a family outing. At one point, we passed a movie bill picturing a man in a rubber suit wallowing in his own shit—and I'm just assuming it was his own, because even now my brain wants to make the best of it. For all I know it could have been a crap collective, which is an adequate metaphor given the situation.

"Look," hollered my brother, Jim, "that theater across the street has a *'Live Vibrator' show!*" My sister Cheryl was unimpressed. "Live vibrator?" she mumbled. "In the States, we call that a penis."

Christ, I thought to myself, clutching my eyes. *Where am I?*

If my father had been alive he would have pulled us out of there by our hair. Let me tell you, it's really embarrassing to walk around with your father's fist ensnared in your hair. So it was a good thing he was not there with us in Amsterdam, because if he had been he would have burst into flames, and left my siblings and me with our scalps blistered where his fingers had once clutched our hair. Even that would probably not have kept Jim from the "Live Vibrator" show.

The Amsterdam Red Light District has since been cleaned up somewhat, but back then it was absolutely saturated in porno. You couldn't *not* look at it, unless you wanted to close your eyes and feel your way through, which I strongly discourage. And the whores were not nice either, so we couldn't ask them directions. They really seemed to resent freeloading onlookers, and one even threw a bucket of toilet-bowl water on a crowd that had converged outside her display window. It missed us and hit some backpackers, who couldn't scramble away fast enough.

"That was close," my mother laughed as we darted down the street. She stopped in front of a bookstore window, where a magazine cover depicted a pile of limbs in the throes of sweaty cluster sex. The close-up photo was so severe the subjects were hardly discernible. "What is *that?*" my mother asked as she peered at it closely. "Do I see a *hoof* in there?"

We wandered into an X-rated magazine store, where the locals were shopping for sex toys with the seriousness of a politician's wife picking out vegetables for an important dinner. From a distance I could hear my mother talking to the clerk in loud, slowly pronounced English, "I don't get it; what's so sexy about a big rubber fist?"

We lost each other soon after that. Cheryl and I stayed together, bound by some black Afghani hash we had bought in a coffee shop. It came balled up in dark chocolate fudge and was listed on the menu under "Bom Boms." The waiter recommended it to us with the following endorsement: "Honey, they gonna knock yo' tits off." We ate some and then spent hours laughing and listening to an old man retch at the end of the bar.

Later, at the hotel, we heard that my sister lost my mother at the Sex Museum, a four-story structure near the train station that chronicles the history of pornography. Kim became engrossed in an arcade video titled "Jocks in Socks," and evidently the video was tucked out of view, because my mother thoroughly searched for Kim before approaching the man in the ticket booth to ensure she wasn't missing a section of the museum. "Young man," she said to him. "I've been up and down the four floors here, is there any more?" To which the man, his eyes sweeping the scores of exhibits devoted to every sexual fetish you could imagine (and scores more you couldn't), responded, "Lady, isn't that enough?"

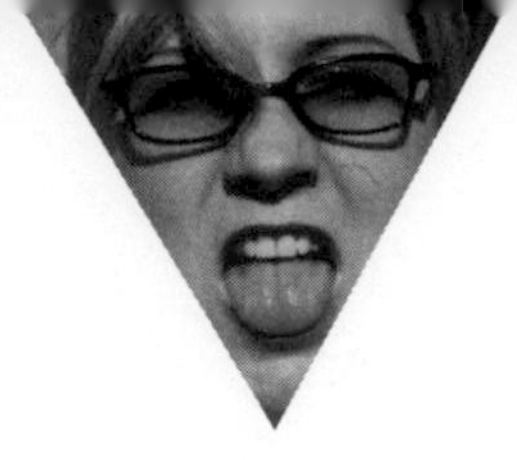

Hanging on in Zurich

The last time I was mugged, I could have let go of my purse and saved myself some decorum. But no, my fingers fastened on the strap like the jaws of a little pit bull on a pork chop. You should have seen the thief's face when she looked back to see me still there, hanging on. I was surprised myself: I didn't know I was that quick, but because I hung on, I did a face plant in the sidewalk. Even then I didn't let go, and I was dragged behind the thief in an incredibly undignified manner.

The mugging occurred in Zurich, and traditionally the Swiss reserve their crime quotient for thievery on a much more massive scale—such as the jillions in Jewish assets their banks have hoarded since the Second World War—but lately miscreants of a trivial nature have threaded themselves through the country's cracks, probably enticed by the easy game, as I can't think of a single Swiss citizen who would value a wallet over suitable social behavior.

But me? I hung on, and while I was being dragged, I remember thinking, *Yes, I bet this is very attractive, especially since my entire body has been blessed with the flexibility of a redwood with the single exception of my elbows, which are double-jointed and can bend inward unnaturally.* When the thief doubled back to try yanking and twisting the purse from my grasp, my arm simply flopped about and contorted like an angry eel, yet I still hung on. Finally, the thief gave up, and the disgusted onlookers recommenced their strolling. One gentleman and his companion sidestepped me like a pile of poo. "Her bag must contain something very valuable," he said in a tone that revealed he thought the opposite.

I'd have been angry if I didn't concede his point. Essentially, I'd just risked my life for a small wad of foreign money, two tampons, and one half-masticated, fuzz-covered peppermint pellet. "Hanging on to crap will kill you," I've heard Grant say a zillion times, which seems appropriate, because he is always divesting himself of his stuff. He's accumulated and dispersed the contents of at least a dozen households since I've met him. His present house is little more than a funnel for furniture—a big colon, kind of—as things are put there just to be passed through. To know Grant is to know his mantra: "Let it go. Let it go."

I try to remember that when I find myself suddenly still furious over offenses from the distant past, such as the time my college roommate fucked my useless boyfriend, or the time I think my grade-school teacher was trying to secretly dry-hump me while we stood in line for the cafeteria, or the time my older sister beat the crap out of me with a wooden spatula, or even the time some bitchy plebe gave me really bad service at the photo-processing counter. You can harbor an entire catalog of slights like these, resentments you thought were long gone that suddenly bubble into your brain one day while you're driving. Pretty soon there you are screaming and conducting imaginary arguments with people who are probably long dead. So what possible good comes out of hanging on?

But it's not always that easy, knowing when to let go of things. Take hope, for example. I have this insane hope that the world will one day be relatively free of people pissing out their territory—religion-wise, values-wise, otherwise—and that there really might be a universal plateau we can reach. Lary says I should let that go, and start stockpiling weapons. But I can't, and I really wonder whether that weakens or strengthens me as a person.

In Zurich, the thief gave up on me, and simply walked away. *Walked*, with a curious look on her face. She had severely plucked eyebrows and braided hair the color of highway hazard cones, and she didn't speak German. I know this because I saw her again as I turned the corner, talking to the rest of her ratty gang, one of whom started to make his way toward me before she stopped him. So we watched each other, the thief and I, and then something funny happened.

We laughed. We just did, somewhat sheepishly, and as I continued on my way she said something to her friend. I don't speak their language, but I have an idea what it was. "That's the one," she was saying, "who won't let go."

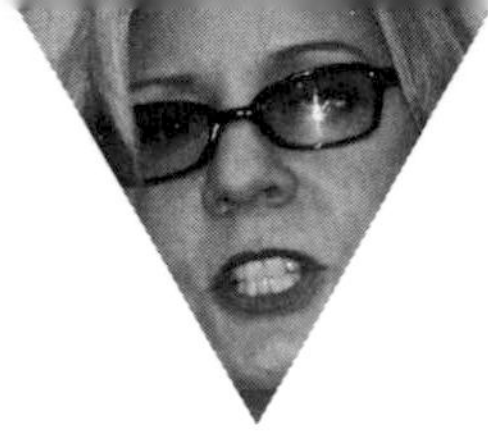

A Pool of Piss

Twice in my life I have awakened in a pool of urine—and it wasn't even mine. That's what happens when you own a new puppy, and fail to understand that the incessant whining you hear at 2 A.M. doesn't mean she wants to be taken out of her cage and cuddled while you continue to sleep. People are a little harder to train than puppies.

Take gambling, for example. Gambling was a big bonding thing between my mother and me. As a mathematician and missile scientist, she was addicted to blackjack, and thus those junkets to Vegas became our common family outing. My mother even took pride in the fact that she was evicted from the Golden Nugget because the pit boss discovered her ability, like Dustin Hoffman's in *Rain Man,* to keep track of dealt cards, even if the dealer was using a six-deck shoe. "I'm a threat," she'd beam. "They're afraid of me." And they were, because she usually won. Usually. Sometimes she followed the odds and they bit her in the ass. At these times she'd end up busted but always ready to bounce back, reasoning, "What was I *supposed* to do, back away from a good hand?"

She'd try to coach me sometimes. If the dealer dealt me an eleven, she'd insist I double my bet, even though I'm a timid gambler. I mean, I can't even count. I'd have to hold my cards out for the dealer to count because they always hate it if you take too long. So it intimidated me to slap more money down on the odds I'd win. *But those were the odds*, and my mother's philosophy was always to play the odds rather than cover your losses. "You gotta keep puttin' your chips on the table, kid. Don't be afraid," she'd say. "But if you lose three times in a row, I don't care how much you like the dealer, find another table."

My brother never learned to leave the table. He would sit there stubbornly, losing hand after hand, convinced that the more he lost the more certain it was that he would eventually win it back. He usually busted, and would end up tracking my mother down at another table hoping she would pitch him a few chips from her winnings. "He won't learn," she'd say, "you got to leave a losing table."

Words of wisdom, I say. Because sometimes it's hard to leave a losing table. You get comfortable there. The dealer might be nice, he counts your cards for you, the other players are nice, they laugh at your jokes. But you keep losing and losing just the same, and then you give it your last shot and you have nothing left. At that point, if you ever acquire any more chips, it's hard to put them on another table because you don't want to risk losing them. I mean, everyone usually experiences some loss in their lives: They trusted someone who sold them out, they loved someone who lied to them, they lost someone who was dear to them. It happens.

But, unlike puppies, we can't be trained not to make the same mistake over and over. The best we can hope for is to recognize the odds, and to be brave enough to back up a good hand if we have it. According to my mother, if the odds are in your favor, grab at 'em.

"You got to put your chips on the table, kid. Don't be afraid." Don't get suffocated by your safety net. That way, if you lose you can't say you didn't try. You read the signs, they said "thumbs-up," and you went for it. Who could fault you for that? It's like she always said, "If you're gonna fall on your ass, it's best to land on both butt cheeks."

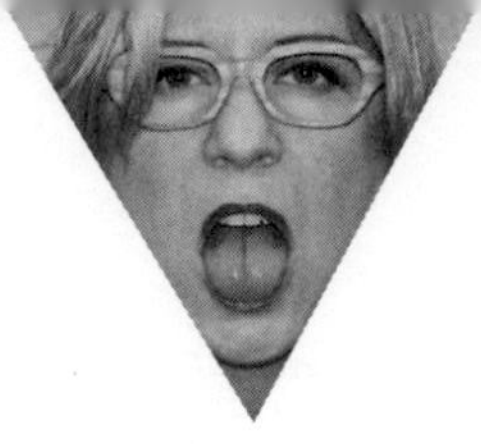

Born-Again Booze Weenie

I miss college. Not because of the gaggle of creatively starved fascists who were my professors but because back then I could *drink*. My favorite cocktail in college was this concoction called "Smith & Kearns." It contained, as I remember, brandy, Kahlua, cream, vodka, soda, some other stuff, about a bucket of fermented potatoes, frog parts, ground glass, and two cans of lighter fluid. The bartender needed protective goggles to mix it. He then poured it into a large trough and we, the future of America, would soak our heads in it until it was time to take midterms.

I *think* that's how it was, anyway, seeing as how my memory is kind of foggy. There's probably video footage of it somewhere, and I'm sure it'll show me having fun (and probably explain all those little mystery bruises people wake up with after a bender). Now, though, I can't drink more than two glasses of wine without having to stop and look for my liver, which by that time will have escaped from my body out of self-preservation and can be found on the road hitchhiking its way to a healthier host. "Get back in my body!" I'll have to yell to it, and my liver will just keep walking, waving me off. "I warned you," it'll say. "I've had it. The Chinese'll pay good money for me." Eventually we reunite, but not until I promise to remember I'm not in college anymore.

Because in college, for example, I could start out with tequila ("I'd like the worm extra bloated, please"), switch to kamikazes, and by the end of the evening be rifling through the cabinets like Kitty Dukakis looking for hair spray to mix with my Mountain Dew. The next day I'd bounce out of bed, read a book by Joan Didion, and have the report finished in time for my one o'clock class.

But by the time you get into your thirties, sometimes your body basically decides to issue a stop-loss order against any more alcohol damage, without warning or asking your permission or anything. It does this by suddenly making your hangovers so hellacious that they couldn't hurt more if your brain actually had, during your sleep, transformed into a toxic ball of molten poison that shoots volcanic acid from your eye sockets every few seconds. This is your body's way of saying, "Time for a new lifestyle, lush bucket."

But the cruelest part is it takes a while before you figure out just how much your body will allow you to get away with. Sometimes you can have that second margarita and feel fine the next morning, and sometimes you feel like your head has been left on a stick outside for eight days under a shower of axes. Essentially it's up to you to find the balance, so you keep playing hit-and-miss with your puny level of cocktail consumption until you find a happy medium. It's either that or stop drinking altogether, which I did once . . . until one day I woke up to find my liver staring at me sternly. "What are you, *dead*?" it said.

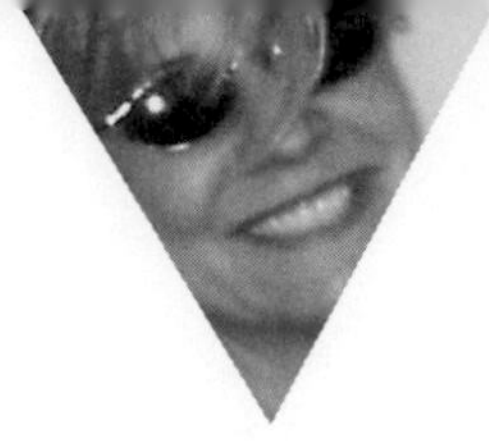

An Ode to Crappy Cars

When I came to Atlanta eight years ago, it was in a '69 yellow VW Bug with the door panel held in place by a roll of duct tape, with French fries permanently bonded to the floorboard under a crust of dried coffee. It cost me two hundred dollars, and it was barely above a moped in the motor evolution. The seatbelt left a streak of rust across the front of my clothes, and if it was raining outside, I got wet inside. Since then I've upgraded to Japanese, but when, in a department store parking lot, I saw a woman use her car door to accidentally scrape a thumbnail-sized piece of paint off the passenger side of my relatively new Honda, I thought to myself, *God, I miss my Bug.*

There's a certain power in driving a crappy car. Take Lary: He drives the rusty, broken, rolling ball of Bondo that used to be a BMW in better days. As an added touch, of course, he has those big plastic biblical characters propped up in the backseat. His car is *worse* than a coffin on wheels, because a coffin would presumably provide you some protection from the elements. If you get in Lary's car, insects and birds—thinking you'll be dead soon enough anyway—will assume permission has been granted to scavenge off your body and will dive at you through the broken skylight, the broken window, or any of the saucer-sized gaps rusted through the frame.

"What are you doing?" I asked him once, when I found him sprinkling potato chips in the backseat.

"Gotta feed the woodland creatures," he answered.

Once Lary watched through his rearview mirror as some fool in a Saab with a cellular phone stuck to his head backed into his car. The Saab was unscathed but there was a dent the size of a cigar box on Lary's rear fender, and, get this, Lary *didn't care.*

"I could have honked," he said, noting that the accident was avoidable, "but it was worth getting hit just to see the expression on that guy's face." The Saab driver insisted Lary take a twenty-dollar bill for the damage. Lary used the money to buy a hundred-pound sack of birdseed.

"You don't own a bird," I reminded him.

"It's for the pigeons so they'll stop eating the Friskies I leave out for the alley cats," he said.

The other day Lary looked out his living room window and saw his car sitting in a puddle. Upon closer inspection he discovered that the puddle was brake fluid. "I guess I better get that fixed," he said, conceding that a car's ability to stop is almost as important as its ability to go, "or maybe it means I need another car."

I didn't bother to point out that he already *has* another car—a perfectly preserved vintage Beemer he keeps covered in his carport—because I know what he means. He needs something disposable. It's like that millionaire folk artist who, when asked why he lived so simply, answered, "If you own too many things, they start to own you."

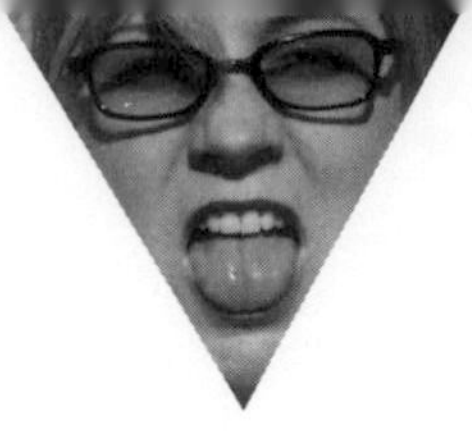

Confessions of a Festival Whore

It all started with the Tuscaloosa Folk Art Festival in October 1995. I went there with Daniel, up until this time referred to as a "real" artist, who was on his way to exhibit his work for the first time in a . . . well, I guess you would call it a "booth." Also with us was Grant, the notorious proprietor of "Sister Louisa's Worldly Possessions in the Church of the Living Room," who makes his living by just touching things and having them turn to gold. "Dinner's on me, honey!" is a common phone message from Grant after another of his mysterious, wallet-fattening transactions comes through. None of us know exactly how Grant stays in the black, but we're almost positive it doesn't involve the illegal sale of vital human organs.

Grant drove us to Tuscaloosa, with Daniel's art stacked in the back of his truck and Al Green blaring from the CD player. When we got there none of us knew how to put up the borrowed vendor tent, so I struggled with it on my own until a veteran festival troll took pity on us and supervised. Soon we were set to go, with me and Grant ready to hock art like carnival barkers, and Daniel . . . well, Daniel began reciting a mantra that would last him for the rest of the festival. It went something like this: "I hate this. I hate this. I hate this," said in varying degrees of bile-spitting vehemence.

I guess it wasn't until Daniel was actually there with his artistic vision displayed like an Amway exhibit for thousands of funnel-cake-greased fingers to fondle that he realized he had posted a huge dollar sign on his artistic soul. Here he was, an artist with pieces in galleries and museums across the country (as well as Mexico and Prague), shucking his work from under a striped awning, across from a man selling candleholders made from bent forks. After the first five minutes, Daniel wanted to tunnel underground. He was a good sport about it, though, nodding approvingly as I excitedly displayed the poodle-shaped toilet-paper cozy that I'd bought a few booths down and laughing when Grant pretended to bellow through a bullhorn, "Come see the artist formerly known as Daniel, now known as the 'Festival Whore.' "

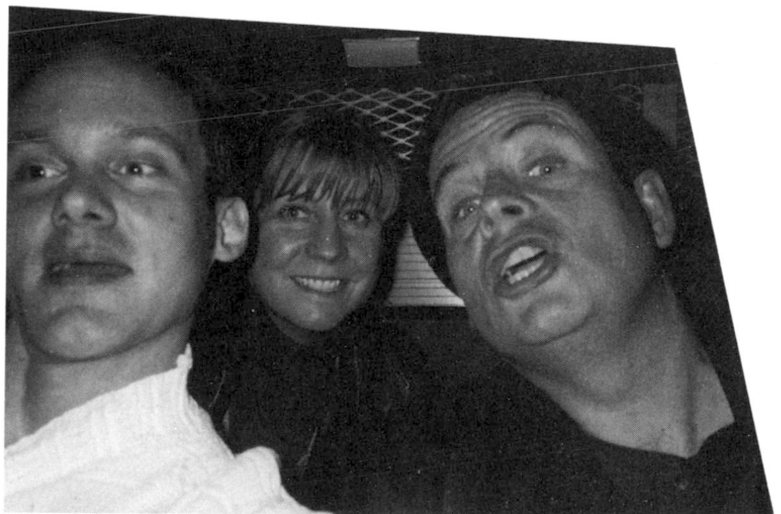

Daniel, me, and Grant driving to Tuscaloosa Art Fest in Grant's truck

It was a juried event, and on the last day one of the judges bestowed a ribbon upon Daniel's booth. Probably because he was almost completely deaf, this judge spoke in a booming voice that carried for blocks. "I think you're the best artist at the whole festival," he told Daniel, shouting it loud enough to be heard all the way across the pond. The judge stayed a while, telling us about how he became an ordained minister through the classified ad of a tabloid newspaper. He specialized in performing weddings that expired after one weekend, and once declined a request to perform a ceremony for a marriage that would expire after only one hour. "I'm not gonna marry any premature ejaculators!" he shouted, turning heads all around. We were quite tickled by it.

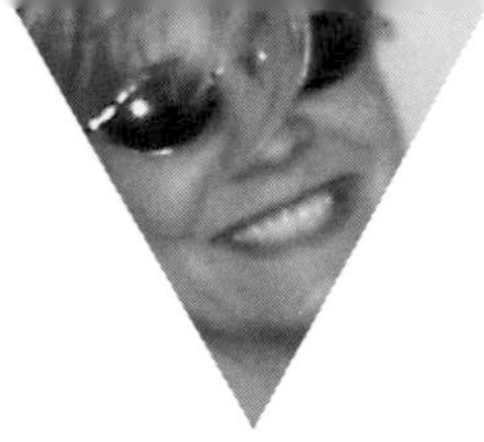

Hell Is a Festival

Fuck festivals. I've felt that way since I went and became a bona fide festival-booth art pimp myself not long ago. Chalk it up to being a little lost, career-wise.

I had a booth where I sold photography and begged friends to bring me beer because I felt trapped, fearing to leave lest some Dunwoody housewife let loose her inner klepto and pilfer one of my framed photographs, which I'd end up practically giving away by the festival's end anyway. "Take it! Christ!" I'd grumble, funnel-cake flakes in my matted hair.

To this day my friends marvel at the bad luck I've had weather-wise at every spring festival I entered, which totaled a whopping two before I packed up my entire frostbitten ass and vowed never to return. Grant didn't even last that long. I'd talked him and Lary into reserving a booth next to me at the festival. Grant's contribution featured his Sister Louisa pieces, among them a collection of "Rapture

Shields" touted as protection against the inevitable gang of marauding pagans in the event the biblical prophecy of the Rapture came to light, along with a rack of old aprons. Lary sold gilded shrines.

In truth, the Rapture Shields were a collection of trash can lids, and they got a lot of laughs, but I don't remember anyone actually getting out a wallet for one. In fact, we were experiencing the coldest weather in spring festival history and couldn't even take our hands out of our pockets. I swear it must have been thirty degrees, *in May*, and I am completely positive the dark side of the moon had warmer weather than Atlanta that weekend.

Lary is mad at me for making him enter that festival, which is saying a lot, because Lary, though he may be lost like me, and evil, and happily admits he's a thief, doesn't hold grudges. But this is different, because he's pretty protective of his art, and here I'd talked him into hawking it at a spring festival, and not just any spring festival, but the very spring festival that the Gods of Freezing Rain and Wind and Gray Skies and Suffocating High Atmospheric Pressure all picked to converge in the heavens and crap on.

Daniel, Grant, and me on a tram in Prague

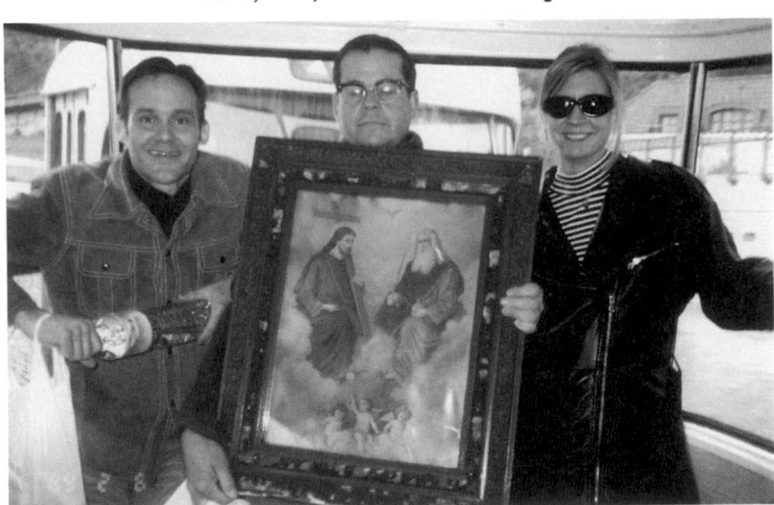

Because of the terrible weather, there were maybe one and a half customers at the whole fair, and we'd catch glimpses of them from our abandoned vendor tents, wandering about in the abyss, bundled up like lost Eskimos. "Over here!" we'd shout, like castaways trying to flag down distant rescue efforts. By the end of the first day I'd sold one item, a thirty-dollar sympathy purchase from one of the event coordinators. One guy acted interested in the most expensive piece I had to sell, though, and he even told me he'd go to the ATM to get the cash to pay for it. But the other artists all nodded jadedly when I told them about it. "The ATM getaway," they sympathized. "They all say that."

Of course by the second day Lary and Grant had pretty much abandoned their booth and urged me to follow suit, but I refused. So I stuck it out the next day, which is when the monsoon struck. People were leaning into the wind like old ladies trying to push through a stiff revolving door. Grant's entire rack of aprons blew down the street, along with the sign I had hung on his booth that read "Please Steal This Shit." By the time the flash flood started, the other artists and I were so exhausted we simply shrugged. *Good,* we thought, *now we get to drown.*

Luckily I'd borrowed my vendor booth from my friend J.R., who is a metal artist. He designed the booth himself, and it was about as easy to put up as an Australian opera house, but just as sturdy. The other artists ran to it for cover, including J.R., whose new store-bought booth was leaking so bad he had to cover his art with a tarp. From there we watched the water roil down the street, sweeping people's wares along with it, including a rusty tailgate from Grant's Sister Louisa collection with the words "Get the Hell Outta Dodge" painted across it.

I probably would have curled up and cried right then if not for the guy from the day before, who picked that time to pop in and hand me a wad of wet money fresh from the ATM. "I was afraid you'd be gone," he said, tucking my most expensive piece under his arm. *No, not gone,* I thought as I took his money, *just lost is all.*

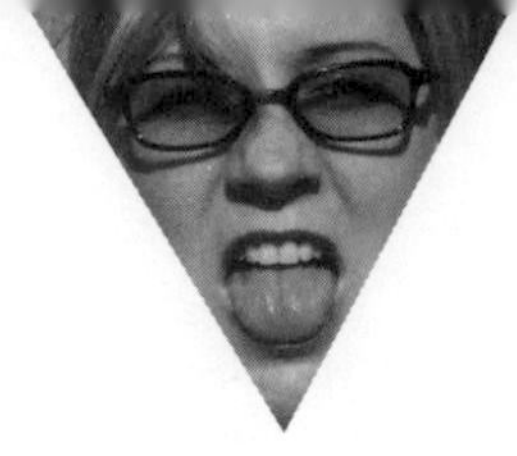

Lost Things

I got lost on the way to Monterey once. It was years ago, and my sister Cheryl and I were driving there from southern California. The route was simple, an eight-hour shot down the freeway, but we were at that monstrously invincible fake-I.D. age, that sun-baked, silver-ring-on-every-finger age. In short, we were drunk and drugged, and basically lucky beyond measure that we ever survived to become the craggy, bleachy-haired ex-beach tramps with matching laugh lines that we are today. God, we were idiots.

Such amiable idiots. We started the road trip on a whim in the middle of the night, and I keep remembering the quiet lightning that fractured the blackness in the far-off horizon. Every few minutes there was this staggering display of silent radiance, like a big wizard in the distance was performing powerful spells. "Did you see that? There it is *again*!" we'd holler. I guess that's what got us lost—

looking for the lightning—because eventually we decided that we wanted to be in the middle of the storm.

But we lost the lightning and never got close to the storm. Weird, I remember thinking from the front seat, no matter how fast we drive, the clouds are always ahead of us. Eventually the sun rose and the sky became evenly brilliant, and after much meandering we decided to follow our original plan, which was to track down one of our childhood homes, a place we simply referred to as "the pink house."

I have trouble remembering why the pink house held a particular fondness for us, because by that time we had moved, literally, every year of our lives. I was five when we lived at the pink house. It was there that our little sister, Kimberly, lost her shoes, and we made her a new pair from fabric scraps in hopes of keeping our father from kicking our asses when he found out that her good ones were gone. Kimberly's new shoes looked like plaid biblical sandals, and our father wasn't fooled for a second. "No, really," we cried as we dodged him between the moving boxes that were like permanent furniture at all our addresses, "She outgrew her other pair."

"Dad was always getting pissed at us for losing things," we laughed while we were lost that day. He even used to blame us for getting *him* lost during all the cross-country moves we made. We proved to be bad map readers on car trips, issuing random instructions like "take a right at the red dot." After that, we were relegated to the backseat. "You're a disgrace to the daughters of traveling trailer salesmen everywhere," he chided us affectionately.

Driving around, Cheryl and I finally, via Iceland, I think, found the pink house. It had lost its original paint and was now a sort of maple color, but we recognized it from a small set of concrete steps imbedded in the grass that circled the terraced front yard like a little arena. "This is where Dad sat, right here," Cheryl said, pointing to a specific spot on the concrete. She was referring to the only intact family photo we have to this day, which was taken while we all sat on those steps. "Kim was on his lap, I was next to him, you were on Mom's lap, and Jim was next to you," she sighed, finished.

I guess it was important to her to find that exact spot. I'm looking at that picture right now, and in it the sun is beaming on the six of us, and Kim is wearing the shoes she later lost in the park. My father is the age I am today, and looking closely, I can see that on his left hand he wears a ring. I recognize it as his signet ring from the army. I wonder what happened to that ring. I didn't even learn he'd served in the army until after he just up and died one day. Soldiers attended his burial, and they handed me the folded flag from atop his coffin to keep.

I wish they hadn't done that. I wish they had handed it to my brother or someone else, because it wasn't even two months later

Family photo

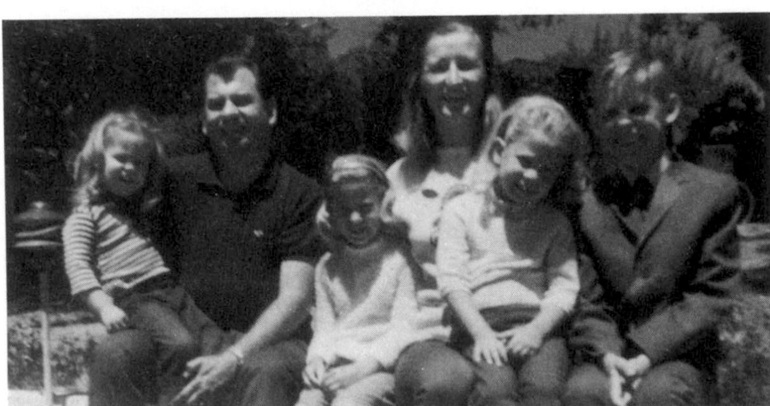

that I was moving again and that flag fell off the back of my friend's El Camino while we were driving down the San Diego freeway. The flag billowed like a patriotic parachute as it caught car grille after car grille. His Bible was in that box too. I lost my daddy's Bible too. Jesus God, looking back, I realize how I was always losing things. I lost my father's flag and his Bible and probably that ring too. I lost every opportunity I had to find my way back to the bond we shared, like the one we had when we lived together in the pink house. I lost the lightning and never got close to the storm, didn't I? I lost the point of it all, didn't I?

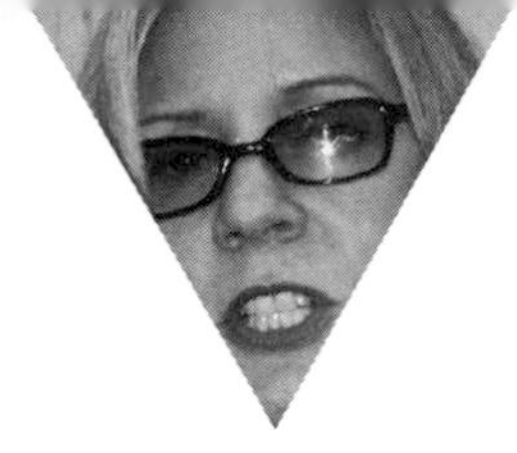

Bare Breasts

It's not like me to flash my tits in public—and I'm still suspicious over whether this actually happened, since I consider the three friends who testified to the act totally unreliable sources—but in my defense I'd like to say that we were in Key West. Key West is a place where people party until their senses are so deadened they wake up days later crusted to the bottom of a dock like human barnacles, and where, in some places, very well-muscled men tend bar in their boxer shorts, and where, on Halloween, it's not uncommon to see tribes of totally naked women walking the streets wearing painted-on costumes. So the sight of my unimpressive chest is really *no big deal*. If it happened at all.

"It happened," laughed my friend Jim. "You had to be there," he continued, knowing that, in any real sense of the phrase, I wasn't. We were sitting at Harpoon Harry's, one of the more popular breakfast spots on the island, probably because it's easy to crawl there, crab-like, from the Schooner Wharf bar, a dockside party mecca frequented by the barely ambulatory bunch of salt licks that make up the local crowd of "regulars." Nearby is another wharf bar and restaurant, Turtle Kraals, the place where my reported peekaboo occurred. If it happened at all. Accompanying me for breakfast that morning was the same cohort from the evening before; my other friend Paul; and a new acquaintance named Scott, a waiter at Margaritaville who was the person through whom Jim and I were to contact Paul, because a few days before Paul had left an ominous message on my answering machine that went something like, "Hollis, I'm in Key West. I'm hungover, homeless, and broke. Help."

So, a few days later, Jim and I went to Key West and found Paul sitting on a bench, disheveled and unshaven, with a cigarette casually pinched between his thumb and forefinger. He had been living in a hammock on a boat for two weeks, showering out of an elevated plastic bag filled with sun-warmed water. He looked like one of the walking lost toys that that tropical land is famous for attracting. There's a well-known danger to visiting Key West—you may get hit with a kind of blissful island dementia and melt into the crowd of colorful seamen and tall-talkers, drinking and dreaming, never to return home again. Everyone is susceptible.

A few days after we found Paul, at the culmination of a collective Key West–wide debauch, we were all sitting at Harpoon Harry's, where Jim and Scott were exaggerating the number of mai-tais I'd belted the night before. "She had seven or eight just while I was sitting with her at Boston Billy's," exclaimed Jim.

"I counted twenty," said Scott, a statement that made me snort with a disbelieving guffaw. Let me put it this way: It's more possible to pass a planet through the birth canal of a fourteen-year-old Olympic gymnast than it is for me to consume twenty cocktails without waking up to see my bloody, severed head at the foot of my bed. On that morning I had been completely hangover-free, I pointed out, which was incontrovertible proof of my frugal alcohol consumption the night before. My foggy memory must have been due to a delayed bout of jet lag.

"It's the Keys," explained Jim. "The closer you get to the equator, the better you feel after a bender."

"Besides," said Scott, "you could still be drunk."

After much investigative backtracking on my part, I determined that the boob-baring incident was nothing more than a tall tale evolved from the fact that the knot on my sarong was loose, making way for the possibility that, in a very demure, understated manner, an excess amount of cleavage could have been uncovered. That's my story, anyway, and I'm sticking to it. If it happened at all.

With that mystery solved, Paul, Jim, and I bid Scott good-bye and hit the highway back up to Miami, where we got on the plane and patted each other on the back for staging such a successful escape from the alluring, velvety warm grip of Key West, the most enticing place on the planet to drop *off* the planet. One and a half hours later, when the plane descended through the clouds, we saw the cityscape of Atlanta, and reentered its atmosphere with all of our ensuing responsibilities, obligations, and other soul-sucking burdens still in place. When the plane landed and ground to a stop, we sighed and gathered our belongings along with our strength to face reality—and that's only if we ever got on the plane at all.

Jim in postcard photo

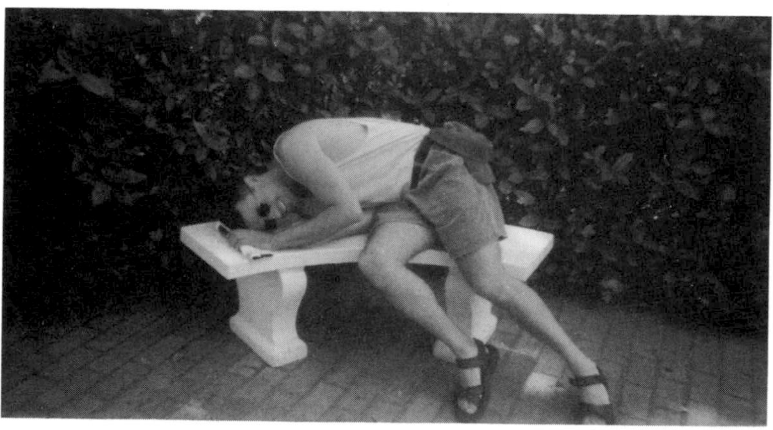

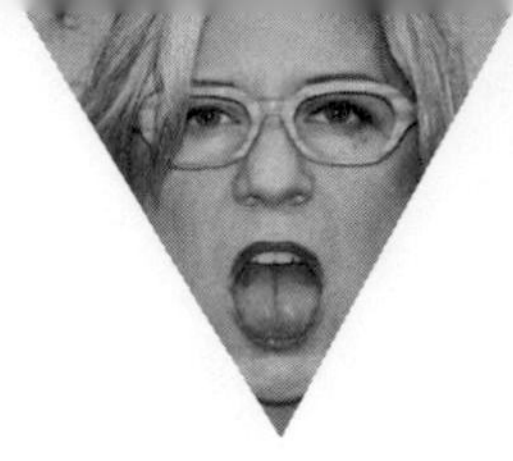

A Dead Cat

Thank God Lary's cat didn't die. This is the second day in a row I forgot to feed her, so I realized I better get off my ass and pass her some kibble, because Lary prides himself on his absolute lack of attachment to anything on earth except that cat. If he came home to a carcass he'd have to track me down and rip my face off my skull.

I raced over to Lary's place all worried his cat would be scratching at the doorjamb in little kitty death throes, sputtering and stuff, and who wants to walk in on that? And then there's the maggot factor. When, as a totally unsupervised seven-year-old walking home from the liquor store with two packs of Salem menthols for my mother, I once came across a dead cat in the gutter. Being seven and propelled by insanity, I decided to find a stick and flip it over.

Jesus God. It was all furry and fine on top, but underneath it was boiling with maggots like that piece of meat on *Poltergeist*. I'll never forget it. Before I flipped it, I was thinking maybe I could take it home and present it to my mother as the perfect pet on account of its being dead and not needing expensive vaccinations or anything.

In the past she had reacted favorably to such offerings, like when I presented her with that poisoned fish wrapped in toilet paper I found floating in a polluted tributary behind the park. She was so attentive as she took the fish straight to the trash pail, graciously thanking me. That type of consideration was a rarity in my household, and I was hoping to score some more. But those maggots sucked all the fun out of everything. For days afterward I'd spontaneously break into shivers like a little alcoholic in detox.

I finally got Lary's door open, and I say "finally" because he lives in that former candy factory with a complicated iron gate for a front door. Thank God I got in, because Lary loves the shit out of that cat. If anything bad happened to her he would be boneless, I mean just a big, boneless, jibbery mess of flesh. And I know how he feels. I've known Lary since back when we both thought there was nothing that could keep us tethered to the world. We were free and unfettered, with a big ball in our court called "nothing to lose." Then he got himself that cat, and I got myself . . . well, him, I guess, and Daniel and Grant. If anything bad happened to them I would be boneless too. Just a quivering, useless bag of boneless larvae. Jesus God, that is scarier than an entire pit of ticks.

Finally I found Lary's cat, alive but a little shrunken on account of her fast and all. She puffed up fine after I forced three cans of food down her throat.

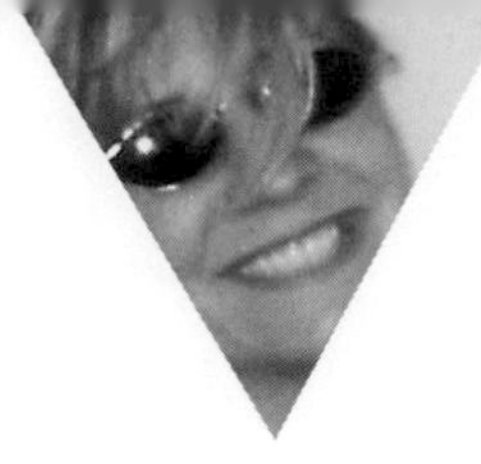

A Clean Slate

I wasn't happy when Grant said that he wanted to hang human babies. His inspiration came from his refurbished crack house, which is empty—like a clean slate—and usually he wants to keep it that way. But, other times, he says he wants to host the occasional art installation, and that's where the *ideas* come in. "We should take a bunch of babies," he said excitedly, "and just hang them on hooks. It would be *fabulous!*"

He swept through the vast living room, his face alight with enthusiasm, his sandals shuffling on the polished wood floor. "There could just be babies all over the walls!" His voice rises and echoes off the cement. "Babies hanging like hams! I *love* it! Are you not loving this idea?"

I was not loving the idea. But Grant was unfazed, and he continued to soak up inspiration from his empty house. Thank God he finally got off the hanging-baby brainstorm and went back to entertaining minimalism. "Nothing!" he spouts breathlessly. "Can't you just *see* it? Bare walls, nominal possessions. A clean slate! I'm loving this idea."

Who wouldn't love it? A clean slate is the ultimate possession. My own slate looks more like Lary's place. Lary lives in an altogether different warehouse than Grant, and has tools and torches strewn about. I've found that, these days, I enjoy it there more than ever. I hang out while he's out of town, feed his cat, and eat his pistachios. It's almost peaceful, sitting there amid another man's junk, free from my own junk for the time being.

That's the real hazard: my own junk. I've been trying to avoid it lately, pushing it into places like the closet in my office, and not even stacking it neatly. There's my broken treadmill, two plastic trees, old area rugs, a large plywood sign Grant, Daniel, and I pilfered from the roadside, and a wind-up plastic penis with clown feet that hops. These are just a few items in my galaxy of crap, a precariously teetering danger zone that is the mirror of my own cluttered brain, which is painfully littered with memories of my perceived past atrocities.

Atrocities such as the time I allowed my classmates to taunt my little sister, who was fat. That memory murders me: I should have protected her. I should have been a better person. Instead I am who I am. Sometimes, just to rescue myself, I'll rewrite the bad memories. If there's ever a moment I wish with every atom to take back, it is the moment when my little sister looked at me to save her and saw that I wouldn't. Her eyes rounded with the realization that she was utterly alone, and she held back her tears by pretending to pluck pills off her secondhand sweater. In my mind I go to my little sister, who is trying not to nervously pick at her sweater, trying instead to fold her hands with heartbreaking dignity atop the cafeteria table, and I take one of her hands and bring it to my cheek. In my mind I see her eyes smile with relief, and I dream for a second that maybe a clean slate is possible after all.

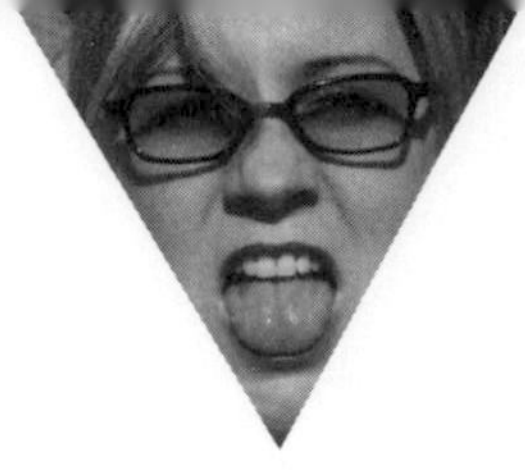

Ample Breasts Bursting with Desire

Fifteen years ago, I took a boat to Greece with my typewriter stuffed in my backpack. My mission was to write a novel packed with insights on female angst about sex and other important stuff. But mostly sex, because some months earlier I'd read one of those epic romances in which the heroine gets her clothes ripped off and raped every other page, then she ends up falling in love with the man who treats her the crappiest. In these books the main character always has "ample breasts bursting with desire" and she's always "awash in an unfathomable sea of pleasure," when really she's just being used like a toilet seat by the man camp.

I went to Greece to write the "anti" of that. Exactly what it would consist of, I didn't know, but I knew I couldn't write it at home. I had to roam, because I thought characters and adventure couldn't be found right in front of you. So off to Greece I went—Corfu, to be exact—where immediately I was accosted by two yelling, foul-mouthed, greasy-haired hobbits who clutched at me like evil puppies fighting for a chew toy. It turns out these two men were rivaling night-club owners, and it was common for them to pluck potential customers fresh off the bus like caged roosters waiting for a food pellet.

I was saved from this fracas by a spiky-haired guy named Dax, a charming part-time petty thief who worked the ratty parasailing ride in the lagoon at the bottom of the cliff. We became good friends. He was living out of his sleeping bag on the communal balcony of a nearby villa, and I rented a private room there on the third floor. The villa would have been the perfect place to write if I'd ever got around to it, but I was too busy being with Dax. He squired me about the island on the back of his rusty Vespa and talked me into consuming copious ouzo shooters and tiny fried squid with the eyeballs still attached.

Then one night he stumbled into my room, drunk. Due to a small act of larceny ("It was just a crate of melons," Dax insisted, "and they were rancid!"), he had to leave the island at sunrise and wanted me to come with him. I told him no, because I had this here book to write, you see, about love and sex and stuff. He stopped swaying for a moment to stare at me intently, then shook his head sadly. I'll always remember exactly that, the shaking of his head sadly, because you acquire moments in your life that come to signify certain regrets, not the agonizing variety of regret, like the "if only I took the toaster off the edge of the bathtub" range of regret but the other kind—the nagging little pangs you feel when you look back and wonder what you were thinking.

That morning Dax had tried to comfort me because I'd encountered a crippled man selling fried dough on the beach and—being the bleeding-heart little plebeian I was—the sight had left me bereft. "Don't be sad. He loves his life," Dax said of the invalid. "He lives on the beach, doesn't need shoes, eats all the doughnuts he wants . . ." and on he went, listing all the reasons why this particular person need look no further than the sight in front of him for untold delights.

But my gloom persisted, mostly because later that afternoon I got caught in a fight between nightclub owners again. This time one of them threw a boulder at the other, which hit me instead. It struck my shoulder blade and numbed my right arm all the way to the fingertips. Typing would have been hard if I had picked that point to get around to it. That's why Dax stole the rancid melons. He'd smashed them onto the courtyard of the nightclub owned by the odious man who hurt me, taking care not to hit anyone. He'd just wanted to make the floor slippery to hinder any reveling in general and dancing in particular. Afterward Dax was identified almost immediately, though, owing to the freckles on his face and bright flames tattooed on both forearms. "Take *that,*" they said he'd hollered as he hurled the melons, "for my *friend.*"

Later he stood in my room, shaking his head, dismayed that I would pass up true adventure for the sake of a fake one I'd never get around to inventing. After I turned him down he paced the room a few times, looking ready to argue with me, then picked up his satchel only to throw it down again and fiercely hug me good-bye with his brightly burning arms. He left without another word. At the time I was surprised Dax chose not to quarrel with my conviction, but today I remember precisely the sad shaking of his head, and I realize that right then he saw how I was crippled, blind to the sight of untold delights right in front of me.

In Greece at age twenty-two

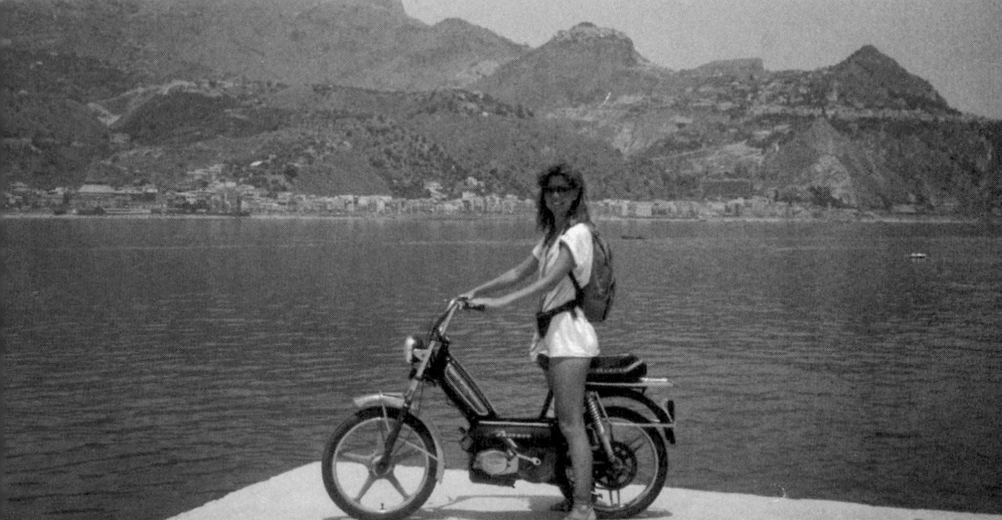

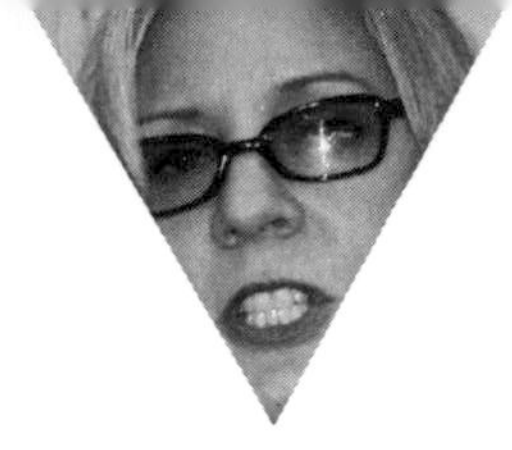

In My Head

I can tell when the holidays arrive, because my hypochondria becomes completely activated. I become convinced my liver is the size of a sea elephant, living inside me like an angry unborn twin with teeth and everything. I wish there was a way I could take a look to make sure, I mean other than with an X-ray machine, which would be hard to steal. I could make an appointment at the doctor's office, I know, but my reputation there is still tainted after my tapeworm panic on Christmas Eve 1998.

One year I felt this pain in my side. It wasn't my appendix, because that was cut out of me on Christmas in 1996, a monumental event that proved that sometimes *this was not all in my head.* I mean, seriously, they wouldn't have opened me up and taken out an *organ* (would they?) unless there was something really wrong with it. So the newest pain was not my appendix, so it must have been another organ, and I figured it must be my liver, seeing as how I'd been drinking like a frat boy at a beer fest lately.

I admit I'd been partaking in a lot of festive elixirs, but it was the *holidays*. I had to survive them somehow. In fact, that's what made it all so difficult. How do you separate crazed panic from perfect reality? How was I supposed to know that the flesh-eating ass cancer I freaked about a few Thanksgivings ago was really just the result of sitting all day in my underwear on top of a lost earring? On the other hand, the 1997 incident was easy, because that year I got accidentally stabbed in the head over the holidays. It's not like I was *imagining* that. It happened, I tell you, and the coworker who did it (with the pointy edge of a metal cabinet door that had flown off its hinges) was super sorry, and still sends me cards sometimes. I walked around for weeks afterward, with stitches and everything, looking like a Tijuana cocktail waitress. See? Sometimes this is *not* all in my head!

My hypochondria started back in grade school when, the day before Thanksgiving, my life sciences teacher showed the class a close-up of a bisected clogged human artery. "This is what happens when you eat crappy food," she said in her crone voice, holding the photo aloft. "When this guy died, his arteries were so stiff you could snap them in half like a piece of dried pasta," she added, thrusting the photo forward, which caused her upper arms to quiver like two turkey wattles. "Dried pasta," she reiterated, and I swear it was years before I could eat SpaghettiOs again.

It didn't help at *all* that my parents dropped me and my sisters off at the cineplex that year to watch *Scrooge* and *The Aristocats*, chaperoned by my big brother, who took the tickets and accidentally on purpose walked us into the wrong theater, where we sat through four showings of *Tales from the Crypt* instead. He kept telling us the cartoon was coming on next, right after this part showing a lady getting her whole arm hacked off by a mad magician for the twentieth time, or whatever. That night I had to invent an earache just so I could sleep in my parents' bed, and believe me, my parents were not cuddly people, and their bed was not comfortable either.

For one thing it had *ashtrays* in it, and books, tons of books. One in particular was *The Exorcist*. Jesus God, I wish my mother had hidden that book a little better, because after reading it I have never been so scared of a book in my life. *Oh, my God,* I remember thinking, how can this happen to a little girl? A pretty, pious, sweet little girl who went to church and everything? If that could happen to her, then what about me?

So that's the year it started. That year I was possessed by the devil for the holidays. I began twitching my shoulders and thrashing my head at odd moments, because I could feel Satan simmering inside me, and I thought if I stayed still too long I'd barf up a big nest of snakes, which would be very embarrassing. Finally my mother confronted me one night—I was hard to miss, twitching and thrashing, right there in bed with her—"What is the goddamn matter with you?" she shouted.

I told her the truth, that I was afraid I was going to Hell, that Lucifer's minions would drag me down through the butthole of oblivion to the heart of all awfulness, where devils will poke at my festering sores with fondue forks for all eternity. At that my mother eyed me keenly over the top of her book before muttering just one sentence. "Kid," she said, "Hell is all in your head."

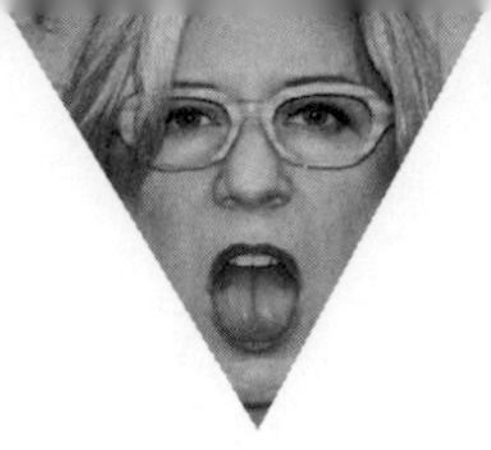

My Outstretched Hand

I woke up last Saturday fairly comfortable with my own mediocrity, not knowing what was in store for me at my friend James's Christmas party. First of all, James should know not to invite me anywhere. It wasn't so long ago that I showed up drunk and in my underwear (practically) at a party thrown by the Democratic Leadership Convention held in New Orleans during the jazz festival. I came because James invited me, and I danced until my hair unfurled in a lacquer-matted cascade, threw myself at a few men—including, I think, the governor of Indiana—and left clutching a tropical cocktail and a fistful of those little quiches some poor server was offering from a platter. I remember little else of that night, except that James didn't seem embarrassed by me. He keeps inviting me places. What is *wrong* with that man?

Like why didn't he *warn* me that Peter Gabriel was coming to his party? How could James let me walk right into his house not knowing I was about to shake hands with a dapper-looking man whose face I didn't immediately place and whose name I didn't immediately hear, but to whom I nodded my greeting anyway, only to discover, midhandshake, that this was *Peter Gabriel!!! Peter Gabriel!!! Jesus God!* standing right there at the end of my outstretched hand, smiling at me like he has any business at all being flesh and bone.

"Peter Gabriel?" I said.

"Yes," he said.

"*Solsbury Hill?*"

"Yes."

Let me give you some background. When I was a kid, I wasn't a music junkie. On the contrary, there was just the one song, and I didn't hole myself up with my headphones and rebel against my parents and lament over the big tub of turd the world was turning out to be. Instead, I was confused and timid, and I pretty much had the personality of a cornered rat. My father, the largely jobless alcoholic with big dreams and even bigger fears, and my mother, the missile scientist who took night classes in cosmetology because her own dreams were inversely simple, created a home atmosphere as comfortable as a sealed chamber full of whizzing Ninja blades.

Our household seemed like a sad dungeon for my parents' faltered hopes, and you couldn't sit there very long without hearing those broken aspirations flap around the room like trapped bats. This situation was unbearable to a budding romantic like myself, so to escape I'd sit in my sister's rusty Celica and play Gabriel's "Solsbury Hill" over and over on her car stereo, running down her battery and getting the crap beat out of me because of it. But it was worth the reprieve, because when you're young like that, and sad, you have your hand outstretched, metaphorically speaking, and you're searching for a string to pull you through. And for reasons more corny than the importance I'm placing on it now, my hand found that song. Does that make sense?

Later, after my parents' inevitable divorce, I moved to Zurich with my mother, and it was there that I realized the true frailty of her health. During the day she seemed like a perfectly normal weapons specialist with a hankering for beef jerky and Salem menthols, but at night she was crippled by coughing fits, barely able to keep from drowning in the pools of fluid forming in her own lungs. Unable to sleep, I spent nights watching obscure music videos, including the one with Kate Bush and Peter Gabriel clutching each other and singing "Don't Give Up."

"Don't give up," I'd mentally implore as I sat outside my mother's bedroom door and waited for her suffering to subside. The day came when I realized that the not giving up wasn't up to me, and two facts about my mother became apparent: One, that she would be dead soon unless she quit smoking, and two, that she would never quit smoking.

A year later, after she died in my arms, it was one of those times I could have given up but didn't. I was rescued, I guess, by the safety net I'd woven over time with the threads I'd collected from when I had my hand outstretched, metaphorically speaking, searching for a down payment on the possibility that life might not be such a basket of crap after all. So the *least* James could have done is let me prepare. I mean, *Peter Gabriel.* Jesus God! There was Peter Gabriel, at James's party, at the end of my hand—my outstretched hand. "You, you, you . . ." I blathered to him, but then the woman who had brought him extricated him from my grasp and led him away. I continued to sputter even after he was gone.

"You helped pull me through," I finally finished.

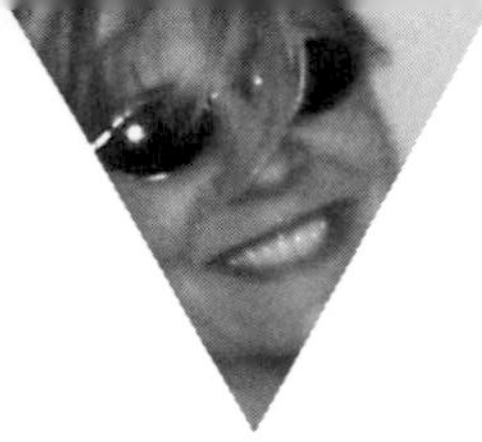

The Long Good-bye

Since when did watching two people tongue each other in public make me so *angry?* When did I get so caught up in this misanthropic, mole-flecked emotional crust that I can't handle two college kids practically copulating right there on the plaza in Barcelona? What is *with* me?

I mean, there's other stuff to look at. Even though I'm only here for the day, I don't want to be blind to beauty, because it's too easy to tote your personal sensory-deprivation devise with you wherever you go, to grow your own little layers of rust around the cracks in your heart, and heartbreak is the whole purpose of life. Without it we wouldn't cherish anything. I once had a kindly professor who, in spite of my inner oath to prioritize good grades above ever actually learning something in college, made me understand the poems of T. S. Eliot. "April is the cruelest month," he quoted from Eliot, and to demonstrate the meaning behind the verse, he led me to the courtyard outside the classroom. There he pointed to a tree, its branches as brown as old photographs.

"Do you see that?" he asked, indicating the minuscule blossoms forming from the deadness of the branches. "*That* is why April is so cruel."

I sensed then that later I'd become familiar with how painful it is to bleed life back into an atrophied part of yourself, to come alive after the comfort of deadness. It's a rite of passage you can't avoid if you expect to reach levels of enrichment in your life. The passage is easy to bypass though. For example, if my hotel room didn't happen to smell like a jailhouse toilet I might not have left it at all, opting instead to spend the few hours until my flight home in my usual manner: flicking the porno channels in perfectly timed, three-minute intervals so the hotel wouldn't bill the movie to my room. But instead I bounded to the street, heading straight for a huge plaza packed with people, including at least four Peruvian flute bands and the before-mentioned young couple dry-humping each other on a street corner next to my bus, where I watched them from a window seat as I waited for the bus to make its timed departure from the plaza.

Get a room, I silently fumed at the two lovers. I mean, Jesus God! If I wanted a porno peep show I could have stolen it from my hotel. Look at them! Undulating like two electrical wires, attached by their tongues as if their taste buds were capable of keeping each other alive. It's easy to stare at people like this, because, believe me, they don't see you looking. So I wasn't the only one on the bus beating them with my eyeballs. And then the girl extricated herself from her lover's young tentacles and boarded the bus along with the rest of us. *Oh,* I thought, *so that's what this is all about.* It's good-bye.

But Spain isn't famous for its timely precision, and the bus stayed there with its engine idling long after its scheduled departure. The girl sat two seats in front of me with her hand pressed against the window, with the boy on the other side, his hand opposite hers, separated by the glass. They stayed that way, with eyes large with longing, angering people all around them until enough time had passed to make it obvious the lovers weren't putting on a performance. These were, simply, two young people who hadn't yet learned to lock a chastity belt around their chests, so their hearts were all out there, exposed and flailing like little crabs without their exoskeletons.

As we watched them silently reach for each other, our faces softened. They were two fools with their toes sticking over the ledge of their teens, about to jump, ass first, into the fantastic crap fest that is their twenties, and about to be hit with the brick of knowledge that the world is not their personal balloon on a string after all. Why ram that home ahead of time? How does it harm us to let them sweep through life in ignorance of any true agony other than their longing for each other? How does it harm us to let them not be blind to their own beauty?

The bus lurched forward and began its journey. We watched the boy grow smaller in the distance, his arm outstretched like all your lost hopes trying to remind you they're not so lost after all. And then we felt it, that stinging of the eyes, and, What is that? That ache. It's the ache that accompanies the cruelty of coming alive after enjoying the comfort of deadness for so long.

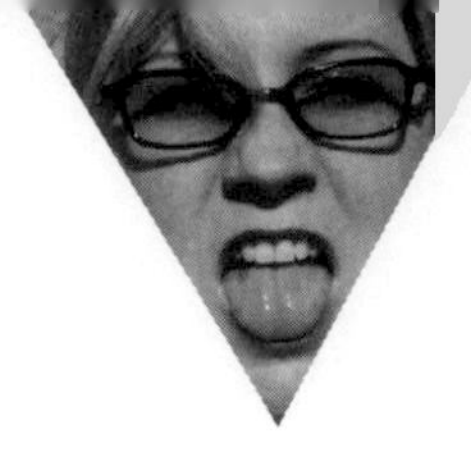

It's All About Safety

Just because I'm a flight attendant doesn't mean I'm not nervous when I fly. I'd hate it just as much as the next person to have bloody chunks of my body shower down on complete strangers. So I try to remember to wear pants when I work, as opposed to the dress option of my uniform, because if the plane crashes, I want to lower the odds of my corpse ending up inside the pages of *Newsweek* with my skirt over my head. And the thought of having to be cleaned up after kind of creeps me out as well. I'd hate to have my kidney end up on someone's car antenna and not even be able to *apologize* to those people.

I'm not kidding. I really worry about this stuff. That's why I'm such a safety freak when I fly. Even as a passenger I always put my tray table up, turn off my CD player, and narc on people who don't put their bags in the overhead bin. A guy once sitting next to me tried to tell me the rules were not about safety but were just arbitrary commands to keep us occupied since we would all die on impact anyway.

Ha! He better die outta my way. I don't want to be tripping over his shit while I'm trying to outrun the ball of fire roaring through the fuselage. I count the number of rows to the closest exit in order to feel my way out of a smoke-filled cabin if necessary, and I bitch at people who use their cell phone after we back away from the gate. I don't screw around.

Because, you know, safety is important. People think it's our youth we try to resurrect as we age, but actually it's the feeling of childhood safety and security we spend our lives trying to recapture. Try to recall the last time you felt really, really secure. You were, like, *eleven*, right? I remember back when I believed in Hell, I used to sleep with my father's Bible under my pillow. It was around then that any illusion that I was somehow protected from evil by my youth and innocence was dispelled.

I think I can trace it to the Hillside Strangler back in the seventies. Two of their victims were pre-teens—tortured horribly before the killers snuffed them out. I lived in their crime territory at the time, a Los Angeles suburb called the Hollywood Riviera, and after the killers were caught I remember hearing they had taken surveillance photos of future victims from their van, and that some of the photos the police found featured a classmate of mine.

Back then it wasn't customary for throngs of psychologists to descend upon schoolchildren to buffer them from the horrors of the world after reality has reared its hideous face too close to their innocent eyes. We were left to form conclusions on our own, and mine led me to the belief that there is an intrinsic awfulness in the world. Something inside me set about forming the emotional exoskeleton I thought I'd need to survive it. Why dig under levels of magma to reach Hell, when it's right outside the door?

But I wish I had that early feeling of security back. I do. I wish I had more evidence in my life that I once felt perfectly secure, that I used to run barefoot out the front door to catch blowfish off the end of a pier. My friend Art has a booth at Antiques on Amsterdam in Virginia-Highland, and I walked in there the other day and spied a sixties Hans Wagner folding chair and just froze. "That *chair*!" I cried. "We had that chair in our living room when I was growing up! I used to sit in it and watch *Match Game*!" I had to have it. I had to add it to the growing throng of secondhand impostor tokens from my past I've been collecting in an attempt to re-create a world in which I once felt unfettered by all these pedestrian fears.

I'm no different than almost anyone. Why do you think eight-track tapes are so collectible? It's not like people *play* them. Instead, they cherish them like a surviving light that leads straight to the magic of their past, to the time when they had buttered toast for breakfast and friends circling outside on bicycles. Back when the world was their personal balloon on a string, before their father's Bible fell off the back of an El Camino on the San Diego freeway and erupted into a tornado of confetti that rained down on cars spanning two entire exits. Before, back when they felt safe. So don't tell me it's not about safety. It's *all* about safety.

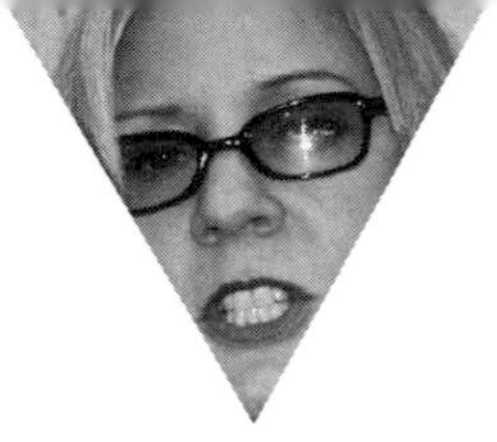

Escaping in the New Year

This New Year, I resolve to be more picky about where I put my tongue. It's the same resolution I make every year in memory of an oceanography professor I heard about in college, who licked a sea anemone (or maybe it was a sea urchin) during a field trip at the beach to show his students how harmless they are. He was wrong. He'd momentarily confused an anemone with an urchin and forgot which one was poisonous and which one needed a good licking. His tongue swelled to the size of a kielbasa sausage, blocked his airway, and he died writhing on the ground, with his fingers clutching his throat while his students laughed at him hysterically, unaware until it was too late that he wasn't just putting on a really good act.

I think about that at the start of each new year because—what with serial killers, plane wrecks, weapons, disease, "acts of God," acts of those who claim to be acting in the name of God, gangs, killer sea creatures, plain stupidity, cholesterol, and those tiny fish bones that can get caught in your colon—I'm just amazed I survived another year.

I'm always amazed by it, and I always prepare for escape in case the above-mentioned survival is ever threatened. I used to keep an army knife in my pocket because I have a fear of being locked in a trunk. My friend told me about a woman who, after her abductors locked her in their trunk, saved herself by ripping out the wires that led to the taillights. The car was pulled over by an alert policeman, and the killers were foiled. "Can you believe she thought of that?" my friend asked.

Hell, yes, I can. I think of stuff like that all the time. That's where the pocket knife comes in. I figure I could chisel my way out of the trunk at an intersection or something, or at least spring up after the killer rapists open the trunk and use the knife's menacing can-opener tool to peck at their eyes. I'd lead the police back to the crime scene hours later, where the killer rapists would still be crawling around clutching at their empty sockets. Am I the only one who thinks of these things?

My pocket knife, though, was finally confiscated by Albuquerque airport security. "I was gonna use that to cut myself free from a malfunctioning seatbelt in the event of a crash," I whimpered as I saw the guard toss it into a box that contained a massive assortment of clippers, files, tweezers, and, oddly, a curling iron. With the pocket knife gone, now I'll just have to think of a different way to escape in order to run away from danger.

Running away brings to mind one day back in high school, which I spent ignoring class and driving down the coast of San Diego. I came to a stoplight and suddenly saw all these people jogging. What are they *running* from? I panicked. Should I be running too? This was the year after the PSA crash of 1978, in which a 727 jet collided with an out-of-control Cessna, sending them both nose-first into the ground and turning a suburban San Diego cul-de-sac into a charred pit of destroyed homes and lives. The wreck happened about a mile from where we had just moved, and I remember hearing about a man who reached for his wife in bed that morning only to notice that her breasts were much bigger than they should have been. Of course it wasn't his wife he was embracing after all, but an unlucky dead woman who had fallen through the roof because the plane she was in had disintegrated in the air over his house.

If you go to that section of San Diego today, there is no trace of the crash, other than a marked newness to the homes that had to be rebuilt in comparison to the ones that didn't. There is no sign, no ceremonial marker that I know of, that distinguishes this neighborhood as a place of painful history—a place where, among other things, a man dozed with his wife one minute and awoke clutching the corpse of another woman the next. It is over. It is smooth. It is smoothed over.

But I still sometimes panic when I see people jogging. At first glance, they are not just running, they are running *away,* and I don't want to be left behind to face whatever threat they are fleeing. After that initial second passes, though, I realize there is no threat. None you can see coming anyway. None you can point to while warning others. None you can't avoid by staying focused, by not confusing a sea anemone with a sea urchin. To this day I still think about that poor man's flat-chested wife. I always figured she got crushed by a beverage cart or something, and that's why she was gone when he reached for her. But now I look at it differently. She was gone, I like to think, because she escaped.

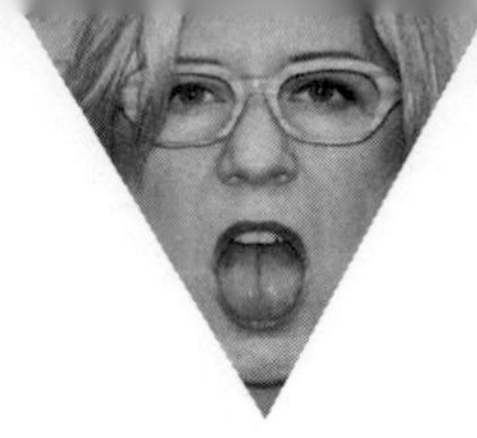

Perilous Climb

My friend is fucking her boss, which I think is a really bad business move. She won't listen to me, though, because she believes she's "climbing the corporate ladder" when really all she's climbing is the sweaty, crass, married ass of a pockmarked, balding bag of bacon fat with, like, a *clipboard* or whatever it is that midlevel incompetent corporate suck-ups wave around these days to exude a false air of importance.

"Are you *insane?*" I ask her. "Are you a drooling, booger-eating *idiot?*"

We are at Eats, a pseudo-edgy chow house on Ponce de Leon Avenue, where a lot of office-badge-wearing people now like to lunch it seems. They line up at the counter and crowd the aisles with their magnetized identity cards clipped to lanyards around their necks, reminding me of tagged animals marked for scientific study. They mill about in their Dockers and prudent dresses, bumping into one another softly with their cafeteria trays before selecting a seat. I used to hate that about this place, but now I think it's nice. Don't ask me why.

"If you don't wise up, your ass is so canned," I warn my friend, but as I said, she is not listening to me. She's got that infuriating, faraway look in her eyes, like she's remembering the bionic blow job she gave her boss before coming here. Jesus God. How frustrating. How do you talk sense to someone in this situation, someone who is so tragically mistaken in her smugness? She thinks she is securing her future, she thinks she's distinguishing herself from the rest of the turd pellets in the pile. Christ, it's like watching a kid nosedive into an empty pool.

Little does she know her shelf life is already eroding. My guess is she has a few weeks, tops, before that selfish diaper wipe dumps her like a load of toxic waste. He's a *guy*, after all, and most guys formulate excuses to bolt long before they even have the actual sex. I mean, seriously, guys will make up early-morning squash matches during the *appetizer course,* thus eliminating the obligation for any cuddle time should their date decide to copulate with them after dinner. So, c'mon, what *guy* wants to hang out forty hours a week with somebody he's balling?

"Canned," I reiterate to my friend, "like a truckload of tuna."

I speak as a witness and not from experience, which is surprising. I mean, of all the wrong moves I've made in my life, you'd think boss-humping could easily be among them, but I was never a corporate-climber type. In addition, of the few office jobs I've had, my bosses were either gay or running the company from a minimum-security prison, and therefore impervious to my wiles. One time, though, when I was waiting tables in college, my boss took me aside and informed me the restaurant was firing half the staff, but I could ensure my position if I partook in acrobatic sex with him on the table in the break room right then.

"Let me get this straight," I said, "if I lay you I get to keep my crappy-ass job?" Then I laughed so hard I nearly coughed up the pitcher of margaritas I had drunk by the pool before showing up for work that day. I didn't screw him and he didn't fire me, but he did can the poor cocktail waitress who *was* sleeping with him. Her name was Becky, and she wore chunky-heel shoes when stilettos were in style. I remember she served us all after work one night when my coworkers and I were sousing ourselves at the bar, everybody young and grandstanding about their design on life, especially me because I'd just been accepted to a program to study literature at a university in Oxford, England, and I had plans for myself.

"I'm climbing out of this tar pit, people," I laughed, clinking cocktails in celebration with my wait-staff friends, each with big dreams too. I remember Becky was widely despised for sleeping with the boss, who was absent that night, but she weathered the sneers anyway. She was my age and had a six-year-old daughter who lived far away with relatives. "I want to open my own place," Becky joined in, "have my own business."

We toasted to her dream but almost broke our eyeballs rolling them at one another afterward. ". . . *have my own business*," we mimicked the minute she turned her back to fetch another round. It didn't occur to me then that she probably had that dream because it ensured her against having to sleep with the boss to climb ahead.

A few days later Becky got fired, and I saw her afterward in the parking lot, sitting in her relic of a Celica, her forehead resting on her steering wheel as she sobbed. I was watching her from the window of the restaurant, as was nearly the rest of the floor staff on duty that day. We all stood there, none of us having ever really needed a job before, none of us with a six-year-old girl we were trying to become worthy enough to raise, none of us trapped in a mess we thought we could climb out of by balling the boss. We all stood there, watching Becky cry, and none of us went to her.

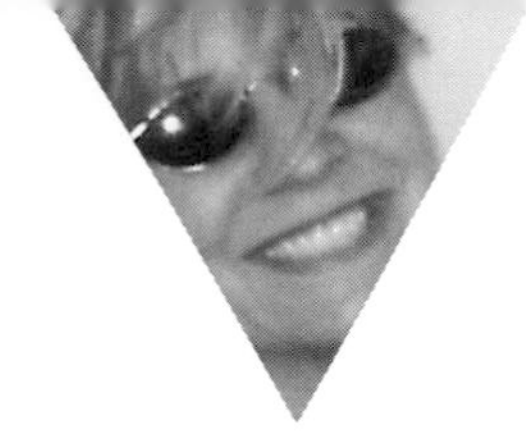

Unconnected

Lary told me I needed drugs. He said I was way too upset about my phone connection, or my *lack* of a phone connection, to deal with the situation lucidly, so a few tabs of acid were in order. "You should try it," he said, sounding like a bad actor with a bit part in *The Cross and the Switchblade.* "It makes you feel good."

"What're you, my *pusher?*" I yelled. Lary had been trying to foist acid on me a lot. He even stashed it in weird places all over his house because he knew I'd hang out there when he was gone and I bet he was hoping I would ingest it accidentally. Once he even accused me of stealing some acid buttons he had hoarded in his freezer. "They were right here," he kept saying, staring at the icy abyss, "wrapped in tinfoil and plastic. Are you sure you didn't eat them? Because if you ate them, I don't care."

Me? Eat acid? Even back when I *did* drugs I didn't eat acid. After having been forced to attend that drug-awareness forum in grade school, in which all those former LSD and heroin addicts recounted their horror stories, I didn't want to end up like them, living in sleazy tenements littered with needles and unwashed underwear. So, no, I didn't take his acid.

"C'mon," Lary still implores. "It'll make you feel connected."

I doubt drugs would help with my connection. BellSouth claimed my phone line was working perfectly, but if that were true I wouldn't be spending forty cents a minute like your average cell phone bovine, in line at the drugstore and such, begging the phone company to fix what's making my land line act like a radio receiver for the construction crane across the street. When I pick it up all I hear is *beep beep beep*. In spite of this, customer service still says my connection is fine.

Believe me, it's not. And because these are the holidays, people might try to reach me, like relatives. But as Daniel has always pointed out, I have no relatives, and that's why I keep old pictures of total strangers on my mantel, to fake friends and visitors into thinking I have a history. His words gave me pause, because I never thought of it that way, that those old photographs might be surrogates for my missing relatives. I just thought they were really pretty, all those sepia portraits of other people's ancestors. There are three wedding pictures of various women festooned with white lace and brooches, a girl of pre-Raphaelite beauty holding a bouquet, and, my favorite, an old lady with a baby on her knee.

So maybe it's true that I like having these pictures because I have no evidence of my own ancestry. Solitude has its perks, but sometimes I wish I had a real extended family rather than my mother's gaggle of asshole siblings and their spawn. She'd estranged herself from them by the time I was nine, but I briefly reconnected with a few at her funeral, where they eyed my sisters and me with misgiving, as if afraid our newfound orphan status would require them to act as real family members or something.

Rather than remain connected to them, I collected old pictures I found at flea markets and thrift stores instead. The genuine articles, pictures of my own family, had long been abandoned, and now they just cluttered the empty corridors of memory. I replaced those photos with new ones. I like to look at the one of the old lady with a baby on her knee—she must have been dead for decades—and I try to see into her sunken eye sockets. I try to envision how she must have sat down that morning to twist her hair into a Bavarian bun at the nape of her neck before tying a gingham apron around her waist. I wonder what she would have thought if she knew that, a century later, her picture would end up in the hands of an unconnected person, her photo serving as an impostor relic from someone else's past. Might she have been happier to remain unfound?

If I were her, I would want to be found. So I look at her now, with her toothless grin and her proud grip on her grandson, and if I gaze long enough I can see that, yes, there is definite possibility there. There is a possibility that the person who abandoned this photograph regrets having done so. That person could be related to me. That person could have *been* me. I look closer and suddenly feel a connection. Yes, I realize, she is mine. I finally found her, and I will never throw her away again.

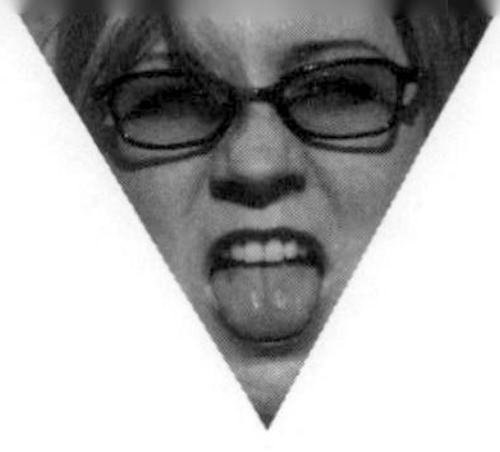

The Art of Fooling People

The other day I was passing pileups on one of the car-encrusted shit smears Atlanta calls a freeway on-ramp when a refreshing realization came to me: One of the big benefits I enjoyed as the daughter of an alcoholic traveling trailer salesman is the heightened sense of driver awareness I acquired in my role as my drunk father's front seat lookout as he lurched home with us in the family Fairlane.

"Dad, *stop*!" I'd yell at red lights.

"Watch *out,* you're swerving!" I'd screech on causeways.

"Police car, Dad, *police car!*" I'd scream. On those occasions, my father would rifle around for one of the emergency packets of peanuts he kept strewn about the front seat. It must have fooled the police every time, because my father drove like an overmedicated mental patient but never got arrested. In fact, the worst thing I recall happening is that time he drove over a lady's foot. She was trying to save the last parking spot at a popular picnic area until her husband returned with the car. My father must have fooled her into thinking he wouldn't run her ass down, because she sure took her time getting out of the way.

"That's my quarter in the meter," she whimpered as she limped away.

"And I thank you for that," he called after her cheerily. By my father's demeanor, you'd be fooled into thinking they were friends.

And fooling people, after all, was my father's forte. His buddies at the bar thought he was independently wealthy, so that's why he could afford to hang out all day. The bartender, Kitty, knew differently. Regardless, there was genuine affection between the two of them, probably because my father tipped her heartily with my mother's money. He always laughed when she called him a useless sack of crap.

And my father fooled me in other ways as well. He had me thinking that he wrote all the words to "Puff, the Magic Dragon," that he could speak fluent German when all he could say was "*eins, zwei, drei*," that he was brilliant, and tall as a tree. I'd run across the yard and meet his car when he came home bleary-eyed and smiling. He'd carry me back into the house under his arm, talking about all the trailers he sold that day when really he hadn't worked in months. I hugged his neck and looked up at him with gleaming young eyes of admiration.

Then one day the school nurse discovered I had strep throat and needed to reach one of my parents to drive me to the doctor. If she was surprised that I gave her the number of my father's favorite bar she didn't show it, but when he arrived I guess he'd forgotten his peanut remedy because his breath was like a blowtorch and she refused to

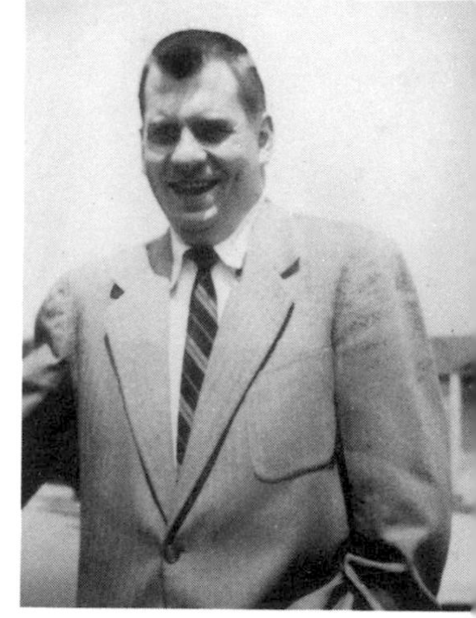

My father

release me to him. Unable to charm her, my father unsuccessfully tried intimidation instead. It fell upon our big biology teacher, who had once fed a bunny to a boa constrictor, to order my father off the property. He was about to argue, but then he saw my face, and right then he knew he couldn't fool me anymore.

Looking back at the sad man he became after that, I remember, instead of coming home smiling, he came home searching because I had taken to hiding when I heard his car pull into the driveway. He died young in a one-room apartment soon after his family left him, and I realize how desperately he needed his children's gleaming eyes of admiration to fool the most important person of all: himself. Looking back, I wish I had known to let him keep his illusions, but I was young, and had yet to learn the art of fooling people.

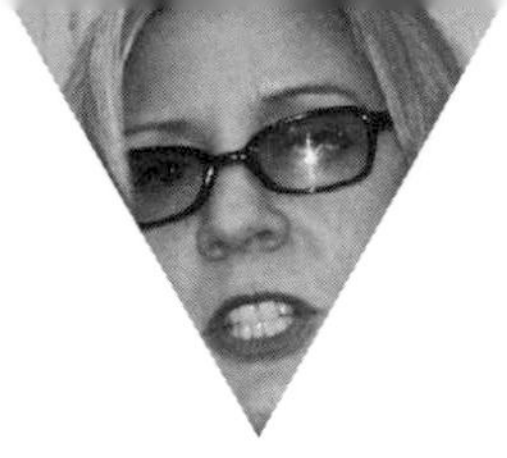

Inner Evil

I have horns. This fact confirms Lary's view of me, as he has been calling me a demon almost since we met. "If I'm a demon then what the hell does that make *you,* nuclear Satan or something?" I ask, but he doesn't even have to answer. He is Lary, and Satan can only aspire.

I found my horns in Grant's kitchen and I've been wearing them ever since. They are red and glittery, sculpted from clay, and Daniel says they are quite a nice accessory to my daily attire. Grant will probably want them back, but they've grown on me. They are mine now, a glorious testimony to my inner evil. Years from now, when I'm super old and sitting in the carport next to my trailer, with my tiny dusty horns on my head, with half my face drooping southward like a mud slide in front of a Malibu beach house, I wonder if Grant, Daniel, and Lary will be there to hear me sputter, "You bastards, you made me what I am."

That's another one of my big fears, to end up alone in a trailer

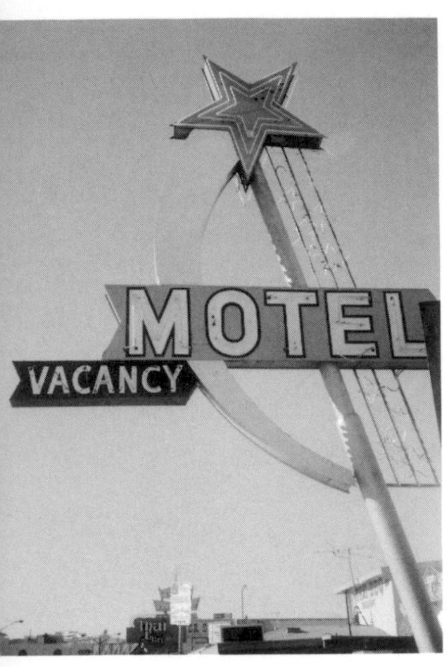

Route 66

park in Arizona, trying to fire up my Hibachi with arthritic fingers. I drove across country twice with my father in the Fairlane, through expansive, desolate stretches of total nowhere, dotted with lonely homesteads and occupied by ghosts who are not really ghosts, just people who might as well be. I wondered what happened to drive those people out there. Did they get there because they couldn't contain their inner evil? Did evil sprout out of them like horns, repelling their friends? Were they banished to these desolate outposts because they couldn't cope with regular people? *Normal* society?

These people could be me, I was sure. They could *easily* be me. When I was six I took a standardized intelligence test along with the other kids in my school, and my results were not normal. Far from it. My mother made my father promise not to tell me, a promise he kind of kept. In looking back at my childhood, I'm totally surprised I endured. Let's not forget while my mother made bombs and could design complicated weapons, she couldn't follow a recipe more complex than "just add water." As a result, she fed me so much junk food, I'm surprised I'm not sitting here right now with a tumor the size of a second head.

And my father, now, he's a whole other sack of bats. For family entertainment he used to like to get drunk and pile us all in the car to cruise through the cemetery and watch the deer eat flowers off fresh graves. I had no idea this wasn't normal.

One Halloween, at my seventh birthday party, I was dressed as a little devil, complete with horns and pitchfork, and my father decided he had a way to tell me but not "tell me" what he and my mother knew about my brain. He took me aside and whispered fiercely, "Never forget this: You are *not* normal, you are more than that. You are smarter than me, smarter than your mother, smarter than anyone you know."

I laughed, because it was so seldom that he was serious with me, and I had no idea what he meant. I tried to turn away to resume my party, but he had me by the upper arms. "Dad," I said nervously, "I'm not smarter than you."

"You are," he said solemnly. "You are better than me. Never forget that. Be better than me," and with that he was back to his old self, drinking Buds and making the other parents laugh.

But they didn't buy his act. By that time nobody did. He ended up alone, like those people in the Arizona desert, with nobody to help him come to terms with his inner evil. He died suddenly one day in a furnished studio apartment next to the Los Angeles airport, as planes packed with strangers roared overhead. "Be better than me," he'd said. But why? He wasn't so bad.

Part of me longs to hang out at those homesteads in the middle of nowhere. I guess it's because I want to know it's really not that awful to be cut off from almost everyone. Maybe you could watch the sunset every night from a lawn chair on your carport, and you could have three crusty old coots for friends, who shuffle over occasionally with boxes of bad wine and a dozen doughnuts. They could help you light your Hibachi. They could help you with the hope that maybe you were wrong about your father. Maybe he wasn't alone after all. Maybe he had friends he could show his horns to, friends like Daniel, Lary, and Grant, who could look at his inner evil and make him realize he wasn't so evil after all.

My parents at the Grand Canyon, 1975

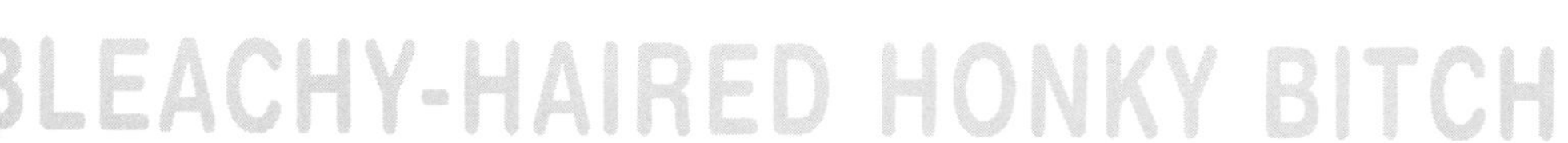

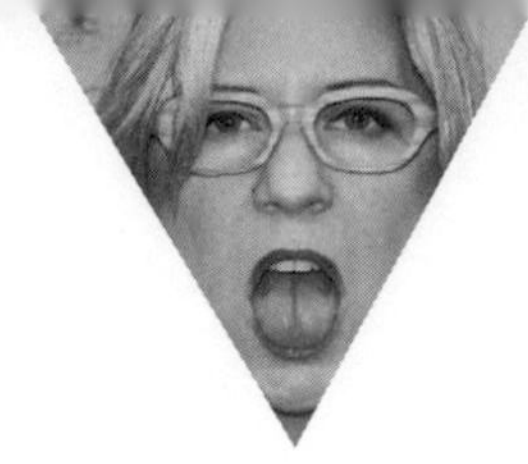

Rock Bottom

Not that this matters *at all,* but Lary finally found the acid tabs he had accused me of stealing. He had been away on a nine-day excursion to Cancún, the Mexican sleaze pit some people sadly mistake for a resort (he was there on a *job,* mind you), and during that time he had let me stay at his place so I could deal with the fallout of a failed relationship. His place is a fortress, after all. It's a concrete-and-steel former candy factory down by the stadium, where, on the back of his TV, he had duct-taped a handgun, and he instructed me to wave it around in front of the windows intermittently in order to keep the criminals away. When he returned he eventually made it to his kitchen and noticed the missing LSD buttons.

Ever since college, I'd bypassed heroin and acid, and gone straight to cocaine, because with cocaine you hit rock bottom quickly—unless you're made out of money, in which case you can buy yourself ten extra minutes. My own personal rock bottom came one day in college, when I took stock of my life and saw that I came home every evening to a house full of unfaithful friends and impolite strangers passing a plate of blow around, and realized that I was sick of this crowd with their tight lips, limp dicks, and bloviating drug-induced benevolence ("I know I don't know you that well, but *goddamn* you are beautiful"). And I was sick of myself, since I was the worst offender. *Fuck this,* I thought, and moved out the next day.

But my former friend Gina has never *not* been a heroin addict, ever since she was sixteen. She attended the same drug-awareness scare fest I had, but for some reason she was unaffected by the prospect of waking up in a nest of her own filth, jonesing for a fix. She had curly blond hair and long legs, and we used to make pot holders together in home ec. Now she was rheumy-eyed and absent, with a Rorschach pattern of ruined veins covering her broken body. A veteran of dozens of government-funded rehab programs, she had yet to reach her rock bottom, and it's possible she never will, proving again and again the new depths to which she can fall. A day rarely goes by that I don't recall the former luster of her hair, and wonder why, with our identical backgrounds, she grew up to face a tormented existence in which it's a burden every day to wake up and find herself still alive and I . . . well, I did not.

So back to the missing acid: Lary found it where he put it, in his freezer. It was stuck to the back of a Precambrian potpie or something, and therefore well hidden throughout the years, so I was off the hook. "Did you eat it? Are you, like, *tripping* right now or something?" I asked when he told me the news, looking to see if his pupils had assumed a gyrating spiral pattern.

"Don't worry, I'm throwing it away," he said. "It's old."

Yes, I nodded, it is most definitely old.

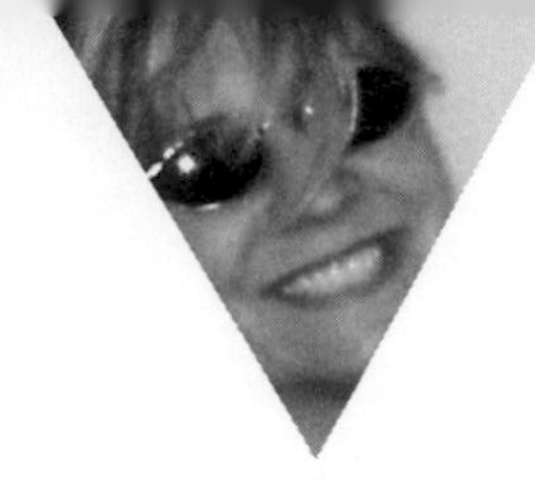

Other People's Blood

I dislike being bled on. I once made Lary drive by the neighborhood in Atlanta where I'd seen my second corpse. I'd seen it earlier that same day, and there was still a puddle of blood on the sidewalk in the shape of Australia. Lary, peering out the driver's side window, said it was a melted Popsicle and wouldn't believe it was blood until I got out, stuck my finger in it, and came back inside the car to give him a closer look.

"Are you insane? I'm not gonna get it on me!" I shrieked. God! You'd think that Lary, more than anyone, would recognize actual blood when he saw it. He goes to the damn emergency room just about a hundred times a month. The most recent was necessitated by injuries sustained after he took acid and dove headfirst off some scaffolding in his living room. That he has scaffolding in his living room should tell you something about him. But I think he was kind of unsettled about the puddle that day. He probably dislikes being bled on as much as I do.

It's a good thing he missed the soccer hooligans in Dublin last month. I'd never been to Dublin before, and at the time I was just hanging around loving the hell out of the place, because what's not to love? There are cobblestone walkways and old pubs everywhere, shrimp-flavored potato chips, eight-hundred-year-old brass accents still shiny from daily polishing, and people *tip their hats* to you. It's so damn finished and seemingly civilized in downtown Dublin that the men even wear pocket watches, for chrissakes, and every other café has curtains made of white lace. It's lovely there, I swear, and it's really the last place you'd expect to encounter other people's blood.

It all happened while I was admiring some silver trinkets jangling from a street vendor's pushcart, when suddenly the air became instilled with a different sort of loudness than before, something more frenetic than the normal business bustle of the day. The onset was all pretty subtle, actually, because the Irish are studied in the art of sustaining tirades. There was no war-whoop, no running for cover, no shouting of warnings. Nobody froze in their steps or crapped in their pants. The only omen of what was about to happen, the only thing that warned of an oncoming menace, was that everyone around me suddenly became extremely intent upon some menial task at hand. The change was immediate. One moment everybody was interacting with one another—commenting on the big soccer match, laughing at jokes—and the next they were rummaging grim-faced through a pocketbook, mindfully picking lint off a lapel, closely inspecting the incisors of an ancient lapdog. Even the pushcart vendor stopped talking to me midsentence to intently study a pebble caught in a crease of his sole. All this alerted me to switch myself to survival mode.

There was no big trick to it. I just adapted the demeanor of the people around me, which basically entailed making myself as boring as possible, thus enabling the hooligans to ignore me and move on to other potential victims, which they did. They chose a hapless, long-haired young man not far from me and descended on him like piranhas on a pork chop. They were so thick on him he was invisible under the pile. It was over quickly too; the thugs lifted like mosquitoes swarming for fresh blood, and they were gone. This is when my instincts failed me.

"Do you think that guy's okay?" I gasped to the pushcart vendor, who looked at me like I'd stepped on a twig and alerted the enemy to our hiding place. The hooligans were gone, but the injured guy, who was being helped to his feet by his friends, was near enough to hear me. Bloody-faced, he was no longer hapless; on the contrary, he was full of hate and pain right then, which he bore on me with the intensity of a hundred suns.

"Leave me alone, you stupid *bitch,*" he shouted, coming closer. *Fucking bitch!*" he hissed into my face. I looked around to see if anyone would intervene, but they were busy brushing dust off their coats or inspecting their watchbands or whatever. Luckily, I'm obviously too pathetic to serve as much of a trophy, even for a guy looking to reclaim his ego after having the shit kicked out of him in public, so he simply called me a bitch a few more times and then limped away, leaving me standing there, blinking. The pushcart vendor handed me a tissue.

"I'm not crying," I snapped at him, angry that he hadn't interceded on my behalf.

"Your face," he said, and I looked in the mirror attached to the cart's ballast and saw that my face was flecked with blood, which the injured guy had spewed on me while calling me a bitch. *God,* I thought as I wiped it off, *nothing like being bled on to dick up your day.* After that I stormed away, fuming so heavily that people began to cross the street to get away from me, and not another person tipped his hat to me for the rest of my stay.

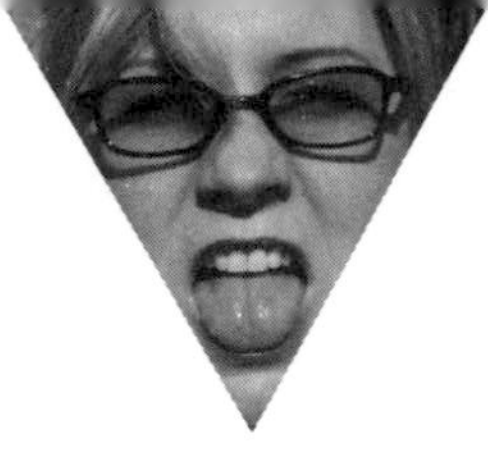

The Dutiful Sister

Last weekend my little sister, Kimberly, renewed her vows with her Swiss husband, Eddie. They wouldn't have met if not for me, as I'm reminded often. They live in a tiny homestead in Arizona, and to attend the ceremony I had to fly to New Mexico and then drive through four hours of nothing to get to nowhere, which is where they live with their three-year-old daughter in a baby-blue mobile home, with a "For Sale" sign on the empty lot next door that touts an installed septic tank. There are some other mobile homes dotting the barren landscape nearby, but none as nice as theirs, which has a wood-paneled front door and an improvised canopy over the carport to protect their truck from the weather. Eddie painted the truck himself, in a camouflage pattern, and it's quite the object of admiration among their neighbors, as is their video collection, which includes the entire *Die Hard* series.

They met in Zurich, Switzerland, when Kim was visiting me

after graduating from college. I'd had too much to drink in a pub one night, and Eddie offered to help Kim escort me home, and they haven't spent a night apart since. She remained in Zurich after I moved back to the States, and married Eddie despite my very vocal objections, which included, but were not limited to, the fact that he was old enough to be her father, that he almost burned down our house after leaving a lit cigarette on a mattress, and that during drunken sprees he would show up at our door waving a gun. What I didn't realize was that my sister truly loved Eddie, and that every word I said, instead of driving her from him, was serving to cement our own separation. And even if over the years Kim would eventually forgive these words, Eddie might not.

They moved to the States after their wedding, and for a while depended on my mother for housing and money. Eddie was always full of ideas—he was going to make a fortune by breeding rare cats, by teaching self-defense, by selling sandwiches—but drank himself stupid almost every night, which sparked my scorn and a fresh slew of appeals to my sister to reconsider her attachment to him. It's easier for me to fly to Moscow than to reach them on that stark dot in the Arizona desert. Eddie quit drinking and now holds a job as a security guard, and my sister has an administrative position with the county. There are no relatives within thousands of miles of them, and I guess that's the point. When I visit, I'm as docile as a circus animal, eager to please the ringmaster in order to be tossed the treasure of time spent with my sister and niece. During these visits, Eddie will commonly lead me out on his porch, gesture to the horizon, and say things like, "We're going to buy three more acres and raise Korean pigs. Isn't that a wonderful idea?" and I'll look at the expanse of emptiness before us and nod, saying, "Yes, that's a wonderful idea."

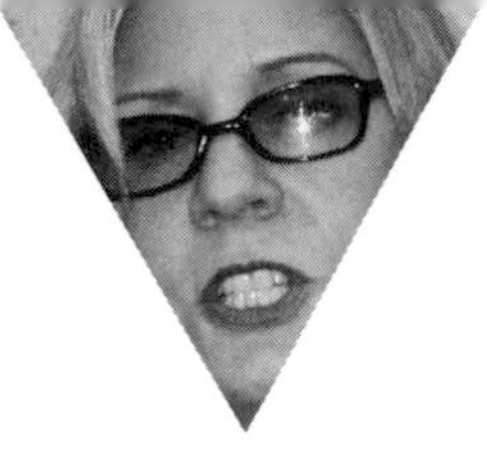

The Pie Approach

My mother was always enthusiastic about Christmas, which was odd for an atheist. "Stop that," she would exclaim in response to my skeptical expression as she decorated the Christmas tree one year. She knew I was in my own atheism phase, and that I faulted her lack of commitment to the club. But she knew that my flirtation with atheism wouldn't take, since her own beliefs had been formed with quiet resolve over the years. Mine, on the other hand, had formed instantly, after a failed affair with an asshole member of the God squad.

"Lighten up," she said in response to my Christmas cynicism. "Did the Bible say Christ had this . . ." she shook a handful of aluminum tinsel in my direction, ". . . lining his little manger?" As a joke I later presented her with a stuffed Santa Claus nailed to a cross, but she failed to see the humor in that. So I concluded it was a bad joke, since my mother never failed to see humor if it was actually there.

The affair I had with the Jesus freak my senior year in college was almost embarrassingly clichéd. He'd made it his mission to save my soul because I kept showing up for class dressed like a hooker. He said he didn't even have to be looking at the door to know when I walked in, because he could tell by the lascivious looks coming from the other guys that I'd arrived. "I can see your *breasts*," he would hiss. "Johnny," I laughed, "my tits are tiny, so you really must be *looking* for them."

His seduction took a roundabout route: First he greased his way into becoming my friend, then he heaped love, salvation, and manifest fate into the fray. It was an effective ploy, and in the end I didn't just take the bait, I swallowed the whole boat. When he inevitably dropped me, I hit the ground like a safe. I placed a call, sobbing, to my mother. She left work immediately to meet me at a coffee shop. (It would be years before I learned that, at the time, my mother faced a looming deadline for a project involving sensitive defense technology. One of her coworkers later told me that my mother breezed by their objections to her departure with, "My daughter's been dumped by some dick Bible thumper. Gotta go.")

She suggested the coffee shop because she wanted to feed me pie. It was her belief that pie was a good thing to provide to brokenhearted daughters. She herself could not make pie—aside from her specialty, tamale pie, which involved cornmeal and came out of a box—but she figured out a way to get her kids what she believed they needed, even though she herself couldn't create it. For example, she didn't know anything about romance, so when I started dating she gave me books—epic romances, with pictures of busty women fainting into the arms of muscular men on the cover—in the hopes they could prepare me for what to expect. When she discovered that it's customary for these books to depict a heroine who gets gang-raped ten times a week, she backpedaled by pouring forth books on self-esteem. Since then, though, she had settled on the pie approach.

Just give her pie and let her cry, she thought, and she was right.

I cried and cried. My mother sat across from me patiently, her deadline ticking away, and ordered more coffee. I catalogued all of my ex-boyfriend's abuses:

"Then he took back the Bible he gave me," I finished, blubbering.

As I said, my mother never failed to see the humor in a situation. "He took his Bible back?" she squeaked, her eyes round like little planets. Soon she was laughing so hard it looked like she might cough up a kidney.

"Well I guess you're going straight to Hell," my mother roared, slapping the table, "and that sure cuts your odds of having to see him again." She collapsed into new peals of laughter, doubling over until she was lying flat in the booth with her feet kicking in the aisle, which upset the passing pie-laden waitresses on their way to deliver solace to other people.

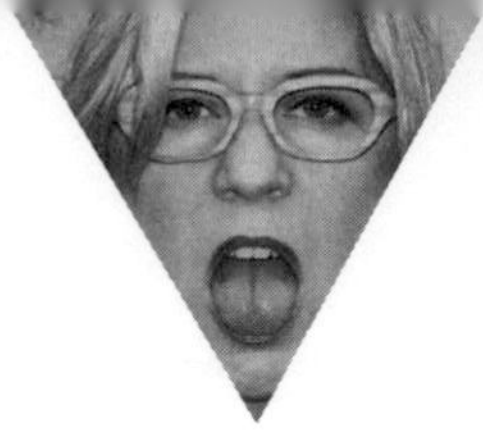

Godless Whore

I envy insane people. I saw one standing on the street corner in Portland once, wearing a sandwich board he'd fashioned by blacking out some panels of a cardboard banana box and draping them over his shoulders. The sandwich board was covered in odd evangelical scribblings, such as "Sex=AIDS=Hell," and he stood there waving his arms and shouting verbal vomit to match. I thought it appropriate that you could still see the outline of bananas on the blacked-out cardboard panels. I must have been peering too closely, perhaps puncturing his little circle of insanity, because as I passed by he interrupted himself, pointed at me, and screamed, *"Filthy, evil, Godless whore!"*

I scurried away, trying not to smile. "How'd he know your pet name?" Lary joked to me over the phone later. Lary enjoys a minor level of insanity himself. He has an entire other personality he calls "Evil Otis," who is always landing him in jail. Otis took over once when Lary was working on the roof of Philips Arena. The next thing

Lary knew, Otis was throwing boulders down at a police car on the street below. Afterward Lary had to get his ex-girlfriend to bail him out of the hoosegow. But Evil Otis has his upside too. Once Lary found himself in the Bahamas on the beach fucking a blonde Ukrainian casino dealer in public. If not for Otis, Lary says, he might miss out on stuff like this, making the occasional incarceration a fair price to pay for his appearances.

But Lary has yet to take up screaming on street corners. "Wouldn't you *love* to do that?" I asked him. "Wouldn't it be great to be that insane and not care if people stare at you?"

"You don't have it in you," he said.

Ha! How little he knows me. In fact, I'm pretty sure I have it in me. My sister Cheryl definitely does. As a kid she was so crazy, even Jehovah's Witnesses refused to enter our house. I remember one came to our door when our parents were out, and my older brother, then fourteen, asked her inside. The lady got as far as the living room, where she was assaulted by the sight of my sister Cheryl in the throes of one of her nuclear tantrums.

"Goddammit!" Cheryl was shrieking, flailing about and flicking water everywhere owing to the bucket my brother had dumped on her earlier in hopes of eliciting a tantrum that would provide the afternoon's entertainment. It worked, and Cheryl was going full throttle; she was a heaving, snorting, snarly-faced, cussing mess of kid-like limbs on the floor, writhing like a pile of dying snakes. The lady lasted one nanosecond before turning on her heel and dashing, ashen-faced and screaming, back to the street. My brother laughed so hard he almost lost a lung. The lady's retreat was exactly what he'd hoped for.

"Godless!" the lady screamed. "Awful, Godless little beasts!"

Jehovah's Witnesses never knocked on our door again, I mean *never*, even after we moved across the country to Melbourne Beach, Florida. On the whole I was mildly disheartened, because I was hoping one day someone would take it upon themselves to save our souls, but I figure we must have been branded network-wide or something, as if our household, no matter where it pitched itself, could not escape the earmark as a haven for Satan's spawn. Our family pastime of hanging out at cemeteries to watch the woodland creatures eat flowers off fresh graves didn't help either.

On Sundays, when our friends were at church, my sisters and I could be found barefoot at the splintery old town pier, trying to catch sailor fish by using clumps of canned shrimp cocktail as bait. I loved that pier. I remember the three of us, tanned and salty skinned, happy and languid, oblivious to our Godlessness, dragging the shredded shrimp bits along the surface of the river hoping to entice feebleminded fish to bite.

I went back to that pier once, decades later, after I'd moved to Atlanta and the rest of my family had fanned out, disconnected, all over the planet like tribeless nomads. It was exactly as I remembered: The pier was splintery and decrepit, beef-jerky colored, and you almost needed a tetanus shot just to set foot on it. I couldn't believe I ever frolicked barefoot on that thing.

So I walked with covered feet to the end of the pier, where some kids were fishing. They'd catch one, reel it in, toss it back, and start over. They were barefoot and the sun was warm as a womb, baking them like little angel cakes. I sat on the edge nearby and dangled my legs over the water, attempting to impersonate a benign entity just sharing a pier with some carefree kids and not the lost lemming that I was—needful, searching for the scattered fragments of my heart, looking for a way to reconnect them to pass my Godless self off as whole—but I couldn't manage it. Instead, the kids ended up staring at me, wondering who this person was, this insane person, shoeless now, blubbering on the end of a pier, with nothing but her sock to wipe her snot away.

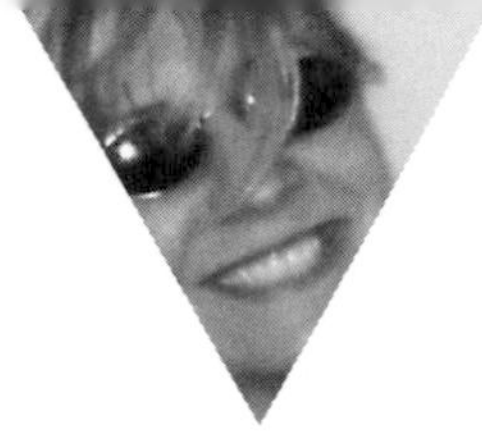

Freak Like Me

I find it infuriating that my friend Michael refuses to admit he's a freak. First, at six-foot-seven, he's so tall he doesn't fit in a lot of places. He didn't fit on the cramped upper floor of the first restaurant he bought here in Atlanta ten years ago with his two siblings (both of whom Michael likes to believe would be living on abandoned mattresses under a freeway overpass if not for him, by the way), and he doesn't fit in the bathroom of my loft either, complaining that the only way he can sit on the toilet is to fold up his mantis-like legs and hang his feet in the tub.

I'm adamantly unsympathetic. We were both equally poor when we met a decade ago. Lary introduced me to him when Michael was waiting tables at his own restaurant, The Vortex, which thrived and then became the Vortex *chain*. Lary and I used to hang out at the original one, a comfy dive on West Peachtree Street, dreaming about the future and demanding that Michael make us stronger drinks.

Just look at us today, Michael and me; me with my rented loft that has a bathroom as big as my bed, and Michael with his chain of restaurants and his mansion on eight acres with a bathroom big enough to be used as a cult compound. "I swear," I grumbled at him while freeloading at his midtown location, "you are such a freak."

"Retard," he snapped back, hardly distracted from his task, which was to build a big go-go cage. That's right, a *go-go cage*, where girls in fur bikinis can undulate over people trying to dine. Michael all of a sudden figured this was the one thing missing at that particular restaurant location, so he immediately brought in a bunch of electric saws and drills from his truck, and started tearing the place up over by the bar, where there were people *eating*, I might add.

Okay, maybe they weren't eating, but there were people drinking, with menus nearby. Or at least I was drinking, because Michael had bought me a margarita to remind me why I still stand him. That's my boy—just because he's rich doesn't mean he's forgotten about the dregs he left behind in the cesspool. Anyway, the go-go cage didn't fit where it needed to fit, so rather than take my advice—which was to give up and use the failure as an excuse to soak his head in hooch—Michael did what he always does. It's what separates a person like him, who has never easily fit in anywhere his entire life, from the tidal wave of plebes who constitute the average human morass. What he did is this: He carved a big chunk out of an obstruction so he could accommodate his vision of how things should be.

God! I hate to admit I envy him for his ability to just remove obstructions like that. I can't remember ever doing something like that—not consciously anyway. I came to the realization that I'm the great giver-upper after I uncovered an old letter I wrote when I was six that my sister sent me along with a sack of other mementos from our childhood. She'd heard I regretted not saving such stuff myself, having thrown it all away a decade and a half ago because I didn't have room for it in my apartment. I felt it didn't fit into my life.

My letter, written in red crayon, espoused some pretty simple dreams for the future: "I wanna be . . ." I had written over and over, misspellings rampant. I wanted to be a tennis player on TV, I wanted to be a "pricess," a "moofy star," a "book riter." "I wanna be," I finished, "ever thing I wanna be."

Christ, what a contrast to today, when all I wanna do is lie down it seems, because even sitting on the sidelines and watching a friend build something is too exhausting. It's all in my head, Michael says. He has always said that. For ten years he has been telling me that. "I wanna be . . ." I told him way back when. "What the hell's stopping you?" he laughed then, and still laughs now.

I suppose Michael and I are kindred spirits in that we're both freaks, but he'll pound out a place for himself while I'm content to let people purge me from their circle. Remember, at fourteen I got fired from my first job at an ice-cream parlor because of that habit I had sitting around wondering what it felt like to be bit in half by a shark. If that happened to Michael, he would have opened his own ice-cream parlor. He would have served shark shakes. He figured out a long time ago he didn't fit on the same train with everyone else, so he's accustomed to building his own tracks.

I build my own tracks too, but only because I'm one of those people whose search for a person to follow came up empty. See? I can't even take credit for my individuality because I came at it reluctantly, unlike Michael, who relishes his freak status to the point he refuses to concede that he even is one. I'd copy him if I could, but that's not possible, so I make my way with the six-year-old I used to be still haunting my thoughts. *I wanna be, I wanna be*, I hear her whisper in my ear on occasion, but graciously she has added to the list. *I wanna be fine*, she sometimes says now, *fine with my freak-ass self*.

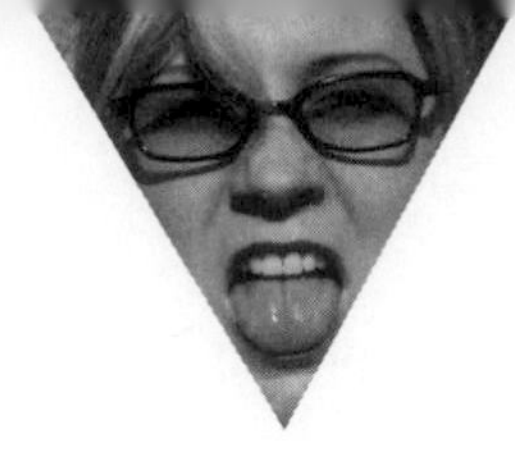

Playing Dead

Twice now—*twice* in the past few months—Lary's cat has had to fake her own death to get his attention. "I swear she's really dead this time," I had to shriek into Lary's voice mail. "I can't find her anywhere, and there's a *smell*. I know that smell, it's dead-cat smell, so get your worthless crusty ass back to Atlanta and look for your poor dead cat who died of loneliness, you selfish walking colostomy bag of cat-killing wasted space. Fuck you."

Lary can't escape, not from me, and not from his cat, Mona. No way. He had to fly all the way back from his work in Chicago, or Wisconsin, or the damn Bahamas (that was the first time Mona played dead), to look for his cat, who usually sleeps on a heated pillow atop a gilded pedestal in his living room, if you can call it a living room. (I personally call it a covered alleyway, but then I have to admit that since he's added climate control it can be pretty nice sometimes, even though there are mosquito larvae living in the fountain in his foyer.)

In his absence, a tribe of feral kittens had moved into Lary's carport, living under the upturned oil barrels. It served him right if you ask me, because Lary is not a kitten kind of guy. Mona doesn't count, because we all concede that Mona must be a reincarnated gargoyle, and probably spent her past life perched above the very same doorway of the very same dilapidated old stone warehouse where Lary now lives. Years ago, on the day she appeared, she was obviously just returning home after a long absence, and she must have liked what Lary did to the place. He's fashioned it into a passable habitat over the years, I must admit.

The feral kittens certainly agree. In the months since Lary's been away on his series of failed escapes the kittens have made themselves at home, even slaughtering a squirrel and leaving it on his doormat like a fuzzy little sacrificial offering, with its fuzzy little throat ripped out. "Thanks for the digs," the kittens were saying to Lary. "If you come home, we promise there'll be plenty more where that came from." But Mona's tactics are more subtle, and more effective. Her practice is to go on a hunger strike and hide in an unused air-conditioning vent above the bathroom until he's forced to return. Lary's home now, probably for good, considering the weak economy, because it looks like no one will escape that.

I'm in danger of losing my job too—or at the very least any semblance of what it used to be—but Lary is much better equipped for poverty than I am. His place is paid for and tricked out like a survival bunker. I think he can even catch rainwater through some brick-lined flow patterns he created in imitation of the ancient Roman aqueducts. And there are a jillion plants in his home too, some of them probably edible, as are the kittens of course.

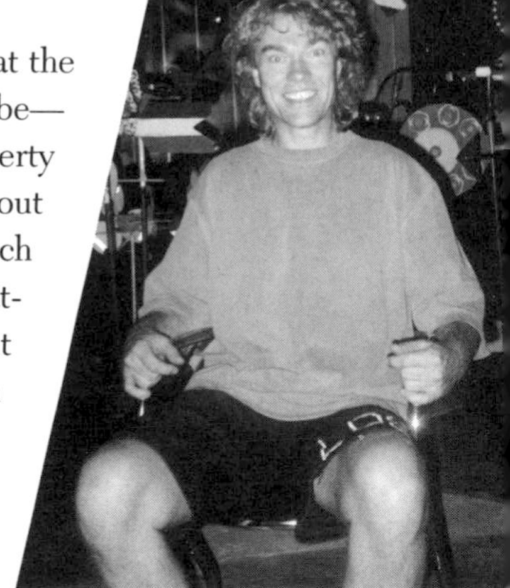

Lary

Lary's been poor before, and it seems he's been priming himself for when it happens again. I should learn from him. I wish I could just fake my own death like Lary's cat did, but I know I'll have to hang in there. Toughen up. Stick it out. My mother was in her mid-fifties when she lost her job as a computer weapons specialist during the government cutbacks of the late eighties, and right away she rolled up her sleeves and got another job selling packaged sandwiches from a catering truck parked at construction sites.

After that she became a junk dealer. She sold big-eyed ceramic beagles, old turntable parts, macramé owls, angel-shaped toilet-paper cozies, and all kinds of random crap at swap meets in the San Diego sports-arena parking lot. The local newspaper was so impressed with her tenacity it printed an article about her, entitled "From Missiles to Miscellaneous," which featured an unflattering photo of my mother in a coin belt, standing next to a secondhand Catholic confessional priced at just seventy-five dollars. If I think hard enough I can still see her smiling back at me in that bad picture, smiling with steely resolve. "Don't you dare," she is saying to me. "Don't you dare roll over and play dead."

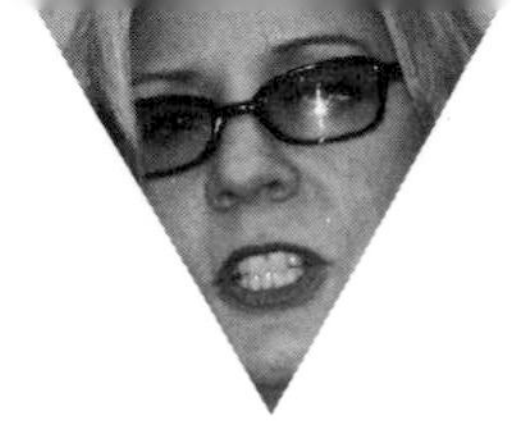

A Big Shock

My neighbor George looks damn good for someone who was electrocuted last year. I saw him yesterday with his wife, Judy, smiling like he always does, and I would never have known that, fairly recently, he fried the holy hell out of himself trying to fix an old air conditioner. I still feel a little bad about laughing when I heard the news, but you have to understand I'd been nagging those two for missing my birthday party for an entire *year*, and it wasn't until now that Judy finally told me why.

"Well," she said, almost sheepishly, "George got electrocuted."

How do you *not* laugh when someone says that? That is a funny-ass reason for missing a party, and there George was, sitting right next to me, smiling and looking about as unelectrocuted as can be. I hugged him very tight right then, which is what I hear you're supposed to do with shock victims.

George and Judy live upstairs from me in the old telephone factory. They used to sell furniture out of their truck, and now they own Paris on Ponce, a giant antiques and retro-furniture labyrinth that reminds me of what the attic of Andy Warhol and Madame de Pompadour would have looked like had they ever got married and birthed a brood of poets and circus performers. George and Judy always put out a big tray of complimentary cookies and cider for paying customers, and considering how rarely I fall into that category, I'm amazed they've never slapped my hand away. I've gone in there and chowed from that tray like it was my personal trough, complaining the whole time how hot it was in there.

I now feel guilty for bitching about the heat, because it was when George finally got around to installing an air conditioner (which he probably excavated from underneath car wreckage at the bottom of a dried riverbed or something) that he went and electrocuted himself. Evidently he stood there, bug-eyed, for quite a while, paralyzed by the voltage running through his whole body, before he got tired of waiting for someone to save him and somehow mustered the oomph to wrest himself free from the current. Afterward, his shoes were all melted and it looked like someone had taken a blowtorch to his armpits. "He couldn't come to your party with burned-up armpits, now could he?" Judy said, and I had to laugh again.

I am so happy George didn't die, because until then I always equated electrocution with certain death. As a kid I was terrified I'd one day be falsely convicted of murder and have to face the electric chair. I once confessed my fears to my father. "Damn right they'll electrocute you," he said. "They'll flip the switch as easy as a burger."

My mother yelled at him not to shock me like that. She'd not yet rebounded from the time I was five and came across the childbirth edition of *Life* magazine, which I'd opened to a picture of a naked lady with a big blue head popping out of her poon-tang. "That lady has a head coming out of her pee hole!" I wailed.

My mother carted my crying ass away from the magazine and acted concerned about the possible shock I had just endured. She was forced to explain the facts of life to me right then, and while she tried to make it sound nice, she wasn't all that adept at euphemisms.

"That's just where babies come from, and yes, it hurts like hell, but you'll live," she said, and she hugged me so tight she flattened two bubble-gum cigars in my front pocket.

A decade later, she had another shock to impart. She came home and asked me to sit down. From the look on her face she obviously had something important to announce, and she didn't know how to ease into it. "I'm leaving your father," she blurted out, waiting for my traumatized reaction. When it didn't come, she continued. "When you get back from school today I'll be gone," she said. "Gone."

But I was not shocked at all. Throughout my whole life I had known she would be leaving. For fifteen years I'd witnessed the simmering fury between my parents, hanging in the air like heavy smoke, each blaming the other for the calcified casket of emptiness their lives had become. Every day I'd seen my mother long for the life she felt my father denied her, and every day I'd seen my father marinate his sorrow with booze and bold proclamations. But my mother felt she had done a good job of protecting me from this, and she hadn't realized her misery was as transparent as a shattered windshield. "I mean it," she said. "I'm gone."

"I know," I said lucidly, and at that, my mother crumbled like an autumn leaf. All the tears she'd kept hidden behind the basket of broken dreams in her heart broke free right then, and she lowered her head to her hands in shame. "I'm so sorry," she wept, her shoulders shaking with the weight of her regret. I wanted to ask her what she was so sorry about, because I didn't see how this was anyone's fault, but instead, I hugged her very tight, which is what I hear you're supposed to do with shock victims.

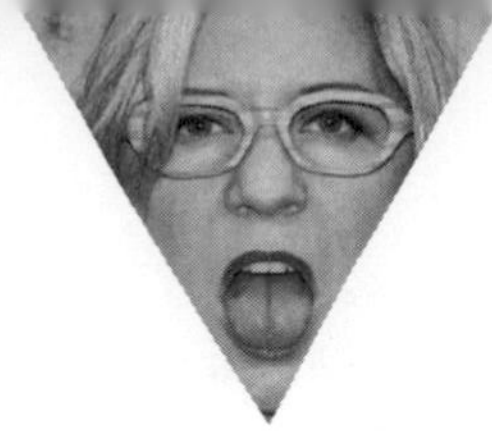

Puppy Love

Nothing like stumbling over a dead puppy to dick up your day, so thank God *that* didn't happen, but it *almost* did.

First, the puppy was not really a puppy, but one of those perpetual puppy-type dogs, one of those furry button-cute kind of pets, with long ears covered in curly fleece and legs that are the canine equivalent to one of the Budweiser Clydesdales. This is the kind of dog an ex-boyfriend of mine used to refer to as a "pussy pet." If this guy saw that kind of dog, he would smirk dismissively and say in his Brazilian accent, "You cannot throw that dog against the wall," because, to him, the inability to be thrown against the wall and emerge unfazed was a grievous shortcoming in an animal.

So you could not have thrown this dog against the wall . . . I'm thinking, but I really don't know for sure. I've never had a pussy-pet dog. Once I temporarily inherited two Labradors named Gracie and Amber. They were sisters, and both of them were the most comical, slobbery, eye-booger encrusted, walking wads of psoriasis you ever saw. Having birthed three litters, they each had hefty leftover dugs that dangled from their underbellies like big balls of soft warm dough. Amber had a problem with her left ear too, which occasionally swelled up like an eggplant and stuck straight out from her skull, making her look like she had a furry party balloon taped to her head. They also had some kind of skin allergy that, for some reason, caused them to chew all the hair off their hind parts. The eye-catching result was that they both sported big shiny red baboon asses. God, I loved them, and I still miss them too, even though I could never get Amber's ear to go down.

Then I had Cookie, an incontinent pit-bull puppy with a deformed tail that reminded me of a carrot pushing up through a crack in the sidewalk. She was routinely so happy to see visitors that she'd squat right there and pee at their feet. Believe it or not, it was a step up from her earlier puppy behavior, when people thought she was undisciplined just because, given the chance, she would chew on their skulls. The immensely tall Michael was always amazed to find her teeth in his head.

I didn't know what to make of this new dog I'd found wandering on Memorial Avenue near Oakland Cemetery. He was about to be made into a furry piece of street pizza by a passing semi when I rescued him. And this was no stray, because someone had obviously loved this animal, probably brushing his black terrier hair every night, and now they were left wondering what happened to him. He wore a blue collar, his green nylon leash was broken, and it looked like he'd been lost for a while, because he was sporting a layer of dirt that didn't look customary on him. I brought him home, cleaned him up, and discovered that he was as mellow as a monk. He wasn't even getting spooked by my big cat, Lucille, who was fifteen and missing her upper teeth but could still kick any dog's ass, even (and probably especially) Cookie's. I started calling the new dog "Scooter," because that's what I call all cute things whose names I don't know, including small children.

Scooter reminded me of a black dog my father brought home when I was seven. We named her Bonnie, and she was quite a slut, but I loved her anyway. I was sent to fetch her one morning and found her getting humped on by a neighborhood mutt. I had no idea what the hell was happening, so I set about trying to pull them apart. I did not know, nor should I have, that dogs get stuck when they're doing it, because it's part of their whole procreation process. So I could not separate them, and the most I could do was turn the mutt around so he was facing the other way and not actually on top of Bonnie. But all that accomplished was to turn them into a freakish set of whining Siamese dog twins fused at the ass.

So the only thing I could do at that point was to sit on the curb beside them and commence wailing. I mean, here my Bonnie was stuck to another dog, probably permanently as far as I knew, and now I'd have to bring this mutant double-dog monster back home and try to explain it to my father. So I sat there and sobbed, occasionally shouting to the mutt, "Get off Bonnie!" but he just looked at me like he was extremely uncomfortable and stayed stuck.

Eventually, a long-haired man emerged from the house across the street and rescued me. He was barefoot and bare chested, freshly roused out of bed by my wails. He carried a bucket of water and threw it on the dogs, which made them pop apart like a Tupperware set. The man was laughing so hard, I couldn't make out what he was saying. It had something to do with the dogs being "attached," or "attachment" or whatever, and how I was supposed to make sure it didn't happen again. But his words went unheeded, because a few months later Bonnie had her puppies, and I got attached anyway.

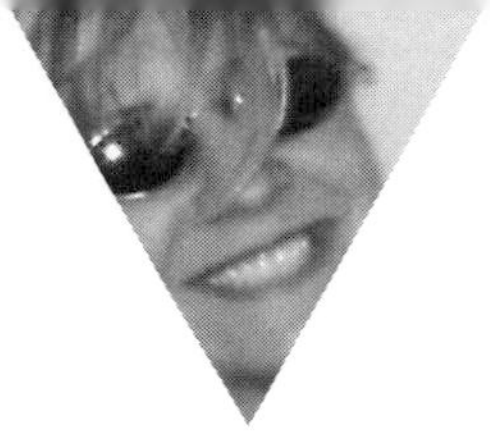

Thank You, Dr. Melkonian

I swear, I thought it was normal to have dreams about your teeth falling out. I thought those kinds of dreams were a universal norm, like the ones in which you're naked on the college campus with nothing but a pot holder to hide your naughty bits. "You mean *you* don't have the missing-teeth dreams?" I asked Daniel.

"It's just you," he said. "You're probably traumatized from the time Grant found the jar of teeth at the crack house."

Hell, yes, I was traumatized by the time Grant found the jar of teeth at the crack house. Who wouldn't be? I'm hinky about teeth. When I was seven I had a baby molar rotting right out of my head. Our family dentist at that time was a nasty ape who always stabbed me in the gums with a needle as big as a dinosaur bone, then used the drill like he was perfecting a Cambodian torture technique. He would literally plant his knee on my chest to secure me to the dental chair. I'm not kidding.

It wasn't until I was a teenager and went to another dentist that I realized you weren't *supposed* to feel the drill during a dental visit, let alone your dentist's knee on your sternum. That's what the needle is for, to administer Novocain, not to punch holes in your patient's head. By then I'd had a hundred cavities, and when my mother heard the new dentist's prognosis, she called him and told him he'd have to hire me so I could pay off my own damn dental bill.

So he did. His name was Dr. Melkonian, and he made me the assistant to his receptionist, who was a kind old woman with earlobes covered in soft whiskers. The light from the setting sun in the office window behind her would sometimes illuminate her lobe fuzz and make it look as though wispy smoke were coming out of her ears. She was the nicest woman I'd ever met, and she used to tell me she could see the goodness in me even though they had to ask me to stop wearing halter tops to the office. I worked there every day after school for almost two years. It's where I learned to type, and I became so deft at typing Dr. Melkonian's name that I used to do it over and over so I would look busy. It's an unusual name, and you almost have to be a concert pianist to punch it out on the keys. *Dr. Melkonian. Dr. Melkonian. Dr. Melkonian.*

The typing practice served well as a bridge to get me through my shift so I could get on with the mess of my life. During that time, my family was falling apart like a piece of stale coffee cake. We were living in Torrance, California, and my mother had moved out of the apartment where we lived and then forced my father to leave before she would move back. Only she didn't move back right away because she'd become too attached to the condo she was renting in the Land of Swinging Separated People to move in the middle of her lease. For a while, my little sister and I actually lived alone. We were fourteen and sixteen, respectively, and I immediately began dating a very handsome heroin addict whose parents were wealthy psychiatrists. Luckily I had that fear of needles, and every day after school—or after I *cut* school—I had my job at Dr. Melkonian's office, where I hit the typewriter. *Dr. Melkonian. Dr. Melkonian. Dr. Melkonian.*

It's hard to miss, that name, so when I saw it in the paper years later it caught my eye. It was in the obituary section. *This couldn't be* my *Dr. Melkonian from Torrance,* I thought, but I read on. He had moved to Atlanta from Torrance about a decade earlier to teach at Emory University. He'd died suddenly in his sleep, having lived all those years probably not ten miles away from me, and probably not even knowing how he had been the bridge for me so long ago and half a hemisphere away. He was the bridge that kept me from falling into a mote of lost hope that threatened my future. I wish I had thought to thank him for giving me a place to go, a place with a sweet old receptionist with a sunlit fuzzy halo, with a kind dentist who paid me for doing little more than type his name.

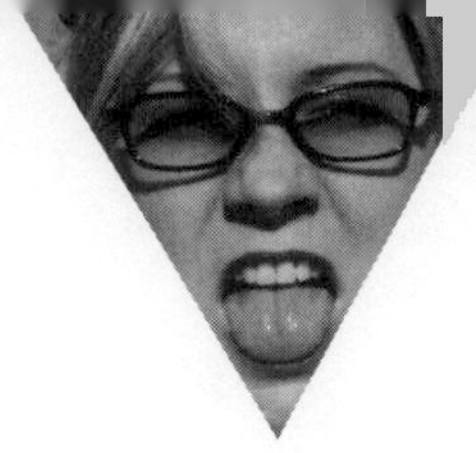

More Inner Evil

A friend of mine got married in a beautiful ceremony, which provided me with a good excuse to partake in a trough of champagne, especially since my date for the wedding, Lary, left with another woman.

"You don't mind, do you?" he asked before bolting.

"You're my *date*, you dick!"

"I knew you'd understand."

"Fuck you!"

And off he went. Grant also watched him go. "Champagne?" he smiled, handing me a glass. He was using his sinister smile, a warning to me that he is very much in touch with his inner evil. He's striving to influence others to achieve that evil, like he's the new Ring Master of the Psycho Circus. I've been trying to trace the birth of this demon in Grant—because I used to know him pre-demon—and, as best as I can tell, it emerged for the first time one Monday night at Fuzzy's, when Francine Reed was performing. That's the night Grant invented "sandwich dancing," which entails three or more people slow dancing in a drunken, undulating conga line. "I wanna be the meat!" Grant yells when it's time to sandwich dance, which is usually every time Reed does her heart-stopping rendition of Etta James. I don't know what it is about Reed, but her singing just seems to bring out the bad behavior in my friends. And I think I mean "bad" in a good way, sort of.

That night, after the wedding, Grant invented "cluster kissing," which I won't describe, except to say that it involves both males and females and it seemed like a good idea at the time, swept up in the sweetness of the nuptials as I was. By this time our group had left the reception to attend a festival party held in a warehouse in the Old Fourth Ward. It was a great party, staged in a massive industrial labyrinth used to build movie sets. Art, music, and interesting people abounded. I drank, danced, laughed, and fumbled into the arms of my friends. "I love you, did you know that?" I'd say. "I *love* you! I *mean* it." Cluster kiss. "I could die right now and be the happiest person in the universe!" Cluster kiss. Group hug. Sandwich dance. "I *mean* it! I could *die*!"

In retrospect it's ironic that—very nearby, and entirely unbeknownst to us at the time—a man *did* die that night. While I was inside the warehouse reveling in a platonic faux orgy with my friends, a social studies teacher and his girlfriend were parking in the side lot on their way to this same party. Soon after they left their car, an armed robber shot them both. The girl was hospitalized and recovered, but her boyfriend died. He was thirty-two years old, and probably the last thing on his mind as he took the keys out of his ignition that night was how little time he had left to live. Did he spend his last day worrying about bills, pondering past regrets, lamenting world affairs? Did he stop, contemplate his life, know that he was loved? Did he leave phone messages for his friends who now agonize over having erased them because they didn't know they would never hear his voice or see his face again?

"It could have been me," I say to myself. And I'm right. And if it were me I would have spent the last moments of my life surrounded by a large number of my favorite people, hugging and kissing them with sticky champagne lips and sentimental abandon, happy to be alive, effectively under the spell of the demon in Grant, whose influence may not be so evil after all. "I *love* you, man!" Cluster kiss. Group hug. "I *mean* it." And I do.

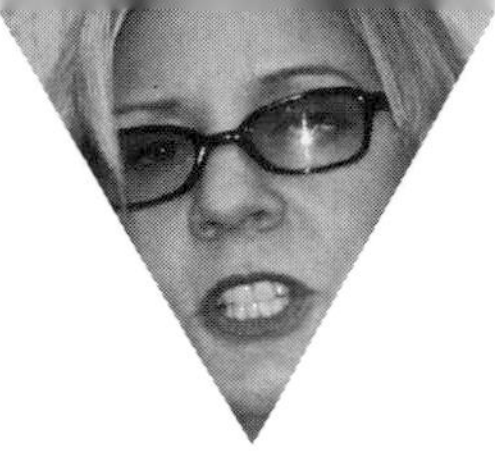

Broken

There must be something really wrong with the world when you can't get a buzz off your codeine cough medicine. Christ if that doesn't just suck all the fun out of being sick. I was chugging that stuff like shooters at a Hooters bar and I was still so lucid I could pilot a plane, plus I kept coughing like a late-stage lung-cancer victim. I had a good mind to go back to my pharmacist and accuse him of switching my prescription with pancake syrup, hoarding the good stuff for himself, because it's not every day I get to do drugs. What rotten luck to have gotten my clutches on a legal narcotic, and it didn't work! I had to find another way to fix myself.

I could have called Lary. Not for drugs . . . though he seems to have drugs in his house he doesn't even know about. Though Lary couldn't cure me, he could fix my broken furnace. My loft was cold, I was cold, and that was why I had that bionic flu bug to begin with. I noticed something was wrong one morning while I was poking myself in bed, wondering why I felt harder than usual—since hardness isn't a quality I would attribute to my body—when suddenly the reason for my condition occurred to me: I was frozen. Frozen because my furnace had done a death rattle in the middle of the night, and in the ensuing hours I basically got crusted over with ice, leaving me a bleachy-haired, flannel-clad, phlegmy Snow White after she bit into the bad apple and lay there preserved for eternity with woodland creatures coming from miles around to weep at her feet.

Okay, not *exactly* like that, but I was cold. So to stay alive, I set about calling people to come and fix my broken furnace. I called Lary because when something is broken my first step is always to charm him into fixing it.

"Goddammit, you walking pocket of pus," I croaked into his cell phone, "get your meager ass over here and fix my furnace."

"Hi, whore," he answered gamely. "I'm in Colorado."

"Huh?"

"Been here all week. You're supposed to feed my cat, remember? How's my cat?"

"Love ya,'bye!"

So with Lary inconsiderately unavailable, my options fell to Daniel and Grant. Daniel was vetoed immediately because he couldn't fix a broken furnace any more than he can perform eye surgery on himself. He's an *artist*. He creates, he doesn't *mend*. His own garbage disposal has been broken for more than a year and he has yet to begin the highly technical process of dialing the building manager's phone number so she can dispatch the superintendent to fix it.

So I called Grant. Grant could fix almost anything—not with his actual own

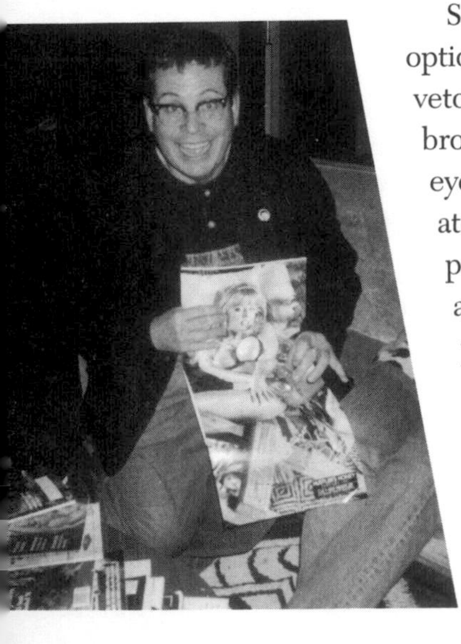

Grant

hands, mind you, but he knows *guys*. There was his hardwood-floor guy, his electricity guy, his HVAC guy. What he can't fix he leaves broken and figures it's better for it. Like that time he found an ancient wooden pie chest on the side of the road. When I asked him if he planned to replace the rusty torn screen, he looked at me like I just asked him to eat beetles. "Its brokenness is what makes it so fabulous," he gasped.

But Grant sounded sad when he answered the phone. I'd been gone and hadn't heard the news: That day he was on his way to a funeral with his daughter to grieve the deaths of her three friends who died together tragically over the weekend. Two of them were children. "She used to baby-sit those kids, Hollis," Grant said, his voice thin. "She can't stop crying."

Grant's daughter had just turned eighteen, and adulthood didn't waste time introducing her to the hardness of life. "She keeps sobbing, she keeps saying, 'But Daddy . . . ' " Grant grieved. "God, why does it break my heart so horribly to hear her say that?"

I think I know why. It's because the child in her was barely veiled by her new womanhood, and Grant heard his child appealing to him to make it all better, to wave a wand and make the world the way it was a few days ago, and he felt utter powerlessness to provide her that. "God, Hollis," Grant lamented, "I couldn't do anything but let her cry. I couldn't *fix* it." Instead he realized a tiny piece of her will have to remain broken, and she won't be better off for it, just wiser and stronger as we all eventually become through the course of life, and a little less dependent on her father.

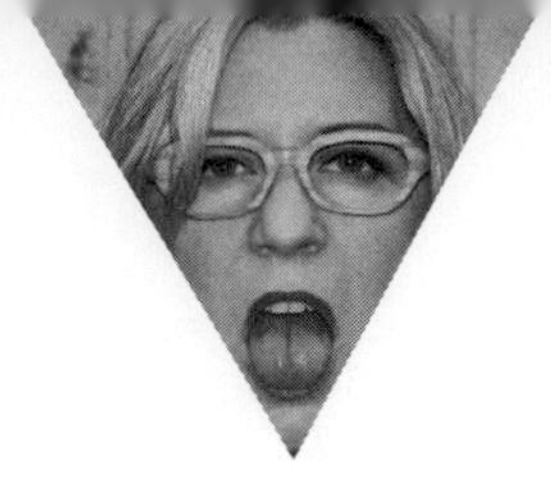

Severed Head in a Sack

It was the night before I was about to close on the house I had under contract when I discovered that the police had recently found an unidentified decomposing human head in a plastic bag *on my new street.* And not only that, they found *seven other* plastic bags full of cut up legs and limbs and crap in the same neighborhood, and they figured, okay, mystery almost solved, sort of, since they have the rest of the body, *you would think. But then the head in a bag didn't match the body in seven bags,* so now they had a bunch of bags of body parts and one bag of head parts that *didn't belong to each other!!!!* So this not only meant that *some sick amateur Frankenstein* was killing people and tossing their parts around in Baggies like leftover chopped broccoli *in my new "up and coming" in-town neighborhood,* but that there was still out there, *in my neighborhood,* the decomposing torso to match the first decomposing head, and the decapitated head to match the bags of people parts found not too far from the head that *didn't belong to it.*

Got that? Good. Because, considering all the above, there are lots more sacks o' surprises—all smelly and teeming with maggots—presumably still waiting out there in my new neighborhood for me to stumble upon in the dark, probably in back of my newly purchased home in that cute carriage-house garage that I never even bothered to have the seller unlock. I looked in the garage window and said, "Yeah, fine, whatever," and didn't even *think* it might be wise to investigate for piles of plastic bags settled into soft biomorphic shapes, with maybe some *seepage* or something—because if I had found that I would have offered a lot less for the place.

But why be greedy? Because the house was "in town," and therefore subject to the real-estate "frenzy" in which people were clamoring for in-town property like feral hogs set free in a field of sleeping newborn babies, and I got it for a good price, so there's at least one bonus to house hunting in a neighborhood littered with so many unidentified human limbs it could pass for a looted Peruvian graveyard. What bargains! The house went up five thousand dollars in value just during the time I had it under contract. *Woohoo!* I thought to myself. I finally have a chunk of the city of Atlanta all to myself! Bummer about those dismembered corpses and all, but hey, at least I won't have to spend hours of my day in line at some *suburban* Starbucks—mainly because Starbucks hadn't yet been brave enough to open a franchise in these parts. In fact, I was so *in on the ground floor* that there wasn't a coffeehouse to be seen in this section of southwest Atlanta where I would soon live. It was, however, the area in which the city's biggest mass murder of the century recently occurred. How about that?

Also in my new neighborhood were a couple of cool-looking thrift stores and a crack whore on crutches, who should not be mistaken for the other neighborhood whore, who was much healthier until she got shot dead while running naked down the middle of the street, four blocks away from my street. One good sign is that her killer didn't dice up her body, which I take to mean that this neighborhood is definitely on the upswing, and that I definitely made a really good investment. Yep, I did.

Another good investment for this neighborhood was Cookie the pit bull. The downside was she was three months old and weighed only twelve pounds. But the upside was that ten of those pounds seemed to be teeth. When she grows up, she'll be able to rip the jugular out of the necks of all chainsaw-wielding killers bent on making a bag of human hash out of me, but for now the most pain I'd seen her inflict was one morning when I was smothering her with kisses and she accidentally bit my nipple. That *really* hurt, but I doubt drug-crazed killers will be deterred by me brandishing a puppy and threatening, "Get back or say good-bye to your nipple!" So I sure hope she grows fast, because—bargain or no bargain—it'll be really hard to reap the rewards of this in-town investment with my severed head in a sack.

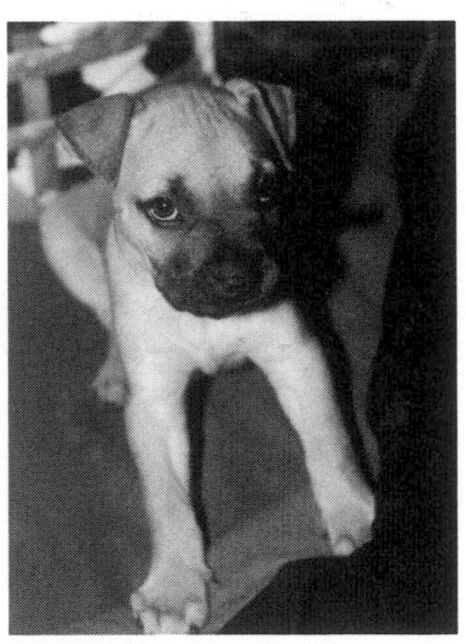

Cookie the pit bull

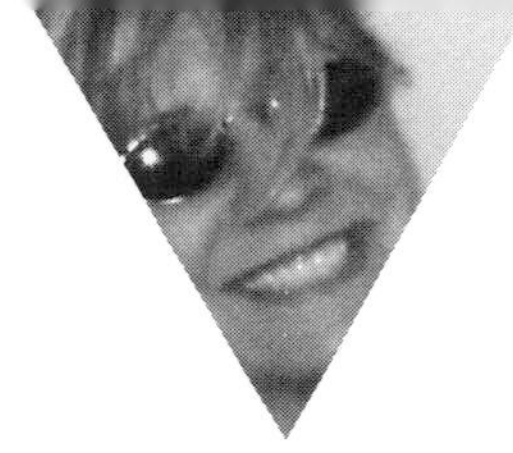

Butthole to Hell

Needless to say, I was scared to move into my new house. I was afraid, now that it was all mine and things seemed to be going smoothly, that all of a sudden I would find the butthole to Hell in my backyard like what happened in *Poltergeist* or something. I wish I was more like Grant, who is fearless. He bought that house in Kirkwood with a dead chicken nailed to the door, and he didn't blink an eye. He didn't look at the holes in the floor, the crumbling walls, or the shifty bar across the street where prostitutes with botched gang-insignia tattoos were beaten by their pimps. He was looking at the house's price, which was, like, five cents. He took a month to make it livable, and then sold it a year later for enough profit to pay cash for two other houses and live like King Tut ever since. He keeps telling me, "Honey, you gotta have vision."

Like I said, Grant never picks the established neighborhoods. He bypassed East Atlanta, the city's darling of the "up-and-coming" communities, for Peoplestown, which is where he lives now, in that former crack house. Peoplestown has since ripened in value, as Grant knew it would, and now it's time for him to move on. His neighborhood has become "fringe," and Grant likes to live on the fringe of the fringe. He's picked out a house in Atlanta's Pittsburgh area, on the West End, which was good news for me, because the house I had under contract was in Capitol View, just a few blocks away.

Grant was proud of my purchase. He thinks that because I bought there I have "vision," when the truth is I don't. I'd heard that Capitol View—just five miles away from where I live now in Poncey Highlands—was a neighborhood gem-in-the-rough situated around a pristine park. I'd heard that a lot of gay people and artists are buying there, and I'd heard it touted as "Grant Park five years ago," which are all really good signs if you ask me, just not super *visible* signs as of yet. So I did not have vision when I picked my house there. I had the opposite. I had to *cover* my eyes—to the crack addicts, to the ugly food store that's just a front for alcoholics to lean on, to the rusty auto graveyard at the end of my block—and just sign the offer.

I liked it when Grant drove me through my future neighborhood, because he didn't see the bad things. He saw what I paid for the house, which was, like, five cents. He sees original wood molding that's never been painted, tiled fireplaces, wraparound porches, hardwood floors, eleven-foot ceilings, French doors. He sees "activity" in the neighborhood, which is code for investors buying abandoned houses and renovating. "Look," Grant said, pointing to a wooden tripod perched on a front lawn, a telltale sign that the boarded-up house behind it is getting rewired and rehabbed, "I *love* this neighborhood!"

I'm glad Grant loves it, because I'm not ashamed to admit I wouldn't have bought there otherwise. I might not have vision, but at least I know enough to pick another better pair of eyes to lead me. Once I made a move on my own and chose a house in East Atlanta that I thought was perfect. Grant gave it the thumbs-down, but it seemed so marvelous I had it inspected anyway. Turns out the main joists were completely rotted through. The inspector pointed out the uneven doorjambs and the inch of space between the bathroom sink and the line of grout that formerly attached it to the wall. Without the joists to support it, the house was, in effect, getting the bottom sucked right out from under itself. Grant just grinned when I told him. "That right there is your butthole to Hell," he said.

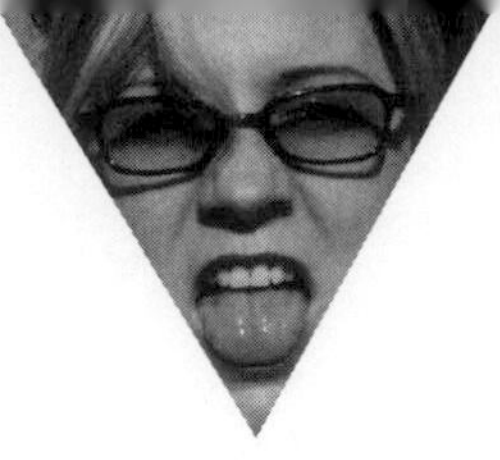

I've Always Been a Bad Whore

The big, hard thing in my bed one night was not a man but a book titled *The Stanley Complete Step-by-Step Guide to Home Repair and Improvement,* which my contractor friend Roger gave to me. After I slept with that book I was hoping it would grant me a favor, perhaps suddenly become decipherable, because I was about to move into my house and it still had a lot of broken parts in it. My new neighborhood, Capitol View, seemed a little squalid, and so did my new two-bedroom house.

The problem with the home repair guide was that it didn't provide a step *low enough* for me to start my climb. For instance, my bathroom didn't have a shower, just a bathtub with a spigot. No overhead shower. None. Nowhere in this book does it have a chapter on how to install a showerhead where there is no shower. There is a chapter on how to *repair* a showerhead, how to *replace* a showerhead, but, like me when I bought the house, this book naively assumes that even the lowliest home in need of repair comes equipped with certain basic amenities. But not my house. It's funny too, because the lady who sold it to me looked really clean. I wonder how she got that way.

The plumber estimated that to turn my bathroom into a real bathroom it would cost $1,100, which led me to conclude that I'm sleeping with the wrong things. I should be sleeping with a plumber or, better yet, my contractor friend Roger. But I've always been a bad whore. I've never been able to "work it," as Daniel likes to put it, or "ride the poon-tang tide," as I like to put it. The most I can do is flirt, which doesn't get me that far (though it does get me out of speeding tickets sometimes).

Lary is really handy when it comes to home repair, but he's impervious to my flirting. I've left twenty-eight messages on his answering machine begging him to help, all beginning with endearments like, "Hey, you worthless stain on the butt end of the world" or "Hey, you turd-encrusted puckered poohole," because to Lary that is flirting. But for ten years he's been helping me fix things, and now he probably figures it's time to pass on the home-repair hammer. Lary doesn't even protect me anymore from the festering nest of big-butted spiders that live in the holly tree by my driveway. At night, when the spiders weave a giant web right in front of my car door and wait there for me like a dozen evil eight-legged Buddhas, I have to create a clear path for myself by flailing my arms around like Michael Stipe in that "Losing My Religion" video, sending web pieces and spider asses everywhere. *I am my own Sir Galahad,* I sigh to myself. That pleases me pretty much, and for a while I forget that in a few days I'll have to wash my hair with a garden hose.

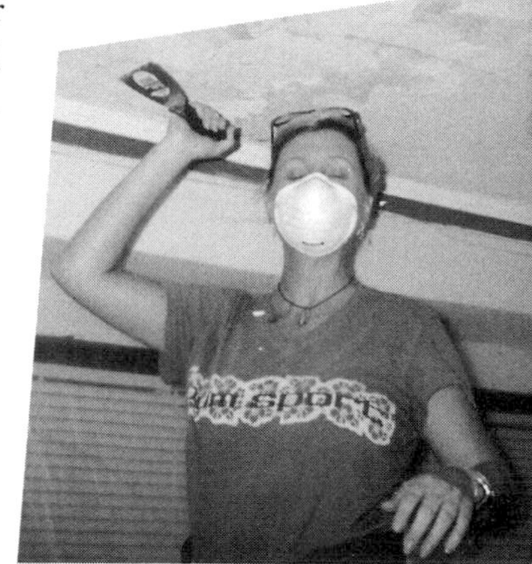

Fixing up my old new house

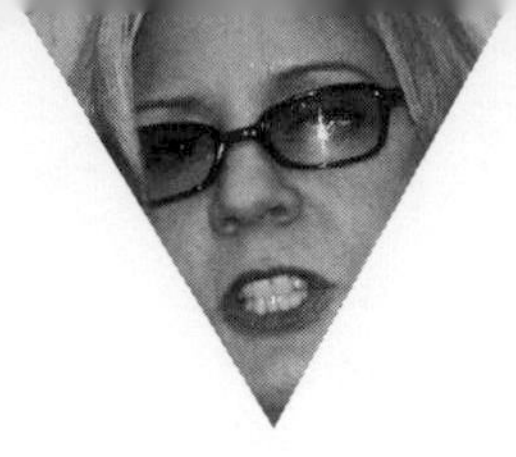

What Are Friends For?

Jesus God, what do you have to do to get people to help you around here? I mean, there I was, my muscles so sore it was agony just to go about my daily routine of wallowing on the couch like a walrus with a bellyful of fish, and, like, *nobody* would massage me. I mean, God! What was I, such a snarly-haired hag with halitosis that my so-called *good friends* couldn't make a team effort to massage my body continuously until I was able to walk again without looking like I was undergoing a nerve-gas experiment?

And talking about "good friends," where were mine when it came time to move my huge-ass houseload of furniture from my rented apartment into my newly purchased house? Scattered, that's where. Scattered like a batch of freshly hatched spiders the second they saw me hauling a load of empty Chiquita banana boxes back from Kroger. They knew my philosophy about banana boxes, how they're the absolute best score for packing all your crap when you need to move (because they're big and have the handle holes on the sides and everything), and I estimated that the *instant* they saw me backing a truckload of those suckers up to the loading dock they started *conspiring* as a group, creating excuses to be unavailable when I was scheduled to move.

Daniel actually bolted all the way to Florida. He had to put a whole *state line* between himself and me, his friend in need. And Grant! As always, Grant had something planned with his teenage daughter. His daughter is a permanent "Get Out of Jail Free" card. He always has something conveniently planned with her every time my life requires a showing of hard labor from my friends. "She's eighteen," I shouted, "she can lift boxes. Get both your asses over here!" But he had to drive her to her SAT test or something, as if her future is more important than my avoiding the prospect of ruining my manicure. Honestly, can we get some priorities here?

Lary, of course, came through, but only after I left twenty-eight messages on his answering machine begging him to help: "Stop pretending like you have a life without me and call me back, you booger-eating retard!" Finally my heavy flirting paid off and Lary showed up at my door with a hand truck.

This is the third time Lary has helped me move, and you'd think he'd ask for a blow job or something in return, but I can't think of anything I've really done for him except once, on the flight home from Amsterdam, I let him have my business-class upgrade, but that was the morning after I'd accidentally locked him out of our *pensione* all night. I mean, sure, maybe I should have been a little worried when he hadn't shown up by 5 A.M., and maybe I should have paid a little more attention to that shouting outside my window, but one of the last audible sentences I remember hearing him say that night was, "Hey, this place is packed with prostitutes and they're serving Afghani hash on the menu!" So I figured he was off getting a tongue bath from Russian hookers in a Jacuzzi of bubbling bong water or something. I mean, God, this is *Lary* we're talking about, the blond equivalent of Kramer on *Seinfeld*. Surely he was off spending the night at a genital piercing parlor, not throwing pebbles at my window. I was wrong, he was locked out, but he still showed up at my door with a hand truck last weekend.

"Try to stay out of the way," he said.

"Sure," I replied. "What are friends for?"

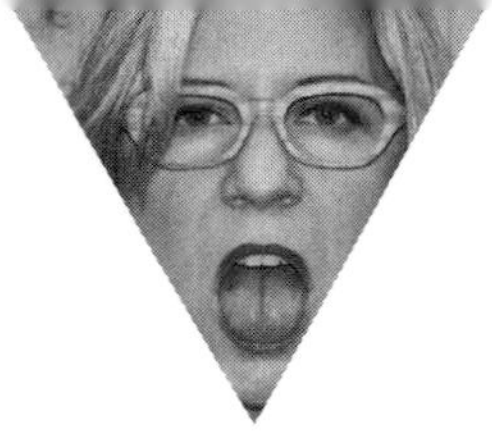

The Road Home

I never really thought about Lary having come from an actual family until recently, when he asked me to accompany him home to New York to attend his sister's wedding. Okay, maybe he didn't *ask* me, maybe I invited my own damn self when I heard he was going, just like I had to invite my own damn self when I heard he and Grant were headed on a road trip to Thomasville. Evidently, Lary needed to get some lady down there to sign over the warranty deed on the decrepit cinderblock mausoleum he calls home.

His home is a weathered old warehouse right downtown on a strip of road that used to be industrial until it got invaded by developers a few years back. Lary awoke one morning to discover that most of his neighboring buildings had been torn down and replaced by candy-colored Victorians with wraparound porches and loft projects with balconies that boasted "sweeping cityscape panoramas!" After that, Lary tried diverting the frenzy by taking to the street and waving his gun like a lunatic, thinking he'd frighten away prospective neighbors, but all that did was help clear his community of real criminals—who evidently have a better-honed aversion to dangerous maniacs—which in turn made the place even more attractive to real-estate caravans. So Lary gave up, and now he lives in a crumbling old ex-factory in the center of a gentrified vista just south of the Capitol. Occasionally, though, he still stands out front to growl at his neighbors like Frankenstein's monster, refusing to be banished by the meddlesome villagers.

I always thought Lary owned the place free and clear, having paid next to nothing for it years ago. And I always imagined him like the kid in the old Cracker Jack commercial, emptying his pockets on the previous owner's counter to reveal a musty pile of pennies, paper clips, hermit crabs, and other sediment, then pointing to the old warehouse, "Pretty please?" Turns out that's almost literally how it happened. "Take it," the guy had said, scooping Lary's offering into his palm, but then they left it at that—a handshake deal.

That's why, a decade later, Lary needed to make a trip to Thomasville, to see the woman there who needed to sign the actual warranty deed before Lary could call the place his actual own. Her fourth husband from forty years back had lost the factory in a card game or something and had neglected to sign it over before the cement dried around his ankles and he was tossed overboard, I'm betting. Whatever the case, the situation provoked an actual adventure.

Grant joined Lary on the road trip because it just so happens Grant is a notary. Grant is always pulling stuff like this out of the lovely shit basket that is his past: He's also a licensed real-estate agent, a licensed social worker, a minister ordained through the tabloid classifieds, a landscape architect, an antiques dealer, a bartender, an ex-seminary student at Princeton, an ex-husband to two ex-wives, a loving *father*, and, basically, the all-round show host of his own psycho circus that stretches all over the Southeast. For example, it turned out his mild-mannered father lives not far from Thomasville, and this trip would be Grant's opportunity to drop in on him and pretend he and Lary were lovers.

Of course, when I heard what they were up to I horned in on their plans like a pesky rash. "Goddammit," I shrieked at Lary over the phone, "don't you dare think you're sneaking off without me. I'll be back Thursday, got that? I'm good for anytime *after* that. My life is *wide open* after Thursday, so don't you dare leave before then."

The following Wednesday, Grant, who is gay, and Lary, who is not, happily headed south without me, and, what's worse, Lary's own ailing father had died days before, thereby robbing me of the self-appointed right to be the official shoulder Lary could cry on, in case he had it in him. I never knew much about Lary's father, except that he was a fairly productive drunk who had divorced Lary's mother when Lary was ten. It took me a decade just to get this out of the guy, because I seriously believe Lary prefers people to think he just happened onto the earth by crawling out of a tar pit somewhere rather than emerging from an actual family. In fact, another of his younger sisters wanted to visit him at home with her baby son, but he advised her against it on account of how he lives in that run-down warehouse, and her kid stood a good chance of accidentally ending up with rusty fishhooks imbedded in his head.

It's in keeping with his personality that Lary, now fatherless, tells me it doesn't feel any different than before, which makes me think I might not have been the right person to accompany him on the road trip after all. Sometimes your friends need something other than what you can give them, and sometimes you've got to let them look for it. Before Lary took the road home last Wednesday, he bid farewell to Grant's father, who gave him a lasting hug. "I like you," Grant's father told him. "You and my son seem very happy together."

It made me think about my own father again. A year after my mother divorced him, I moved to San Diego to begin college. I lived in an apartment on the beach with three untrustworthy, cocaine-addled roommates, and I spent the last year of my father's life ignoring school, doing drugs, and falling in love every fucking day. One night, a friend of mine invited me to accompany him on a private plane to L.A., where he had to pick up a "package." My dad lived right by the airport, and I figured I could drop in on him while my friend ran his errand. So I went on the flight, but when we got to L.A., I didn't go see my father because the prospect of a party loomed too irresistibly. That night at 12:03 A.M. my father died. He was fifty-two.

I'm sure you've heard people use the term, "You just don't get it." Well, I figured out that the "it" is the point in life. I believe I was supposed to have been there when my father died, but it was a point in life I just didn't get. I'll always regret it, especially since, two months before his heart attack, my father told me the story of how his own mother died, and it was one of the only times I remember him communicating with me face-to-face, as an adult. He told me he was in college in Birmingham, and his friends were on their way to New Orleans and would be passing through my dad's hometown, and they asked if he wanted to come along. He said he went and he was glad he did, because that weekend his mother had a heart attack and died in his arms.

Sometimes I wonder, though, if that's how it really happened or if that's how he liked to remember it. Sometimes I wonder if he made the same mistake I did: Instead of going home to his mother, he continued on with his friends, thinking he could catch her another time and leaving her to die alone.

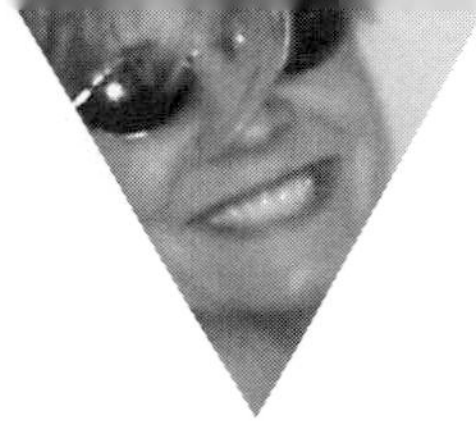

Hot Neighborhood

My neighbor Honnie found a dead dog in the front yard of her recently purchased home, and she took it as an omen. It was a weird morning for her anyway, what with the mystery man who lived in her crawl space, which in itself wouldn't be that catastrophic, because Honnie and her husband, Todd, wouldn't actually move into the house until later when he was gone and they were finished with the renovations. But the stranger had left piles of chicken bones and Pabst Blue Ribbon bottles strewn on the back porch every morning. He didn't even stick around to say, "Hi, thanks for letting me live under your house while you fix it up." He just bolted at sunrise and left his crap behind for Honnie to clean up.

I'd say Honnie and Todd officially had it worse than I did when I'd moved into Capitol View. I never found anything dead in my yard, or in my house either. I was looking pretty hard too, because the week before I closed on the house the police found that decapitated human head in a plastic sack *on my street,* and they had yet to find the rest of the body to go with it. Which meant it was still out there. Somewhere. The headless body. Waiting for me to stumble on it in the dark. I was pretty sure it wasn't actually in my house, since I'd searched high and low. And it was probably not under my house, since my contractor crawled around down there recently and all he found was the bottom half of a dead cricket. Actually, I found that. It was clinging to his hair when he emerged.

The reason I hired a contractor was because I needed a bigger house. Try as I did to buy a bigger house in the neighborhood, they all got snatched up faster than fat caterpillars at a crow orgy. Dead dogs and dead people aside, I guess this neighborhood officially qualifies as "hot." Five minutes from downtown and still cheap, the houses sold before the signs could go up in the yard. Even my friend Chris's grandmother's Jamaican ex-caretaker from New Jersey knows Capitol View is "hot." Now, that headless body could turn up nailed to the front door of a house for sale down the street and it wouldn't deter prospective buyers. "It's just cosmetic," the real-estate agent would say, "easily fixed."

There were bigger houses nearby that I liked, and each time I didn't even haggle over price, I just said, "Sounds good, I'll take it." The problem was the sellers always changed their minds later and wanted more money—one time as much as $25,000 more. I guess these sellers were not sufficiently enlightened about the "hotness" of this neighborhood until they were effortlessly offered their asking prices, at which time they decided they weren't asking enough. Those houses went to other buyers, who became my neighbors. They seem very nice. In the end, I decided to simply enlarge the house I already have.

Another neighbor of mine, a twenty-year-old young man named John Brown, died while in police custody. Witnesses—more neighbors of mine—said an officer beat him to death with his service flashlight, though preliminary autopsy reports are still ambiguous. Reportedly, Brown was helping a friend who'd been evicted from the boardinghouse next door to his when the owner of the property called the police to report him trespassing. The police arrived, a pursuit ensued, and now Brown is dead. The next day the boardinghouse was ransacked and burned down, and the following day, Honnie found the deceased dog in her yard. In the end, though, she decided not to take it as an omen after all, deciding that if it were meant to be a message, the bearers would have placed the carcass right on her porch.

It was a weird morning for Honnie, and what made it even weirder was the burned-down house up the street. At the time, Honnie didn't know why it burned down and neither did I. We chose to believe that it must have gone up in flames because this neighborhood was just so damn "hot."

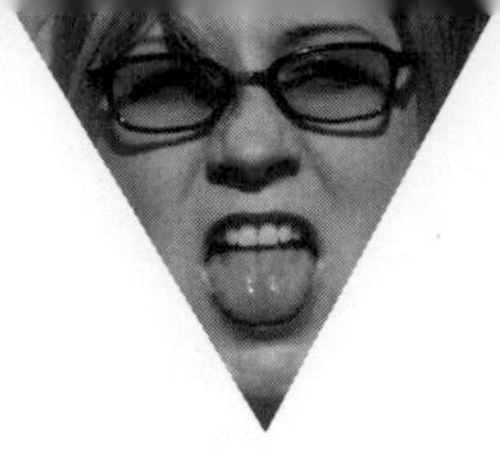

The Bandwagon

I've taken to calling Michael "Mr. Midas" because everything he touches turns to gold, which still pisses me off—and not just because he won't open a bar/restaurant in my neighborhood even though he bought a building there.

"God! How selfish *are* you?" I occasionally yell at him. I like to hit him too, because at six-foot-seven he doesn't even feel it. When I visit Michael's building, a warehouse that is slated to become a studio and art gallery and is within walking distance of my house, I point to a perfectly good section that would probably only take up almost all his space and I say, "Here, you could put the bar here. And the restaurant part could go over there, and you could serve blue-cheese dressing."

In fact, that's really all he needs to serve, just big bowls of blue-cheese dressing with stuff to stick in it: carrots, whole heads of cauliflower, my face. I could eat my own arm if it came coated with blue cheese, and Michael's blue-cheese dressing is my favorite. I tell him he should keep a tank of it on hand so I can wallow in it like a porpoise. But Michael, even though he calls himself my friend, does not think opening a bar/restaurant that serves only blue cheese is a sound business plan, and let's face it, even though he looks like a craven beatnik, he's never made a bad business move that I can see. It's like he's got this, I don't know, window seat inside the force field against all evil and it's infuriating. He has *never made a wrong move ever*! God! I just want to hit him again.

"Whatcha got there, Michael?"

"Life by the balls, Hollis."

Slap, slappity slap, slap.

But my luck could be changing, because it just so happens that Michael bought his loft here at the same time I bought my house, which makes me think I must have made a right move for once. Woohoo! What's this thing I feel under my feet? It's the *bandwagon*! And I'm among the first to jump on it for once. So with Mr. Midas in my neighborhood, all this place needs is a cool restaurant to serve as the binding cornerstone of the community, because, charming as this place is, what with the crack whores comingling with budding yuppies looking for low house payments, there's no getting away from the fact that the nearest Starbucks is *six minutes away*. I can't have that. I need a place closer, a place I can crawl to once my arms evolve into flippers. Michael is the obvious answer.

"No way," he says. "This neighborhood is not ready. If I opened a restaurant now, you would be the only customer."

"Come on," I plead, "you say that like it's a *bad* thing."

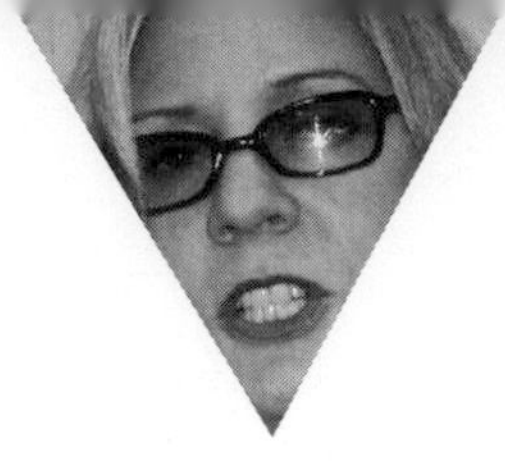

A Bog of Odors

I wondered why my kitchen smells like cocaine. I was sniffing the air in there once, thinking, "What is that, *narcotics*?" when Daniel told me I should clean something while I'm at it. But I don't want to disrupt the comingling of different states of decay that had randomly come together to create this bouquet. I like how it reminds me of college.

Because that's how it is with smells, and this place is a total bog of odors. Not only has the room that serves as my office smelled funny since the day I moved in—like shedded skin, I would think, or the car seat of an old German cab driver—but it's got this mystery moisture that steams the place up every once in a while. It attacks my supply of office stationery and seals all the envelopes. I wonder if this weird atmospheric effect could be caused by a decomposing dead body in the boarded-up fireplace, because the police never did recover the rest of the torso to match that severed human head. And I can't think of a worthy reason to wall up a perfectly good fireplace other than to create a tomb for human remains. I thought about tearing down the wall to uncover the fireplace—because fireplaces do wonders for property value—but I decided to let it rest. Maybe the smell will go away.

I prefer smells that remind me of stuff. For example, I love the smell of clean concrete because it reminds me of the cinder-block bathroom at the Via Paraiso Park in Monterey, California, where I got bit on the nose by a bulldog when I was five years old. I remember I had to remain perfectly still—crouched on all fours, with a bulldog on the end of my nose—until he finally relaxed his jaws and let me go. I like to say that's why I have a big nose to this day, but the truth is I was born with it, and that's probably what attracted the dog in the first place—maybe he thought it was a sausage. Another time, I went to the park and found the trees clustered with monarch butterflies. My sisters and I plucked them off the trunks and put them in our hair. We walked around with our heads all aflutter, like sweet little Medusas. Whenever I smell clean concrete I think of monarch butterflies and bulldogs kind enough to let me keep my nose. Not a bad trade, since it's a common enough aroma.

So is the mothball smell in my closets. I need that smell in my life. It reminds me of a trip I took with my mother to Palo Alto when I was six to visit her aging friend, who embroidered doilies and kept a supply of yarn covered in mothballs in her cabinets. The smell made my eyes melt sometimes. One day the three of us went to a restaurant with a hundred cuckoo clocks that all chimed madly every hour. We stayed there all afternoon so I could catch the show over and over, and the waitress didn't even seem that irritated with us for taking up her table. "I promise I'll bring you back," my mother had said. I never saw the place again, but every time I open my closet, I am brought back.

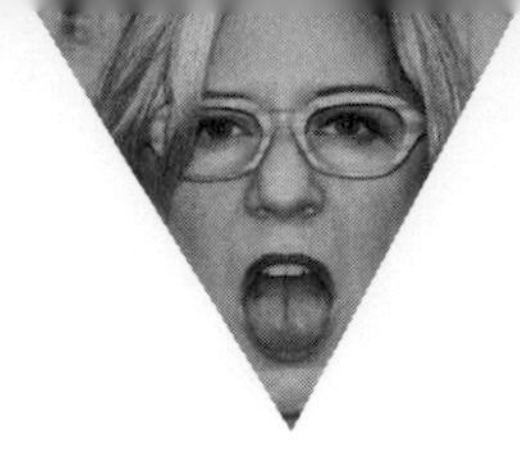

Minor Details

Considering my neighborhood, it's almost alarming that, in my entire time there, I've only come across two corpses in the street. The second was that poor boy, or really I just saw his legs and arms . . . and the blood. Christ, I should have paid more attention to details.

When I saw my first street corpse, the police were already there. They had covered the woman, who had been hit by a car as she crossed the road, and she lay where she was struck, in the center of the street, and I remember her bare foot sticking out from under the sheet. And groceries. She must have been walking home after shopping.

The memory of her bare foot always reminded me of an Argentine pervert my older sister secretly wed years ago. His name was or was not Ricardo, and he was a pimp and a thief, but amazingly he had an oily charm, and, God, could he tell a story. He kept us up half the night one time, telling us about a dangerous strip of road in rural

Argentina known for hellacious auto accidents, and every time the police pulled the bodies out of the wreckage either the left foot or both feet—but *especially* the left foot—of the dead person would be bare.

Ricardo went into such *detail,* describing how even sturdy construction boots could be found on the floors of trucks, still tightly laced but somehow separated from the left foot when the coroner sometimes needed two assistants to pull the other ones off at the morgue. The locals believed the victims lost their shoes because they couldn't take their first step into the kingdom of heaven with a covered foot. "There are hundreds of old shoes along that road," Ricardo said in his hushed Latin accent, "from having flown off the feet of the dead."

That's the detail of the dead woman I always remember: her bare left foot, along with packets of Top Ramen and a torn box of cat food strewn about as plastic bags danced in the wind of passing cars. I always think how, when she left the house that day, the last thing on that woman's mind must have been the possibility of dying on the pavement with dried noodles crowning her head. Maybe if she had paid more attention to detail, like the oncoming car, she would have made it home to feed her cat.

But as I said, the police were already there, so I was not needed in that scenario. The boy is a different story. His blood was so robustly red, practically the color of blackberries, so I could almost understand why Lary mistook it for a melted Popsicle when I brought him there later that day. The boy was gone but his blood was still there.

"He was *dead!*" I shriek. Jesus! I hate how Lary always questions me.

"How could you tell?"

"I could just *tell!*"

It was in the details, even though I wish I had paid more attention to them. When I called the police to report a dead boy on the sidewalk down the street they needed all kinds of details, *sensible* details I didn't remember, such as the address in front of which the body lay, the number of people surrounding him, their genders and what they were wearing.

"Are you sure he was dead?" the officer asked.

"I'm sure."

"How could you tell?"

I could tell by the blood, there was so *much* of it. It was young blood, the color of blackberries. My own is practically the color of marmalade, but it always has been. You could look at a picture of me when I was nine and see that I had the weight of the ages in my eyes. I could tell by the sheet covering the boy's body, and the face of the woman who placed it there, that the boy was dead. Her expression was one of utter frustration, a reaction to witnessing an act of unfathomable waste. "Here was a perfectly good human," her face was saying, "and someone had to go and wreck him."

I continued to recite details, remembering that the boy was face up under the sheet, that his arms were outstretched with palms skyward, that the cuffs of his trousers were rolled, that the blood stain on the sidewalk was in the shape of a map of Australia, that the bedsheet covering him had pink pinstripes and light blue piping along the hem. They were trivial particulars, but it seemed important to honor them at the time so that this boy's dying on the sidewalk surrounded by strangers wouldn't be—in my life at least—a minor detail.

"Anything else?" asked the officer when my voice finally trailed off.

Silence. "No," I surrendered. "There is nothing else."

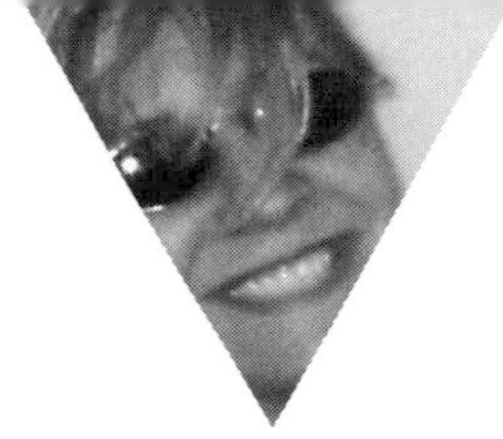

Missing Pieces

God, I can't keep from thinking about those notorious missing torsos in my neighborhood. I don't think they ever uncovered the missing pieces to match the found pieces, let alone figure out who the pieces once belonged to, or for that matter—and probably most important—who was responsible for separating the pieces from their other pieces to begin with.

Today I waved like a parade-float prop as I drove past the crack dealers who hang out down the street. They no longer try to intimidate me with menacing glares meant to make my hand dart for the autolock on the door panel. They know I'm their neighbor, and that my doors were locked long before I even backed out of the driveway. Like it or not, I've stumbled into a home here, guarded by an incontinent pit bull, who will promptly pee on you if you try to burgle us.

But no one has tried to burgle me, and if they did they wouldn't garner much booty because the most valuable item in here is my velvet Elvis collection, which I hear can command double figures on eBay, especially the "crying" Elvis with a shirt collar the size of old Cadillac fenders. I figure I've escaped break-ins because—barring the crack dealers, addicts, and whores—I have tons of other nice neighbors here, and after months of deliberation I'm definitely, without a doubt, just about practically almost certain that none of them are responsible for the cut up body pieces the police found before I moved in, or for the torsos still to be stumbled upon that are probably just bones by now anyway.

Grant and Lary really liked the new place, and claimed I would never be happy because I'm never not longing for something. But I am happy, sometimes. Truly. The other day at dusk we sat in my backyard, and on weeknights the air is always full of the smell of fresh cake from the Nabisco factory nearby. There are tiki torches in my backyard now, and a new fence, which keeps Cookie from escaping to pee on the drug dealers down the street. Even the drug dealers down the street are scarcer these days, and my artist friend Patrick just bought a house a few doors down, which he's fixing up fabulously. Next door, Monty and Greta were mixing strawberry daiquiris and waving us over from their kitchen window. *God,* I thought, *this place is so nice. This place is practically perfect.* And then I remembered what was missing. It's the torsos. The unfound torsos. To me they will always be out there, waiting to be stumbled over in the dark.

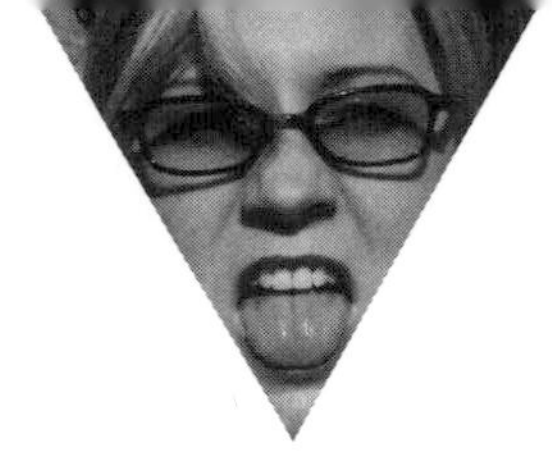

My Mother's Reflection

When I was little, my mother would come home from a day devising weapons, pull together a tamale pie for us kids, and then be off in time to catch the night cosmetology classes at the local community college. She practiced makeup application on my sisters and me, and I was the only girl in fourth grade who wore textured false eyelashes. The notes my teachers sent home made my mother laugh. She never became a cosmetologist, but she did move to Switzerland to construct a missile-tracking strategy.

My usual M.O. for Mother's Day—renting a truckload of animated Disney movies that induce a mental enema—is already failing me. I might have lost my ability to lose myself in fantasy, which is tragic, because I believe it's essential to maintain a fantasy of some kind throughout your life. My mother's fantasy was that she would survive liver cancer, and she held on to it until one day in a Tijuana cancer clinic years ago. The moment she lost it is the memory that's been tormenting me lately.

When we were really young, my two sisters and I were goofing around with my mother in front of the bathroom mirror, but we quit laughing when she suddenly exclaimed, "You're all so pretty, and I'm so ugly." Of course my mother was not ugly. It must have been one of those intermittent moments women have as they lose their youth, the kind of moments I have now. Maybe it's a lapse in fantasy, where we imagine ourselves to be as youthful as we've always felt, and then we have that certainty shattered temporarily, perhaps when presented with three supple replicas of your youth laughing up at you in the bathroom mirror.

When she arrived at the Mexican clinic, where, for five thousand dollars a day, Haitian doctors administered a cancer treatment unapproved by the United States, my mother was so close to death that she literally looked like a corpse, except for the sounds of her laborious breathing. On one of her better days, my sister Kim and I rigged a wheelchair to take her outside, but the excursion was awkward because the clinic was surrounded by unleveled concrete slabs. Another problem, as I remember vividly, was that the outside of the clinic was literally walled with two-way mirrors.

We were facing the clinic, trying to maneuver over the cumbersome paving, when I looked up to see my mother watching herself in the reflection of the building. Her deterioration had been rapid since she had last seen herself. She was bald, and the definition of her skull showed sharply through her thin, blistered skin. Because of her failing liver, her flesh was a pronounced yellow. Deep wrinkles lined her lips like stitching on a baseball seam. Her eyes were sunken and incandescently jaundiced. This is the precise mental Polaroid that continues to haunt me. Not just my mother's face, but the entire reflection in the panel of two-way mirrors. My sister and I, young and robust, were caught once again in the same reflection as my mother, who was watching herself with a defeated lucidity. That was exactly the moment at which she lost her fantasy of surviving. It is an almost unbearable memory.

"Take me inside," she said. Silently, we did.

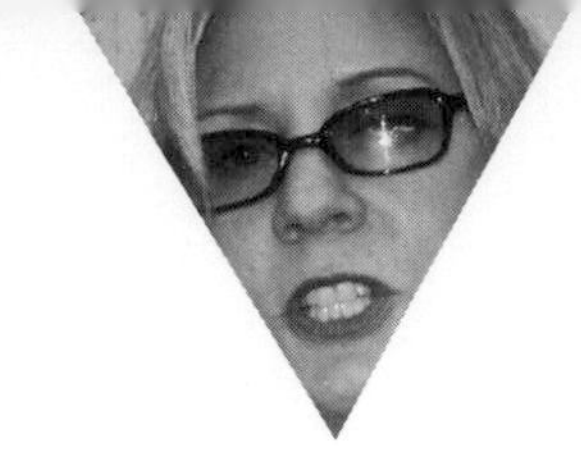

Myrtle the Lesbian Ghost

Most of my neighbors got uncomfortable when I talked about the lesbian ghost that lived with me. I'm thinking it wasn't because they don't believe in ghosts, but because they think mine might be offended if I'm wrong about her sexuality. I don't think I'm wrong, because according to Miss Taylor, who is eighty-seven years old but whose brain is so sharp you could practically get a paper cut holding a conversation with her, "two spinster women who slept in the same bed" occupied this house in the early seventies, and one of them was shot and killed by a fourteen-year-old boy in her own—now my own—backyard.

"It was so sad," recalls Miss Taylor, "because you couldn't find a nicer couple of women."

But even when Miss Taylor told me my backyard was once the scene of a murder, it didn't dawn on me that my house was haunted, even though the ghost had been so active. It finally occurred to me the day my candlestick tipped over for the twentieth time. I don't know why the ghost likes that particular candlestick so much, because there's plenty of other things she could tip over on the bookshelf—rickety, kitschy things—but it was that same solid, wrought-iron candlestick every time. I think she picked it for the noise it makes. When it falls on the hardwood floor it clatters like heavy chains hitting dungeon bars.

At first I thought my cat was the culprit. You'd be amazed at what you can blame on your cat when you have a ghost in your house. In this case, I was in bed in the dark and suddenly, silently, the light in the next room would switch on. Not off, but *on,* which is eerie, because turning on a light in the pitch-dark announces someone's arrival quite effectively. Each time, though, I figured my cat had brushed against the light switch on the wall or something, even though the switch is at chest level and my cat would have to be as tall as an ostrich to reach it.

And, thinking back, there's no way my fifteen-year-old cat, Lucy, who's as fat as a manatee and even less coordinated, could have climbed to the top of the bookcase without pitching the rest of the knickknacks across the room like an angry housewife. But every time I heard the clamor of the candlestick falling to the floor, I'd simply pick it up and put it back without another thought. And there were other signs too, like the cloud of mystery moisture that occasionally still steams up my office, but then one day that candlestick hurled itself *right in front of me!* It didn't just fall, it practically *flew* off the shelf. After seeing that, I stood there, frozen with realization. "Oh, duh," I finally said aloud. "I have a ghost."

I call her "Myrtle." Lately I've been keeping an eye on the candlestick, and when I see that it has inched forward on the shelf, I push it back. In response, Myrtle recently pitched a CD off the same bookshelf, but the effect wasn't the same. But it's okay, living with the spirit of this woman who suffered because of her trust in mankind: She had stepped outside to tell a boy to stop shooting squirrels, so the boy shot her instead. Back then I guess people were unaware of how callous a kid with a gun could be. I imagine she thought he would listen to her and respect her request to stop shooting up her property. He was just a child, after all. So she approached him unarmed and unsuspicious and died because of it. Unable to make her good-byes, she now made noises in my house instead. Recently, I let her knock the candlestick over again, because I know she likes the sound it creates. It's the least I could do, seeing as how she walked out her backdoor one day not knowing she'd be leaving everything she loved behind, forever.

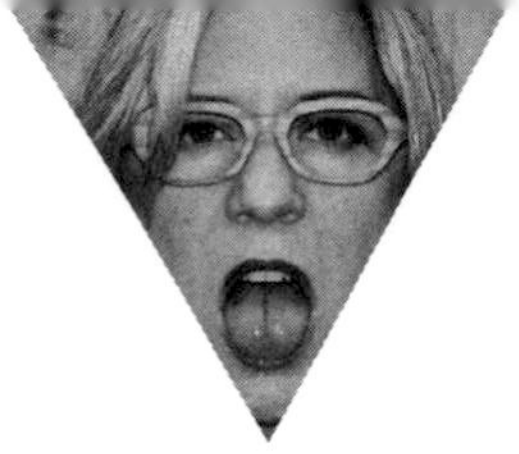

The New Ghost

I often wonder whether more than just the *one* ghost haunts my house, because there have been some departures from Myrtle's usual routine. Take her favorite iron candlestick. I found it not just on the floor but bent up as well. And six pictures came crashing off my mantel the other day. That's not like Myrtle, who has otherwise only been known to throw some CDs that are stacked near the candlestick. Her throwing things was really just her means of reminding me I have company. Destruction was not her point, because she picked only durable items to toss.

Which makes me wonder about the mantel. That's new territory for her, and those pictures *broke,* glass flying everywhere. Before that, the most energy I'd seen Myrtle expend was the time she tried to change the lightbulb in my living room lamp. Of all the tricks a ghost could perform—blood dripping down the walls, a plague of maggots—Myrtle picked lightbulb changing.

Don't get me wrong, it's not like it wasn't scary to return to the living room after only a minute and find a lightbulb on the floor when it used to be screwed into a lamp, *under a shade*. Myrtle must have done that, as she hates darkness and keeps turning on lights in the middle of the night. So after most of them burned out Myrtle must have been at work there, trying to help. That's what I mean, Myrtle was a sweet woman before she was murdered in my backyard twenty-seven years ago. She thought she could walk up to that boy with a gun and ask him to stop shooting, and he would stop shooting and she would walk back inside to finish dinner with her female companion and that would be that. But instead she died on the grass out there. Then I moved in, and Myrtle tried to make herself known but I was distracted. It wasn't until the candlestick flew off the shelf right in front of me that I finally figured it out. After that Myrtle seemed content to know I knew she was there.

I thought I saw her once, a faint apparition alongside me in the dark, but it turned out it was just my own reflection in the Plexiglas of a piece of Daniel's artwork I'd forgotten I'd placed there earlier. Myrtle is not that ostentatious, as I said, she doesn't even like the dark. I personally appreciate the dark sometimes, and can sit in it quietly all night on occasion, but in this house that's not possible. Myrtle can only stand darkness for so long before, *click!*, suddenly a light comes on somewhere. I got tired of getting out of bed to turn them off, so I took to keeping a dim stained-glass lamp illuminated in the living room twenty-four hours a day, and I've learned to sleep with its glow wafting in from the doorway. When you have a ghost in your house, one of the first things you figure out is how to compromise.

But the broken glass—that's a new trick. My neighbor Jim says his house is haunted by the ghost of an eight-year-old girl who died there years ago of leukemia. He thinks she made his basement stairs collapse underneath him one day. I remember thinking that was a bad prank for his ghost to pull, and I felt fortunate that Myrtle has been comparatively mild in her hauntings. But then all those pictures flew off my mantel, and now I'm worried that another ghost has moved in.

Maybe it's the boy who was killed one block over, shot over a game of dice. Or maybe it's the crack whore who was gunned down as she ran naked through the street trying to escape her assailant. That happened the week before I bought this place. Or it could be the addict on the corner who called me a bleachy-haired honky bitch after I accidentally almost hit him with my car. He didn't look like he had much longer to live. What I don't understand is why they would haunt my particular house. If it were me, I would pick a nicer place. But maybe ghosts don't have power over who they haunt. Maybe that's their lot in death, to go where they're assigned, and linger there like a familiar scent forever. Last night, I thought I saw my new ghost in the purple hue of the permanently illuminated stained-glass lamp in the living room, but it turns out that, absent the pictures, the mirror over the mantel is newly exposed. So it wasn't the new ghost after all, it was just me again.

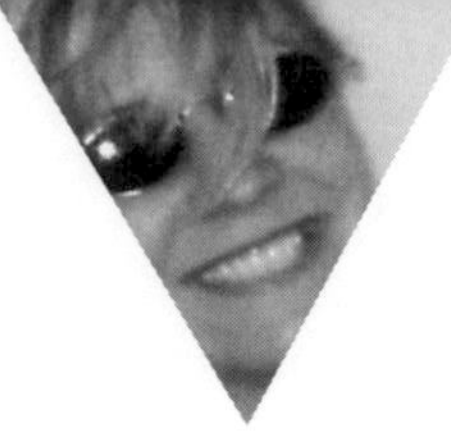

Get Right with God

We were looking for a reason to live after hearing that Petra, the transvestite pizza-delivery boy, had moved to Chicago, where, I hear, they have pretty good pizza. But it was a blow regardless. It wasn't until we dialed Milano's on Ponce to request a delivery by Petra that the terrible fact slapped us in the face like a frozen mackerel: no more Petra. No more horn-rimmed glasses, sagging knee socks, and secondhand sweaters buttoned askew. We were crushed. We had loved her from afar, and we realized sadly that now we would have to love her from farther away, which did not fill the hole in our souls that Petra left behind. We were empty inside, needed emotional nourishment, needed hope—we needed, obviously, to get out of town.

Daniel, Grant, and I headed north, because we heard Chicago is kinda sorta in that direction. We knew we wouldn't make it there; in fact, we hardly made it anywhere. It took us eleven hours just to get to Soddy-Daisy, and I swear to God I have no idea where Soddy-

Daisy is, I just know it's not very far from Atlanta, because when the counter girl at the QuikTrip told us where we were, Grant laughed so hard he bent over double, which upset a rack of Butterfingers.

"Eleven hours to get to Soddy-Daisy!" he kept laughing. Grant told us when we started out that he's allergic to the Interstate, so we let him tool us through whatever side street and highway he wanted. We searched out flea markets, and Grant bought a stack of vented pie pans that he says will make wonderful wall sconces for his Peoplestown crack house, and Daniel was on the lookout for those Popsicle lamp shades that prisoners make. We found a few hanging from the ceiling of the snack shop at one of the flea markets, but they were made by the owner's lifelong friend who had just been executed, so she said they weren't for sale. Grant said we should try to steal them. We still don't know if he was serious.

We didn't steal the lamp shades, but we ended up wandering in the fog, passing a church marquee that said "Courage Is Fear Combined with Prayer," as well as neglecting to stop at a perfectly good bowling alley complete with a karaoke bar in our quest for a place to crash for the night. In Soddy-Daisy we opted to continue driving until Daniel's ass got tired from sitting on the tiny jumpbench tucked behind the bucket seats in Grant's truck's cab.

That decision led us to desolate Dayton, Tennessee, where we booked ourselves into a generic hotel and ate at an Italian restaurant called, curiously, the Golden Monkey. It turns out the name of the restaurant commemorated the famous First Amendment "monkey trial" in which Clarence Darrow defended an idealistic biology teacher named John Thomas Scopes, who was prosecuted for going against the church to teach Darwin's theory of evolution. That was in 1925, and this is the Bible Belt. The teacher lost. Waiting for our spaghetti we looked around the restaurant, which was decorated with about a billion dusty stuffed carnival-booth monkeys. "You know," Grant said absently, "courage is not fear combined with prayer. Courage is fear that said 'fuck it.' "

The next morning we departed Dayton, and remembered why

we started the trip to begin with, and that was to search for roadside religious signs so Grant could use them to panel the outside of the crack house in Peoplestown. Earlier, on a separate decorating whim, Grant had employed the neighborhood handyman's young son to go through the area and collect used crack lighters by the bagful.

"I'll pay him a nickel for two," Grant told the handyman to tell his son.

"I hope you know what you're asking," said the handyman as he descended the outside steps, an ancient foam kneepad heaped around each ankle. "He's an enterprising boy."

A few days later Grant had a two plastic grocery bags full of discarded crack lighters, their metal mechanisms rusty and clotted with dirt, their bright plastic Bic bodies clamoring against each other like large colorful cockroaches. Grant already has two porch chairs upholstered with crack lighters. The lighters are laid flat against the surface of the wood and then drilled through with a screw to keep them in place. It's wild, seeing a chair covered in colorful old lighters, but it's not very comfortable to sit in, and sometimes the lighters aren't all the way used up, so the fact that they have been drilled through lends to the possibility that your pants will smell like propane and be a little bit flammable when you get up. But the chairs are probably not for sitting anyway. They are, truly, something to look at.

The roadside religious signs, on the other hand, were less forthcoming than the crack lighters. We didn't see our first one until the second day, but it was a beauty. Grant and Daniel, who was sitting in the front seat, spotted it immediately and began whooping like frat boys at a beer rally. Grant punched the breaks and the truck screeched to a stop. But I didn't see the sign at first, even though it was bigger than the community satellite dish for an entire trailer park. The sheer hugeness of it is probably why I didn't see it. Roadside religious signs, generally, are no bigger than the top of a coffee table, so when you're looking for something that small sometimes it's hard to see the big stuff. This one had its own post, as opposed to just being nailed to a tree, and it was made out of a great slab of roofing tin, with the words "Get Right with God" cut out of tar paper and nailed to it ("On both sides!" shrieked Grant). It took all three of us to carry it to the truck, and even then it was so big it wouldn't lie flat on the bed. We had to angle it sideways, and that's how we drove home, with a giant "Get Right with God" sign sticking almost straight up in the truck.

I thought Grant wanted it for his crack house. But soon afterward I came home one day to see that Grant had firmly planted the sign in my front yard, and there it remains to this day. It's like a beacon, able to be seen from blocks away. I wonder how I ever missed it the first time.

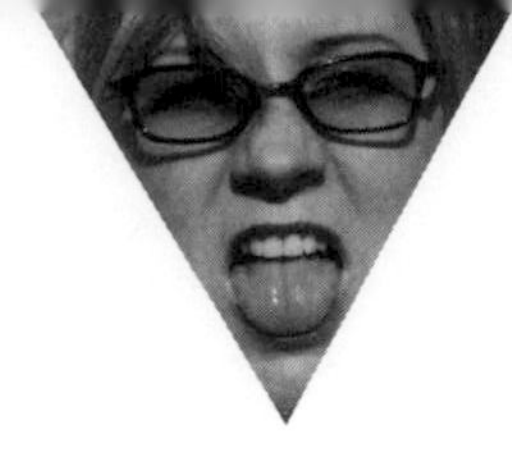

Jesus Loves Atheists

When I was seven I had a crush on Satan. Not that I knew who he was, I just based everything on his picture. In the illustrated children's Bible I remember one picture in particular, in which Jesus had just pushed Satan off a cliff, and Satan is sailing down through the air, a trail of red robes billowing behind him. He looked only slightly irritated at the inconvenience. He had hair as black as octopus ink, styled like Lyle Waggoner's, an impeccably groomed beard, and a deep sunburn. 'Course that cloven hoof was kind of a downer, but hey, other than that I thought he was hot.

When my mother came home from work that day I told her I wanted to marry Satan when I grew up. She looked at me gravely, then said, "Kid, whatever you do, don't get married."

My affection for Satan soon fizzled (he's too possessive). Then came a very brief period during which we were allowed to go to church, my two sisters and I, minus any money for the collection tray. We were all under ten, and I suppose my parents thought it was a good way to get us out of the house for a day. A church bus came by and collected the neighborhood kids every Sunday, and we sang "He's Got the Whole World in His Hands" on the way. Once there, every day, I approached the stage when the preacher called forth sinners from the audience who wanted their souls saved.

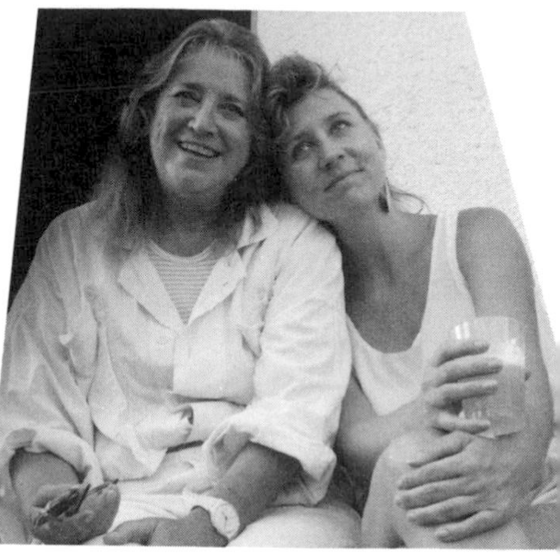

With my mother in 1989—a month later she was diagnosed with terminal cancer

One day a lady usher stopped me in the aisle as I made my weekly pilgrimage. "You were saved last week, sweetie, and the week before that," she said, leading me back to my seat, ". . . and the week before that."

"But it didn't take," I protested as she walked away, her knee-highs sagging around her ankles.

The preacher called my mother to complain about my behavior, and it was this, combined with the fact that we were actually starting to recite some of the stuff we learned in church (like how, after you're dead and buried, devils take an elevator up to the underside of your coffin and kidnap you if you don't tithe properly) that prompted my mother to call a stop to churchgoing. The bus still pulled up outside our apartment building every Sunday and honked, but my mother waved it away. The driver always waited a few minutes before leaving, as if performing a sad little vigil for three tiny lost souls. I worried briefly that I would go to Hell, but my mother said what she always said when I worried about that. "What bigger Hell is there than a heaven full of people like that?" my mother asked, indicating the departing bus. "Your soul, by the way, is fine."

My mother never wavered from her stance on religion. She

would throw herself between her children and any aggressively approaching Jesus freaks during family outings along the esplanade. "Stay back!" she'd hiss, stopping them in their tracks, their propaganda moistening in their palms. They stayed back. As opposed to "the afterlife," she believed in *the only life,* as in, "This is the only life you get, don't wreck it." She died young, her life considerably less wrecked than it could have been. Before cancer caused her to lapse into a coma, she told me her biggest regret in life was writing "bicycle" on her Christmas list as a little girl, knowing her parents grievously could not afford to give her one. When Christmas came and went with no bicycle, she continued to write "bicycle" at the end of her mother's grocery list every week for months. "I wish I hadn't done that," she said with soft penitence, her eyes round and sad, and then she was unconscious.

I laid down next to her on the bed and stroked her blistered head. "I love you, Mom," I said repeatedly, "and your soul, by the way, is fine."

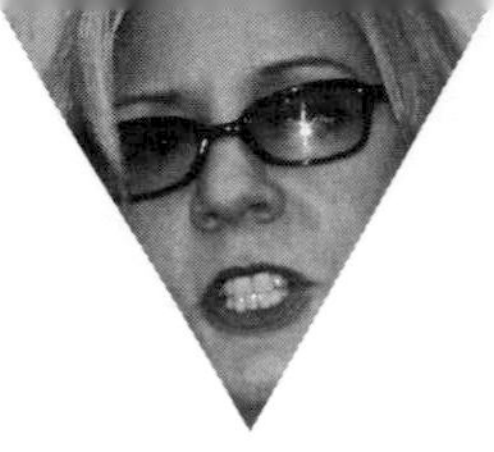

Acknowledgments

I don't know where to begin when it comes to whom I can blame for this book, so I guess I have to start in order of their appearance. First, my parents were the kind of wonderful, just-this-side of insane lunatics who were utterly unable to hide their fears from me, which works out better for impressionable children than you might think. My two sisters, Cheryl and Kim, and my brother, Jim, were the perfect colleagues with which to wade through the days, gathering around me like little life jackets when it seemed imminent I'd sink any minute, then, with the exception of Kim, beating the crap out of me when they figured I could handle it. Later, my friend Jeff Bertram had a bigger hand in honing my sense of humor than he might think, plus I fell in love with his parents, who are from Atlanta, making it seem like some kind of Land of Functional Families to me, which is why I moved there after college. There I met Lary Blodgett, at the wedding of his lovely ex-girlfriend Mary Jane, who that day married another man.

Then I met Jill Hannity. I placed a call to her when she was an editor at *Creative Loafing* to inquire about working for free as an intern, but instead she insisted on assessing some of my manuscripts. Upon doing so she assigned me a cover story, which paid actual American dollars. After that she became one of the best friends I ever had.

Then Jill left the *Loaf* to move to New York to have beautiful babies and continue to be the wife of the now famous, rock-hot TV commentator Sean Hannity (note to Sean: If this book makes me rich, I promise I won't bogey the reefer so much). So I left that paper as well and started writing a column (for free) for a gutsy start-up called *Poets, Artists & Madmen,* published by Patrick Best and Steve Hedberg. By that time I'd acquired two more zimwads to round out my makeshift family: Daniel Troppy and Grant Henry. We were all like a gaggle of hermit crabs without shells, flopping around trying to find ourselves.

Instead we found each other, and that's just as good, I guess. Lary was in there too, but Lary had never been lost. Then four years later *Creative Loafing*, which had grown into one of the biggest alternative papers in the nation under the auspices of managing editor Ken Edelstein, picked up my column after *Poets, Artists & Madmen* lived the last flashes of its brilliant life. They welcomed me back like a craggy uncle who had no choice but to take in an unruly orphan. I can't help but love the hell out of them for it.

But I will truly get crapped on by the Karma gods if I don't also thank the following people: Liz Lapidus, Josh Levs, Sara Sarasohn, Doug Monroe, Rebecca Burns, Judith Regan, Kathy Jett, Laura Geraci, Cassie Jones, Jim Hackler, Michael Alvear, Polly Sheppard, Sam Johnson, Randy Osbourne, Michael Benoit (who hides his pride in me by claiming all the credit for my success), Teresia Mosher, Jan Hickel, Lynn Lamousin, Lisa Hamilton, Corinne Lynch, Thomas Meagher, Suzanne Van Atten, Nena Halford, Jim Llewellyn, Bob Steed, and, most importantly, the readers of my column first in *Poets* and then in *Creative Loafing*. Seriously, if not for these people I'd probably be living in an abandoned truck right now.

One more thing, I can't possibly close without copping to the fact that I'm heavily influenced by P. J. O'Rourke, Dave Barry (who answered the one-and-only fan letter I ever wrote in my life, like, right away), David Sedaris, William Geist, Carl Hiaasen, and Georgie Anne Geyer. I hope I've adulterated my material enough with my own perspective to keep it from being immediately apparent that I rip the hell off out of these people, and I wanna thank them for being so goddamn great at what they do.

Lastly, Judith Regan and Jill Hannity bear double mention, because if it were up to my mojo alone I'd still be working for free, but because of these girls I can now trade in all my thrift-store stuff and buy . . . well, better thrift-store stuff. Thank you both for looking out for me.

OK, I think that's it. Did I mention my column readers? They rock. And my NPR *All Things Considered* producer Sara Sarasohn? Good. That's it, then . . . just about . . . wait, there was a sandbox monitor in my second-grade class named Mrs. Morris who sat me down one day because she could tell I was tortured over the fact that I didn't fit in with my suburban classmates. She stood over me with arms akimbo, and, indicating my classmates with a thrust of her chin, said, "You don't need them." At first all I could do was smell the menthol tobacco smoke on her breath, but then her words sunk in and my brain just lifted above everything like a helium balloon on a broken string. Suddenly, for that moment, I was free.

I still get that feeling. Sometimes, when I look around and realize there's a big sandbox around me, I'll hear Mrs. Morris's words, and suddenly I'm soaring. You gotta thank a person for giving you a gift like that.